PRAISE FOR

Will It Make the Boat Go Faster?

Olympic-Winning Strategies for Everyday Success

"I know first hand the immense pressure of competing in an Olympic Games and the dedication it takes to get on the podium. This book conveys the drama, the heartache and the pride with spine-tingling detail – it will have you on the edge of your seat. The book is also packed full of useful advice, not just for sports people, but for anyone looking to up their game."

Roger Black MBE, Olympic silver medallist, athletics

"Ben describes himself as a normal guy… from my perspective he's a normal guy with extraordinary talent! Not only as an athlete but also as someone who has been able to reflect upon his personal journey and experiences (in sport) and translated them into bite-size life-lessons that will resonate widely with anyone striving for excellence and success! 'Will It Make The Boat Go Faster?' is an insightful and inspiring read… and one that I will continue to draw upon professionally and personally."

Penny Briscoe OBE, British Paralympic Association Director of Sport. Chef de Mission for Paralympics GB for Tokyo 2020

"Ben's colourful storytelling illustrates that teams win together with intense focus, binding trust and absolute commitment to each other."

Heather J. Brunner, CEO, WP Engine

"Invaluable for entrepreneurs. A great mixture of inspiration and sound, practical advice."

Nicola Chilman, Founder, EZ Education

"Every Games has its heroes, but behind every celebration on the podium lies thousands of hours of hard training, relentless mental focus, and choosing to get up each morning before the rest of the world in pursuit of that something extra which just might give you the winning margin in an Olympic final. Ben Hunt-Davis's stories in 'Will It Make The Boat Go Faster?' brilliantly illustrate the dedication required to become a gold medallist, and how the lessons might be applied more widely in our lives. It's a fascinating and inspiring book."

Sebastian Coe KBE, double Olympic gold medallist; IAAF President; British Olympic Association Chairman; former LOCOG & London 2012 Bid Chair

"Want to know what it takes to raise your performance from average to the best in the world? This book provides a fascinating description of both the practice and competition by an Olympic champion (first author) during two years of intense preparation for the Olympics. During this time his rowing team's performance improved from a mediocre level to winning Olympic gold. The book details the changes in the team's practice and preparation that gradually led to increases in the team's objective performance. The two authors extract insights from how practice increased performance and give really useful, practical recommendations for changes in daily life for anyone striving for higher levels of performance."

K. Anders Ericsson, Conradi Eminent Scholar and Professor of Psychology; co-author of 'Peak: How all of us can achieve extraordinary things'

"I loved it. It's a real page-turner - and how often has any management book been called a page turner?! Ben and Harriet have written an uplifting book that convinces you that anybody can improve without having to be an Olympian. It's beautifully written: no jargon, just nice, simple, straightforward English and a lovely informal, self-deprecating style. It's also very practical and sensible - the advice here can apply to anybody in any walk of life."

Harry Gaskell, Chief Innovation Officer and Partner, EY UK&I

"The inspirational story and practical principles translate from sport to cinema and beyond. It's a wonderful book."

Michael Gracey, Director of 'The Greatest Showman'

"An excellent 'Do It Yourself' organising for success book. Essential for full time winners! Personal yet professional."

Kate Hoey, former MP and Sports Minister

"I thoroughly recommend this book, it's fantastic. It captures the intensity of performing at the Olympics, and all the highs and lows of getting there, but it also shares strategies we can all use. No matter who you are, what you do and what your goals are, you'll find a wealth of ideas to help you make your own boat go faster."

Dame Kelly Holmes, double Olympic gold medallist, athletics

"A truly fantastic book. Lots of inspiration from this book went into our World Championship wins."

Frances Houghton MBE, 5 x Olympic rower; 3 x Olympic silver medallist; 4 x World Champion, quadruple scull

"A compelling read; insightful and genuinely useful!"

Sir Chris Hoy, 6 x Olympic gold medallist,
11 x World Champion, track cycling

"To get inside the mind of an Olympian is a privilege. To share the worries and anxieties, the camaraderie and the highs, is rare and this book gives us a ring side seat. But the real bonus is that it is all then made relevant to our lives, to our business space. I challenge every business woman and man in the country not to take something away from this big contribution to business thinking."

Lord Digby Jones, former Director General of the
CBI and Minister of State for Trade and Investment

"A fascinating story of the powerful passion of one man to get to the top of his sport and the winning strategies we can all learn from his experience, whether we are aspiring to be Olympians or simply better managers."

Lord Kirkham CVO,
Founder and former Executive Chairman, DFS

"Will it make the boat go faster? - One simple question that cuts through complexity and helps prioritise, make the right decisions, give direction and increase speed. Truly inspiring and full of concrete actions on how to get yourself and your organization up to the speed that is needed to succeed."

Jan Erik Kjerpeseth, CEO, Sparebanken Vest

"Inspiring & easily applicable. It just works. I have used Ben's story and the tools & techniques he talks about in every business I have worked in. That's how good it is."

Jacqueline Lunardi, HRD, Moss Bros

"Will it make the boat go faster? It's a simple question and goes to the heart of the matter – stay focused on what you're really going for. This book by a supreme athlete - but also a real team player - can show you how. Ben is a naturally modest man but what he has to say has the authority that comes from supreme success. Listen up!"

Ian McDermott, Founder, International Teaching Seminars

"As someone who has spent many years doing research on human resource management and related matters, I have developed a healthy scepticism about much corporate coaching. However, this book is a very pleasant surprise. Written in a totally unpretentious manner, it provides an excellent guidebook for individuals concerned to control and direct their own lives and careers."

Professor Ken Mayhew, Emeritus Professor of Education and Economic Performance University of Oxford; Emeritus Fellow of Pembroke College, Oxford; Extraordinary Professor, Maastricht University

"Easy to read, easy to apply. We've been using these strategies as a leadership team and not only are they helping us to develop as a team, but they are also helping us to transform our business."

Andrew Mindenhall, CEO, Agilisys

"Ben has captured in vivid detail what it took for him, as an individual and as a team member, to win an Olympic Gold medal. The commitment required is immense and so the motivation, focus and belief must be very strong to get to the finishing line and reach this pinnacle of success. I love the way the highs and lows of Ben's personal journey are told in bite size chunks with valuable lessons for achieving in life and at work work drawn out at each stage. There is so much more to this book than I expected. Once read, I am sure you will want to refer back to it many times more."

Liz Nicholl CBE. Former CEO of UK Sport

"This book is an excellent repository of tools , techniques & approaches that are all about people being able to bring out the very, very best in themselves, irrespective of who they are or what they do – what makes it work for me is that these have been developed and put to real use in the context of Ben's great achievement in Sydney, where he & his fellow Olympians did indeed bring out the very, very best in themselves. I have seen Ben speak many times, he brings these things to life in a very personal & compelling fashion."

David Owen, Chairman, Deloitte CIS

"These strategies are changing the life chances for pupils in deprived areas of South Wales."

Justin O'Sullivan, Head teacher, Cardinal Newman School

"Bold, ballsy and brilliant! Whatever your circumstances, this book will help you perform to your potential. I recommend this book to anyone who has a dream."

Kate Pocock (nee Allenby), Olympic bronze medallist, modern pentathlon

"This book is a wonderfully inspiring read, essentially showing that there is rarely, if ever, a shortcut to success. Ben & Harriet clearly lay out the strategies, tactics and ways of working that can be taken from the world of the Olympics and applied to that of business in order to greatly increase levels of performance and the chances of achieving success."

Nick Powell, President EMEA & Asia Pacific, Univar Solutions

"Success is no accident! It's based on hard work, perseverance, continuous learning, dedication, sometimes even the readiness to make sacrifices, but most of all it is driven by loving what you are doing. Harriet inspired us to focus on what is important for our success and gave us simple ingredients to help reach our goals."

Tobias Ragge, CEO, HRS Group

"An invaluable compass for business and life"

Kate Richardson-Walsh OBE, Olympic gold medallist and GB team captain, hockey

"An inspiring story that will motivate any budding athlete. The passion, tears and laughter of training in extreme endeavours jumps out."

Sir John Spurling KCVO, OBE; Chairman of the London Marathon

"Only a very few get to wear an Olympic gold medal around their neck. It takes a tremendous amount of training and perseverance. In "Will It Make The Boat Go Faster?" you'll learn how Ben Hunt-Davis motivated himself to gold. But the real bonus in this book are the many tips presented in small bites that can help you set and stay focused on goals that are meaningful in your life. This book can help you overcome obstacles and achieve that crazy, realistic dream."

Steven J. Stein, co-author of The EQ Edge: Emotional Intelligence and Your Success

"Ben Hunt Davis' book tells the story of how his boat crew transformed themselves from also-rans to gold medal winners. But this isn't just a manual for an Olympic hopeful, it provides solid lessons on how to improve performance whether you are charting the choppy waters of an Olympic lake or planning a critical business project. Buy it for all your staff!"

Dr Richard Ward, Chairman, Ardonagh Speciality;
Former Chief Executive of Lloyd's of London

"An inspiring journey, thoughtfully translated into practical, everyday lessons that can be applied in virtually any situation. The book makes the point again and again that ordinary people can achieve truly extraordinary things."

Helen Weir CBE, Non-Executive Director at: JUST EAT, Superdry RFU, GEMS Education; former CFO, Marks and Spencer

"'Will it make the boat go faster?' has become a well-known catchphrase across Team GB to get athletes thinking about their performance differently. How to perform at the highest level when it really matters, when you have just one chance. This book is easy to read and easy to apply to your daily life. Packed full of game-changing strategies."

Amy Williams MBE, Olympic gold medallist, skeleton

"This book captures the essence of what it takes to motivate individuals, teams and organisations to achieve extraordinary results. These techniques apply both on and off the pitch, whether working on yourself or with others."

Sir Clive Woodward. England's Rugby World Cup winning coach 2003

WILL IT MAKE THE BOAT GO FASTER?

Olympic-Winning Strategies for Everyday Success

Ben Hunt-Davis & Harriet Beveridge

Second edition
First edition published in 2011

Matador
9 Priory Business Park,
Wistow Road, Kibworth Beauchamp,
Leicestershire. LE8 0RX
Tel: 0116 279 2299
Email: books@troubador.co.uk
Web: www.troubador.co.uk/matador
Twitter: @matadorbooks

ISBN 978 183859 296 7

British Library Cataloguing in Publication Data.
A catalogue record for this book is available from the British Library.

Printed and bound in the UK by TJ Books Ltd, Padstow, Cornwall
Typeset in 11pt Minion Pro by Troubador Publishing Ltd, Leicester, UK

Matador is an imprint of Troubador Publishing Ltd

For Harry

In memory of a fantastic coach and an amazing guy

A donation of 10% of profits from this book will go to Maggie's Cancer Caring Centres (SC024414). In each of their beautiful cancer support centres, Maggie's provide a free, professional, evidence-based programme of cancer support for anyone affected by any kind of cancer, at any point in their treatment or diagnosis. You can find out more about Maggie's at:

www.maggiescentres.org

CONTENTS

Contents

Ben Hunt-Davis is a normal guy.

He's also an Olympic Gold Medallist.

How did he and his crew succeed?

By following some simple techniques that all of us can easily apply in our everyday lives.

Here's how…

INTRODUCTION

Why buy this book?

Whatever journey you are on, we sincerely hope these tried and tested strategies help your 'boat go faster.' We first wrote *Will It Make The Boat Go Faster?* to share Olympic-winning strategies which anyone could apply, in any walk of life, to get their own 'gold medals'. Since the first edition, we've been chuffed beyond measure to hear countless stories of how people have used the ideas: From the head teacher in a deprived area, raising pupils' attainment, to the engineering company saving £50 million. From the lady who got back into running for the first time in decades, to the entrepreneurs who started their own businesses, the netball team who won their league, the police officer who secured promotion and the leadership teams implementing compelling goals.

How did it all come about?

I first met Ben Hunt-Davis when we joined the same company at the same time. I'm ashamed to say I was annoyed that he joined – I really didn't see the relevance of him sitting down and paddling a bit faster than his competitors, to me and my world, or our corporate clients.

But the more I heard, the more fascinated I got. Ben told a compelling story about a pretty mediocre team in 1998, who transformed to become Olympic Gold Medallists two years later. And Ben wasn't a psycho either. Put aside the fact that he is a tad on the tall side and you'd never guess he was a sportsman, let alone a smartie-pants Olympic gold medallist. I'd assumed that to be the best in the world you'd have to be superhuman, arrogant, obsessive. To my delight, Ben proved to be a good laugh, he makes mistakes, he can be shy, lazy, an idiot, lose his temper … in other words a pretty straightforward, normal guy. That piqued my interest. How could an ordinary person get extraordinary results? What secrets could I steal from his experiences to get more out of *my* life. Thanks to the tips in this book I have mastered press ups (I am *not* sporty), taken three stand-up comedy shows to the Edinburgh Fringe, written a handful of books, and hopefully been a less than completely rubbish parent. Sorry I was such a sceptical prat when we first met, Ben.

How this book works

Each chapter is divided into two parts. Firstly, there is a narrative bit. This is where Ben recounts episodes on the eight's journey to Gold. Ben has an uncanny knack for making you feel as if you are there in the boat with him, experiencing what it's like to be part of the Olympic team. Memory is a slippery eel, but we've done all we can to check that Ben has remembered things correctly.

Secondly, there is a coaching bit. This is where I analyse how and why the crew did what they did. These sections are packed with step-by-step, practical advice and real life examples. We've stuck to what the crew actually did, not what they ought to have done! It's a warts-

and-all account, complete with questionable grammar. There are no theoretical musings here, it's all been road tested.

It's not an exhaustive description. Our aim with each topic is to pick out key points that made the biggest difference and are easy to transfer to different context. The chapters also unashamedly intertwine – belief, influence habits, habits influence beliefs. Life is messy…

Get in touch

We'd love to hear from you. If you want to get in touch with Ben directly, go to benhd@willitmaketheboatgofaster.com or follow him on twitter at @OlympianBen. I'm at harrietbeveridge.com or @coach_and_comic.

The performance consultancy

The book has spawned a company of the same name. It helps organisations create their own 'crazy goals' and turn them into reality. We bring to life all the Olympic-winning strategies outlined here, so that everyone from the boardroom to the shop floor can raise their game. Head to willitmaketheboatgofaster.com to find out more, and to sign up for our regular 'performance insights' articles.

Harriet Beveridge

CHAPTER 1

LAYERED GOALS

The Morning of the Men's Eight Rowing Final

Layered Goals: Will it make the boat go faster?

The Morning of the Men's Eight Rowing Final

Sydney Olympics 24th Sept 2000

It was 5 a.m., but I was alert as soon as the alarm went off; I knew exactly where I was and I knew exactly what I had to do: "Today's going to be a good day, because I am going to make it a good day," I told myself. If ever there was a day when it had to count, it was today.

Today was the day when Steve, Fred, Kieran, Luka, Louis, Simon, Andrew and myself, coxed by Rowley and coached by Martin and Harry, were going to win the Olympic Gold for Great Britain in the men's coxed eight (8+) rowing event.

The 8+ boat is the biggest, fastest boat in the rowing world. It is 57 feet long and its widest point is just over two feet. It achieves maximum speeds of about seven metres per second. It is fast enough to water ski behind – for a bit!

Most of the big rowing countries put their best people in the 8+: Russia, Romania, Holland, Germany, USA, Croatia. For the 2000 Sydney Olympics – as in most years – GB's selection was done differently. The top four guys went in the coxless four (4-); Redgrave, Cracknell, Pinsent and Foster. The next two guys went in the coxless pair (2-),

Greg Searle and Ed Coode. Those of us left over went into the 8+. We were the guys who weren't good enough to win. Apparently.

The previous ten years had been full of so much disappointment; I'd lost race after race. In ten years of racing I'd only won two proper international Regattas. I'd come 6th and 8th at the previous two Olympics, I'd finished 5th, 8th, 6th, 5th, 7th at the World Championships I'd competed in. All around me my friends were winning medals and the only thing that kept me going was the goal; the dream of Olympic gold.

Every year had finished in bitter disappointment, or had done until the previous year. For the last 24 months we'd been on a roll with a Silver medal at the World Championships 13 months before and we'd won the last two World Cup Regattas. Things were different now; today was going to be a good day.

Luka (my roommate) and I both rolled to sit on the edge of our extra long beds; we gave each other a knowing look. I went to shave. On normal training days I couldn't be bothered and only shaved when I was seeing my girlfriend (now wife) Isabella or when I was racing. I got dressed, put my Olympic security ID pass around my neck and left the room. By now most of the other boys were in the hall of the flat.

We made our way down the stairs. We didn't have to say anything, we all just knew. We knew what we had to do. There were looks and nods, even the odd hand on an arm or shoulder. At the bottom of the two flights of stairs we waited for the last couple of people before leaving the block of flats, out into the cold, dark Australian pre-dawn.

As the ten of us made our way up the slight incline towards the dining hall we must have looked like some kind of oversized gang with a

Pygmy body guard, the eight rowers and Martin, our coach, with an average height of 6'4", and Rowley the cox at just 5'9" in the middle of the group. Our blue fleecy Team GB tracksuits looked like ridiculous pyjamas, but they did keep us warm in the crisp air.

A few minutes later we entered the vast dining hall, a tent the size of three football pitches. I swapped my bag for a ticket with one of the volunteers who ran the incredibly efficient 24 hour bag drop service. At peak times they had to deal with more than 2,500 bags, of which there would be around 300 identical Aussie or American bags and 200 plus GB bags – a challenging task to keep track of them all.

I chose a bowl of cereal, some toast and a banana, knowing it wouldn't stay down very long, but also knowing that I needed something inside me. We sat at the same, black polythene-covered table that we sat at for every meal.

There was so much I'd learnt in the last decade – and I had certainly learnt the hard way about Olympic dining halls. At my first Olympics – in July 1992 in Barcelona – I remember getting an escalator down into a converted underground car park. There was a flashing sign saying that there were 2,500 people in there at the time. I went and got a tray of food, then wandered around looking for my teammates. It was a bit like the first day at a new school with that feeling of nerves and uncertainty, desperately looking for your mates to sit with – but on a much larger scale. For thirty minutes I walked and walked scanning faces. I saw some GB tracksuits, but I didn't recognise one single face. Eventually I sat at the end of a table occupied by Russians and I ate my cold lunch as quickly as I could; I guess that's what happened before mobile phones.

That morning was very different, we knew exactly where we were going and what we were doing. Our attention was totally focused on the goal. I gathered up my breakfast and made my way to 'our' table. It was always good to get something in your stomach the morning of a race, but the important food – the pile of pasta to give me the energy I needed – I'd had the night before.

The nine of us sat in a tense, angry silence all thinking the same thing. I wanted to win so much it hurt. I hadn't been counting but there were probably only 50 nights out of the previous ten years when I hadn't dreamed about it. We had to make it happen. We had to show those bastards who was in charge, whose lake it was. We'd let ourselves down in the heat and we weren't going to make the same mistake again. We'd show them.

Thoughts raced through my head. We'd show them, but would we be good enough? I knew we were, but could we produce the goods when it really counted? Would I hurt myself as much as I needed to? Was I brave enough to keep going when all went black? Would I keep my head straight and back strong? Would I...

"All right, boys?" My thoughts were shattered. We'd been joined by a member of the Judo team. A 54 kilo Glaswegian Judo player who we'd got to know at the Gold Coast training camp the week before. He plonked himself down in our group. He'd been knocked out a few days earlier and his reason for having breakfast at 5 a.m. was very different to ours. He had a couple of Big Macs, he stank of booze and cigarettes; he immediately started to tell us about the amazing night he'd just come back from. It had obviously been a cracker.

He was not the company we'd been expecting or wanting for breakfast, but he did break the tension and made us finish our food quickly so we could get out of there.

We picked up our bags and headed out into the dark. We made our way down the gentle slope, it was already happening. I'd only finished my breakfast five minutes before, I tried to fight it, who was I kidding? I broke off the pavement and ran into the bushes beside the path. The boys took the piss out of me about being pregnant. I was sick most mornings, and this morning was no different. I puked into the wood chippings around the bushes. By the time I'd finished the rest of the boys were passing through the airport-style security area.

I wondered if, next time I was here, my medal would set off the metal detectors. Would I be an Olympic champion? I'd thought the same thing as I left the flat and as I left the dining hall. How good would it feel to come back to the Village as an Olympic Champion?

The other side of the security point was the Olympic bus station with buses going to every Olympic venue, athletes and spectator areas. As I boarded our bus my stomach was screwing into a tight ball again, I pushed off the bus just in time. As I reached the pavement I was bent double heaving – a bit more breakfast in the gutter. As I got back on the bus a few of the guys smiled at me and commented that I must be ready and up for it.

The 50-minute air-conditioned bus ride gave us time to think and to visualise the race. The bus wasn't that full so we didn't all have to cram ourselves into the seats designed for six year olds. My mind was on the race, vaguely aware of the journey as we left the Olympic park area.

Ten years of training – onto the motorway;
Bloody two km rowing machine tests – picking up speed on the motorway;
They'd beaten us at Henley – past industrial units on the right;
How many weddings missed? – speeding along the motorway;
How hard would I go? – past the equestrian centre;
How much would I hurt myself? – still on the motorway;
Five strokes long and then 30 as hard as we could – coming off the motorway;
Another five and 30 strokes – through Penrith, lawns, eucalyptus trees;
All they had to do was turn up!!!! – more light in the sky;
We'd show the bastards – getting closer to the lake;
Chants of 'Aussie Aussie Aussie' – a roundabout with a sculpture on it; I couldn't let the other boys down – past the canoe course;
How would Isabella get here, had she had a good party last night? – the entrance to the lake;
Our Lake, this was our turf, we were going to go out and dominate the lake.

What we had to do was simple, it wasn't about the Olympics. Of course, that was our dream, but all we had to do was win a race, beat people we'd beaten before and to do that we had to focus on performance, then the result would take care of itself. Simply build momentum, one stroke at a time. All we had to do was to keep making the boat go faster.

We got off the bus tense, focused and angry. The hair stood up on the back of my neck as I looked up the lake. There were flag poles beside me encircling the bottom of the lake and in front, to the right, was the lake; our lake, stretching away into the dawn light. Lines of dead-straight buoys dissected the lake into six racing lanes and two spare lanes. The start was 2,000 metres away. We would dominate the lake. It would be ours.

We made our way towards the British tent. The stink of the Portaloos, that disgusting chemical stench, washed over me and I doubled up retching again. Someone gave me a slap of solidarity on my back.

There was not much chatting as we got ready to go out on the water, but the air was heavy with anticipation. Harry and Martin gave us a short briefing. We were told to do one lap of the lake, a couple of starts, we were to paddle with real purpose and dominate the lake.

On the command, we lifted the boat above our heads, lowered it into the water, picked up our oars from the middle of the pontoon, got into the boat and pushed off.

It continued to get brighter and warmer as we did our lap of the lake. As we rowed past the grandstand we didn't have the same experience as the day before when the two thirds full grandstand had chanted 'Aussie Aussie Aussie' at us as we did our last practice sprint for the line.

We came off the water agreeing that it had been a typical pre-race session. It had been tense, nervous and rushed. When we went on the water later we would be more relaxed and looser. We had managed to get the tension and jitters out of our system.

90 minutes to kill before we could race. What did I do in those 90 minutes? I can't remember! Stretching, the rowing machines, wandering around, going to the lavatory every ten minutes, running through every scenario.

We now knew what the weather would be like; warm, dry, no wind, just as it had been all week. I didn't have to run through wet or windy scenarios anymore, I could just concentrate on how we were going to row our race. I'm not sure if the 90 minutes passed in a flash or dragged like a couple years. There were the feelings of excitement, longing to get out there and show how fast we were, longing to punish the people who made us do all the training. If the Aussies, Americans, Romanians, Russians, and Italians hadn't wanted to win I would not have had to hurt myself so much. There were the moments of sheer terror. Would I be brave enough to really hurt myself? Would I let the other boys down? Would I let Martin and Harry down? Would I lose my nerve, and waste four years of my life?

Then there was the rage, the aggression and the anger and my God I was angry. How had we let ourselves down in the heat? Rowing like shit. We'd let the Aussies wipe the floor with us. We'd taken our eye off the ball. My God I was angry, so angry, so aggressive. I was ready to lamp anyone who looked at me the wrong way.

Moments of strength, we were the best crew. We had beaten everyone other than the US and today we would beat them. We were stronger than previous GB eights. We were getting better, day in, day out. Our trajectory was set and we would win. We were here because we were the best for the job, each one a key part of the best crew in the world.

As 9.30 approached everybody got into their racing kit: blue all-in-one rowing suits, a last bit of stretching and bouncing around. Lots of strong eye contact with each other, pats and slaps on the back.

At 9.30 Martin came into the tent with Harry and said, "Let's go." This was it. We were at the end of the journey and what a journey it had been. We'd learnt so much. We were completely different people to who we'd been a few years before.

We left the tent and stood by the lake for our last briefing. There were the nine of us in the crew, plus Martin McElroy our coach, Harry Mahon our assistant coach, Chris Shambrook our Sports Psychologist and Jürgen Gröbler the British Chief Coach. All our focus was on what Martin was saying – his last pearls of wisdom before we raced.

I have no idea what Martin said to us. I went into one of my moments of panic, but his last words woke me up again:

"What are we going to do, Kieran?"

"We're going to f***ing make it happen."

Yes, that was it. We had to make it happen. The aggression, and anger and rage were back. A few boys gave me a slap and eyeballed me. Our eyes bored into each other. This was it, today was going to be a good day because we were going to f***ing make it a good day. The anger, the passion flared red hot. We needed cold clinical minds and skip-fulls of passion and desire.

We carried our boat down to the pontoon, rolled it over our heads and lowered it into the water. This was it. This is what we'd been waiting for. This is what we had been working towards.

We lowered our bums onto the black carbon fibre seats. Andrew made sure he was Velcroed onto his seat so he wouldn't lose contact with it. Our feet went into the trainers that were bolted into the boat.

We did up the three Velcro straps on each shoe, tightened the oars in the gates and we put a little water on the newly brushed wooden laminate handles to make sure they had the right grip. We called down the boat when we were ready… and we were off.

As we pushed off the pontoon I stole a glance back at Harry and Martin. They were standing shoulder to shoulder on top of the small grassy bank just to the right of the pontoon we had pushed off. They had that look on their faces – that look of complete helplessness. I don't really know how to describe it. Martin had poured four years of his soul into this project, he hadn't sweated as we had, he hadn't lifted weights or pulled oar handles as we had, but he had got us together. He'd forced us, helped us, cajoled us to change, to develop, to improve, to learn. Martin had been the co-ordinator, the brains, the bastard who at times we hated, at times we tolerated, but most of the time we had massive respect for. He had fought all the political battles and pulled together the support that had made it all possible, he had resigned twice and there he was now with that look on his face of complete helplessness because now there was nothing he could do to make it happen.

Harry stood beside him. Harry. Harry was dying of cancer. In '97, Harry had been diagnosed and operated on; he'd been given months. In those three and a half years Harry had run his first marathon. He'd coached Greg Searle to a Bronze medal in the single sculls at the World Champs and he had started coaching us.

For two years he'd helped and guided Martin, he'd been the steadying hand and Martin's sounding board. Where Martin was moody and openly passionate, Harry was calming and steady. Harry on the other hand couldn't organise a piss up in a brewery, he couldn't stick to a certain training programme, but he was a technical genius.

Harry had coached crews to be World Champions. He'd coached a crew to an Olympic Silver, but not to Gold. This was his last chance. For Harry, time was running out. It seemed unlikely that he would live to see another Games; he didn't, he died in May 2001.

I looked at the two of them, standing there. They had done their job, now it was up to us to make their dreams come true.

Our warm-up was brilliant. We had got the pre-race nerves out of our system. The warm-up felt strong, pretty relaxed and fast; really fast as we ate up the metres of water in the practice area of the lake. The last burst at 44 strokes a minute and the last start at 50 odd strokes a minute were amazing, the boat simply skimmed across the water. We were going to dominate this lake; it was ours.

The expectation and the energy of the crowds was incredible; we could actually feel it. The grandstand almost had a heat haze radiating from it. It was electric. On the other side of the soon-to-be-furrowed lake was a smaller grandstand, which appeared to be predominantly red with the shirts of British supporters. There was a massive TV screen and a huge press enclosure on the grass, with loads of camera lenses glinting in the sun. I couldn't see the flags, I couldn't hear the anthems, but I could feel the energy from down there. It was an amphitheatre waiting for the show.

Gladiator had been at the cinema all summer and we were going into the 'arena' to lay down everything we had. We'd vowed that if we had enough energy left to stand up and receive a silver medal, we'd never speak to each other again. It had to be Gold. The passion, the aggression, the anger inside me was incredible. I was willing to do whatever it took.

The final of the women's 8+ started. We let them race past us and we paddled down to the start. We rowed into lane two and slowly spun our boat around until it was pointing at the finish line 2,000 metres away and we were looking at the start pontoon.

Under Rowley's instructions we slowly pushed the boat backwards until the boy lying on the start pontoon had the stern of our boat in his hands. Andrew gently manoeuvred the bows until they were in the yellow plastic boot that held them straight and level.

After years of work we were on the start. We were ready.

Layered Goals: Will it make the boat go faster?

Ben: "Being really clear on what we wanted to achieve meant we could always figure out the way ahead by asking, 'Will it make the boat go faster?'"

Chapter summary

We are all heading somewhere whether we like it or not, so create enthralling goals to achieve the kind of happy, successful life you want.

1. Appreciate that clear goals are really useful
1a Have a sense of achievement
1b Focus your time and energy
1c Learn and grow

2. Know how to craft effective goals
Use a layered approach of:
2a Crazy goal
2b Concrete layer
2c Control layer
2d Everyday layer

Ben had an extreme, extraordinary goal. He could only achieve it at 10.30 a.m. on 24th September 2000 and he had to nail it in less than five and a half minutes. How can this extreme experience help us?

The first question it throws up is should we bother having goals? Why not just take life as it comes and stop to smell the roses?

Even when we do something specific, why get all macho and set targets? For example, I ran the London Marathon a few years ago and the question I got asked a million times was, "what was your time?" as if that was the only thing that mattered. When I complained about this to Ben he just countered,

"So your goal wasn't a particular time then, was it something else?"

That made me think. Why did I run the marathon? For me, running was all about proving to myself I could do something I'd find really tough (I am not sporty) and raising money in memory of a friend.

I was still sceptical about goal-setting, though. Wasn't it a bit over-egged? For example, isn't turning 'be happy' into a goal a bit clinical? The dictionary definition of a goal is the 'object of effort, destination'. So stripping it back to its core, a goal is simply where you are going.

This definition makes two things clear:

- Firstly, we're all heading in some direction. For example, someone who smokes 40 a day has a likely 'goal' of a hospital bed. So surely it's useful to think about what goals we want rather than ending up somewhere we don't want to be?

- Secondly, the term goal sounds like something that needs lots of planning and effort, but if it is simply 'where we are going' then it could be round the corner or across the globe. Our goals could take minutes or months to achieve. They might be never-ending – in the same way that you could keep heading west and keep on walking, you might have a goal about wanting to be cheerful and resourceful, which you never cross off your list. Sometimes it's a few one-off actions which will take us to our goal, sometimes it's about embedding ongoing habits. Throughout this book we'll look at both.

Ben: "A goal might be to earn £40k a year or to have a good day, or to have a happy marriage, or to sell more widgets, or to swim the channel. Whatever it is, if we are aware of what we want then it is much easier to work towards achieving it."

Yes, Ben's goal was unusually singular and extreme, but that makes it a very useful comparison to challenge ourselves with. How transformative might it be if we cut through the mountains of 'stuff' we are bombarded with every day and focus on our truly important goals? How many times do we get to a big birthday and think, 'How the heck did I get here?' or to the end of a working week and think 'Yet again I've got caught up in fire-fighting!' rather than progressing as we'd hoped? There are two key strategies from the rowing eight's Olympic journey that we can use in our everyday lives to help make them happier and easier:

1. Appreciate that clear goals are really useful
2. Know how to craft effective goals.

1. Appreciate that clear goals are really useful

The stronger our belief in goals, the more likely we are to get off our backsides and build them, so let's look at why goals are so incredibly useful in everyday life. There are three core benefits:

1a Goals give you a sense of achievement

We are more likely to achieve things if we set ourselves goals. For example, in our consulting work we regularly see corporate teams where individuals who have clear goals consistently outperform those who don't. With achievement comes an incredible sense of pride.

What have you done recently that's made you proud?

- Brought in a project on time and budget?
- Helped a team member get promoted?
- Learnt to play a musical instrument?

What have you done that's given you a buzz?

- Been on a superb night out?
- Negotiated an awesome deal?
- Given a presentation in front of a high-stakes audience?

Whatever the experiences were, wouldn't it be good to enjoy those feelings again? Sadly, most people wait for the experiences to happen to them – they rely on chance – which is heart-breaking, because it is so easy to set goals in order to feel that sense of achievement more often, more deeply.

> I was coaching a woman recently who had written down some goals for the year. She'd divided it into categories such as 'career', 'kids', 'myself', 'husband', 'house'... The 'kids' category had things like 'Go swimming with them once a fortnight', 'Go to Legoland this summer'. There was nothing outlandish or 'big' on there – nothing like winning a gold medal! But can you imagine how fantastic her year was going to be? Compare that with the majority of us who drift along going, "Oh, another year's gone by, how did that happen?"

Great goals aren't about being on a human-hamster wheel, getting through chores. Why? Because great goals are an expression of what is fundamentally important to us. We all have values, things we hold dear. What is on your list? Making a difference? Friendship? Creativity? Goals can translate these into something tangible in the world, and that is richly rewarding.

1b Goals focus your time and energy

When we have a clear goal it acts like a magnet drawing us forwards. For example: getting up at 5 a.m. to drive to a sales meeting we can't be bothered about is a major pain in the backside, but getting up at 5 a.m. to hit a sales target and earn an impressive bonus is a different matter.

I still can't believe I managed to run without stopping for 4 hours 35 minutes (there you go, happy now?!) to cross the finish line in the London Marathon. I am not a natural athlete – I broke a hurdle at school because I ran through it not over it – but I had a goal to raise £50k for Cancer Research and that goal kept me going.

Ben: "People often ask me if the early mornings were really hard and I have to say not really, because I got out of bed knowing what I wanted to do and why I wanted to do it. The same is true today – when I set my alarm I need to know exactly what I'm going to do tomorrow – what my specific goal is – because if I just think I have loads of stuff to do I will hit snooze."

If we haven't got a goal we are much more likely to sink into horrid negativity. Have you come across the saying, 'the devil makes work for idle hands'? Many years ago, Ben and I helped a large retail company to up their game. The shop staff had plenty of negative things vying for their attention:

- The stroppy customer who was having a bad day and being vile
- The piped music that was on its eighteenth loop
- The Energy Vampire colleague who whinged on and on and on about how the job sucked.

It's almost impossible not to focus on these negative distractions, because the mind isn't very good at not thinking. Try it now – don't, whatever you do, think about a purple hedgehog.

Have you managed it? Is your mind completely clear of purple hedgehogs?

It's really hard unless you've got something else to take its place. Replace that purple hedgehog with an orange armadillo and you've got a fighting chance, similarly if you've got a goal of earning £100 commission, it's much easier to tune out the stroppy customer, the piped music and your whinging colleague.

Ask someone 'how are you?' and a typical response is 'really busy!'. How often do we get overwhelmed with what's in front of us? Goals help us *choose* where to focus our energy and attention. There's a massive difference between a conscious choice and drifting.

Because the Olympic crew were so clear on their goal, simply asking "Will it make the boat go faster?" helped them figure out what to do when they felt uncertain, resolve differences when the team fell out and bounce back from difficult times. It's a question you'll find recurring in many of the chapters ahead.

1c Goals help you to learn and grow

Research suggests that we tend to regret what we haven't done much more than what we have done – even if we screwed up in doing it. The psychologist Richard Wiseman suggests this may be because our imagination runs riot about the goals we didn't set and go for – we keep thinking 'if only' and imagine the best possible outcome that might have happened. There's a tendency to create a fairy-tale land in our heads where frolicking unicorns bring us success and champagne by the poolside.

On the other hand, when we take action, we are exploring the actual territory and learning from the challenges we encounter in the process.

Did you ever have a goal of passing your driving test? Did you learn more than just how to drive a car in the process? Maybe it was about the value of money – having to pay for expensive lessons – maybe it was around time keeping – having to fit the lessons into your busy schedule – but isn't it fair to say you got more out of the experience than just a licence?

Ben: "Being in the Olympic crew I learnt a huge amount about mental toughness, resilience, and bouncebackability which has stood me in very good stead for – basically – everything else in my life! When I became a corporate coach in 2001, one of the first training sessions I ever ran was so bad the client said they never wanted to see me again. Not great, but I'd had worse disasters in my rowing career and went on to get gold, so it was much easier to dust myself off and move on – and make sure I really learnt from the setback."

It's incredibly useful to get clear on our goals, to give ourselves some time and ask, "What's important to me? What do I want to be, do and have?" Why not grab five minutes and write some ideas down now? Let your imagination run riot – don't worry about refining your thoughts or editing your thinking, there's plenty of time for that later.

2. Know how to craft effective goals

As well as appreciating the value of goals, the other big learning the crew had was around how to formulate them. The crew discovered that the key to a 'good' goal is that it is layered: there is the crazy goal, then the concrete layer, the control layer and finally the everyday layer.

Spoiler alert! This is an art, not a science. The only point of having layers is to create alignment from the big hairy, scary, exciting crazy goal down to what we need to do on a daily basis. Layering takes away the overwhelm and makes it doable, it challenges the faffing and helps you prioritise and take action. Please, please, pretty please with sugar on top, follow the *principles* described in the following sections – without getting het up about the dictionary definitions of one layer versus another.

2a The Crazy Goal

Ben: "For me to win gold at the Olympics was a crazy goal. There was no way I could do that. Or running my own business – my parents were amazed when I set myself that goal."

Lots of people told Ben and the crew that they were crazy to attempt to win gold, so the crew spun this criticism round and started to refer to it fondly, proudly as their 'crazy goal'. A crazy goal is something that completes the sentence, 'Wouldn't it be amazing if…?' They are bold, extravagant goals, which fire our imagination and kindle our desire.

Does a crazy goal have to be *big*?

Ben: 'No, 'significant' is a better word. A crazy goal needs to have emotional attachment. For example, 'I want to have a good day' might not seem spectacular, but multiply it over weeks and months and it is huge."

This month alone I've supported people with crazy goals as diverse as 'have work/life balance', 'get fit', 'have happy kids', and 'be the best leader in my business'.

The only trouble with crazy goals is that they often seem stupid, naive or simply overwhelming so we never pursue them. We dismiss our dreams because we don't want to be silly.

> I remember a delegate on a leadership development programme who'd wanted to drive a hovercraft ever since he was a kid. He'd buried the desire in that bit of our brains we all have, marked 'don't be silly'. He decided why on earth not and after ten seconds on Google found a local course where he could achieve his ambition for the price of a birthday present.

The other problem with crazy goals is that you can't put them on your to-do list: Monday do laundry, Tuesday take car in for a service, Wednesday achieve work life balance. They are too big and they aren't measurable, so they never get done.

Businesses often have financial targets, but that's not enough to win hearts and minds. The company, Will It Make The Boat Go Faster?, helps a lot of organisations find their 'crazy'. For example, last year we ran a crazy goal workshop with a software company and they decided, 'wouldn't it be amazing if we keep customers and employees for life?'. Now, when you read that cold, you may well think, "Meh! Fluffy words!" but the magic lay in the context and conversations behind it – what it meant to the people involved. For the firm in question it was magnetically compelling. To paraphrase the CEO:

"I think we'd been stuck thinking that business was hard work, so wouldn't it be amazing if *100%* of customers *wanted* to work with us, year in, year out. Where our products and services are so good that they were *eager* to work with us. Wouldn't it be amazing if we were such a great place to work that our staff would love to stay?"

It was an exciting goal, and also one which would prioritise how everyone in the company focused their time and energy.

Which brings us neatly on to the next layer:

2b The Concrete Layer

We need to turn our crazy goals into something tangible. The concrete layer answers the question, 'how will I know when I've achieved my crazy goal?' For example, the crazy goal of 'keeping customers and employees for life' translated into concrete measures around employee and client turnover.

For the crew, they would know they'd achieved their goal when they had gold medals hanging round their necks. But because they could only achieve this goal on 24 September 2000 at 10.30 a.m., they decided to choose concrete goals they could achieve *before* the race, in order to be in with the best chance of success. For example, one of the crew's concrete goals was to row 2,000 metres in five minutes and eighteen seconds. This was faster than World Record pace, so it would give them a pretty good shot at winning gold.

Sometimes concrete measures are easy and obvious, but sometimes it's useful to think of a pragmatic proxy (remember, this is an art, not a science). For example, the crazy goal of 'achieve work/life balance' might translate into concrete goals such as 'spending x minutes of quality time with my kids every day' where quality is measured by a gut feel of 'marks out of ten'. You *could* do a comprehensive, daily, 360 feedback behavioural analysis with your kids. I just venture to suggest that this might possibly get in the way of actually spending quality time with them (unless, of course, this is the very definition of 'quality time' in your household… whatever floats your boat…).

The trouble about concrete goals is that they might be outside our control. For example, the water and weather conditions had an impact on how fast the crew could row. 'Spending quality time with the kids' suggests the kids have to be in a good mood and as any parent knows, that might be a bit of a challenge.

So, here's the next layer:

2c The Control Layer

This layer starts to answer the question, 'What's inside our control – what can we *do* to drive towards our crazy goal?' That can feel like a head-spinning question, so it's useful to start by thinking about the big buckets of stuff, the category areas. The crew's bucket areas were: physical ability, tactical, technical, equipment, mental attitude because they knew that working on these areas would help to make the boat go faster. The software company's were people, products and services, clients, delivery, brand, business controls. The work-life balance coachee I helped recently had things like workload, fitness, family time…

This means that the crazy goal is now translated into realistic chunks and you can put tangible targets in place for each one. Some of these targets are one-off projects – for example, the software company had a one-off project to implement a new IT system – but a lot of the items are ongoing: The crew had times they wanted to achieve on rowing machines, weights to lift on bench presses and habits to manage their moods… All working towards the same thing… all totally geared up to achieving the ultimate crazy goal of a gold medal.

The final layer is:

2d The Everyday Layer

This layer includes the actions needed to achieve the layers above. Again some things might be one-off actions and some might be ongoing habits.

Now we've reached a level where just as we might plan Monday: do laundry, Tuesday: take car in for a service, the crew could make the boat go faster by thinking in terms of Monday: do x bench presses in x minutes, strengthen the relationship with Y by chatting to them. Tuesday: achieve x metres per second over x metres, work on improving and positions.

The software company made sure every employee understood what that meant for their everyday roles. For example, for a customer service rep it meant making more calls (not emails!) and making them more consultative. For managers it meant making sure they walked the floor and recognised their staff's efforts on a daily basis, not just via a stale, high level performance review every 6 months.

The person dreaming of work life balance had some one-off actions like buying some bedtime story books, they also set regular everyday goals such as leaving the office at 6 p.m. three times a week, reading the kids bedtime stories at least four times a week, doing a meal planner and batch cooking on a Sunday night.

The power of layered goals

Each layer does a different job; each layer supports the others. The crazy layer is exciting, but it needs to be grounded in something concrete and something inside our control. Everyday goals are things we can put in the diary and improve incrementally day by day – but, on their own, they aren't massively motivational. For example, out of context, 'batch cooking and meal planning' sounds pretty dull, doesn't it? But if it's going to get us work/life balance then, suddenly, it's interesting. If one of the layers is missing, the whole structure could collapse. Without passion a goal becomes a chore, without specificity a goal is simply a pipe-dream.

Some of the goals on each layer are one-offs – to achieve your crazy goal of being a yoga teacher you'll need to get some qualifications – but many are ongoing habits. We'll keep exploring both types of activity throughout this book.

I was facilitating a boardroom session recently when one of the Directors sighed and said something like:

"It was easy for Ben. They had one goal, whereas I've got a dashboard of umpteen measures and a matrix structure with dotted reporting lines. In the real world it's incredibly complicated!"

Absolutely, I totally get it. And that's just work – throw in personal goals and family goals and it gets even more fun. But I'm still going to unashamedly throw the gauntlet down:

- If you are a CEO or department head reading this, has your organisation got a truly compelling, crazy goal which people can get excited about, and clear everyday actions for achieving it? Or just a bunch of irksome targets on a spreadsheet that don't really mean anything?
- If you have a personal project, like losing weight or getting fit, have you got really fired up about the big idea AND translated it into tangible, everyday actions?
- In your family, do you ever have conversations about what's important to you all, and what everyone wants to get out of the year ahead?

I hold my hand up and confess I've answered 'no' to every single one of these at some time or other and paid the price. I've moaned about people working in silos at work, I've wasted years dreaming big but not taking action, I've whinged that I've become a parenting taxi service with no life of my own... When a bit more clarity about the layers and conscious choice would have worked wonders.

How about you?

Conclusion

We can't help but have goals. Goals are just destinations and, whatever we're doing with our lives right now, our actions are taking us somewhere. Having *conscious* goals puts us in the driving seat to go for outcomes that we truly want and goals also give us all kinds of benefits, such as making it easier to enjoy the journey and giving ourselves the chance to grow. A layered approach to goal-setting helps create a rounded goal that is both motivating and practical.

By asking ourselves, 'Wouldn't it be amazing if…? What do I want to achieve? To be? To have? What is my definition of a happy, worthwhile life?' We can make sure we're heading in a great direction.

But how do we then achieve these goals?

- How do we keep motivated along the way?
- What do we need to actually do – what are the steps along the way?

- How do we deal with other people who might laugh at us, try and stop us?
- How do we deal with setbacks?
- …

That's what the rest of this book is all about. There are chapters devoted to all the key topics that Ben found crucial in achieving his goal and which we need to master to achieve what we want.

Have you ever wanted something and not quite followed through on it? The next chapter is all about how to stay motivated every step of the way…

CHAPTER 2
MOTIVATION

Christmas Eve

Motivation: What floats your boat?

Christmas Eve

A few years before the Olympics

Three days before Christmas Eve we'd had a long distance sculling time trial for everyone who wanted to get into the national team. We'd had to get up at the crack of dawn and drive up to Peterborough.

Some of the universities, Oxford Brookes, Oxford, Imperial, Cambridge and a few others had turned up in coxless pairs, but everyone else had to race in individual sculls. The smallest boat in the rowing world, 15 feet long and too narrow to get your arse in, so you sit on top of them, making them almost impossible to balance.

These were the hard races. There would be three or four of these trials every year. If you didn't do them, you didn't get in the team and you didn't race the rest of the world. If you didn't do them fast, you didn't get in the team and you didn't race the rest of the world.

No one watched, no one pushed you on, no one else cared. The weather was usually awful. They were grim. It was all about how much each one of us wanted to be in the National Team; it was the first step for everyone who wanted to be an Olympic Champion.

I just had to ask myself, "What floats your boat?" to remind myself why I was putting myself through all this pain and tedium. For some sessions it is easy to switch off the pain and just go for it, but some sessions are going to hurt. Hurting yourself for no reason is pointless, but I knew what was important to me:

I was desperate to prove that I could be good at something, to show everyone who doubted me that they were wrong. I wanted to be as good as I could be (as opposed to the 'he might aspire to mediocrity' a teacher had once written in a school report). I wanted to be physically tough. I wanted respect. I wanted my family to be proud. These were my core motivators, driving me forwards.

As it got light, we invaded the rowing club's changing rooms and formed queues that snaked to the toilets. We got into our boats and sculled two kilometres up the canal/river/ditch – whatever it was – to where we would, eventually, finish. We kept going, five kilometres more, to get to the starting point. We sorted ourselves into the order dictated by the numbers pinned to our backs and waited on the windswept water until it was our turn to race the five kilometres back to the finish line.

The only clues to tell you how far you'd gone down the course were a set of overhead power lines at one point, a fence that came down to the river at another point and a very slight kink in the otherwise dead straight, featureless landscape. Then it was back to the boathouse, have a bite to eat and do the same thing again in the afternoon.

From the outside it must have been a bizarre scene, a hundred or so boats, one behind the other chasing each other up the choppy water. Ungroomed oarsmen dressed in various types and ages of sports kits with agony on their faces battling against wind and waves under a low, fast-moving grey sky.

At the finish line a bundle of coaches with stop watches shouted at their rower to keep pushing to the finish. As the oarsmen approached, they looked like well-disciplined human machines, but as soon as they crossed the line they collapsed – revealing just how hard they'd been working.

The trials had been OK. I'd beaten the people I wanted to beat. I was looking forward to being able to get away for Christmas, back to my parents' house in Wiltshire. It wasn't exactly a holiday, as I had to get stuck into my 'homework', one or two sessions a day of running, or on the rowing machine – as laid out in my training programme. This week 'off' would get me ready to move on and strengthen my position in the team. The following year was going to be a better year, I'd go faster and that would start now.

Before I could go home I had to do my normal day's training. As it was Christmas Eve we had our 'Turkey Sculls' race at the club. Everyone in the club did the three and a half km time trial race in single sculls and the prize was supposed to be a turkey, although no one ever got one. It was just for fun. At the end of the day it was just another training session, but making it into a competition for a non-existent turkey made it more of a laugh and helped to build our competitive spirit.

The night before had been our Christmas party; I have no recollection of the evening. I woke up on the floor of our living room wearing what I'd been wearing the night before with an imprint of the rush-matting flooring on my face. I've no idea how I woke up, it was just lucky that I did. I had to 'flick the switch', get up and get on with it.

I forced down my usual eight Weetabix and my usual pint of Tesco value coffee. If I didn't get my caffeine intake I couldn't stay awake long enough to make the 40-minute drive to Henley. There had been a couple of occasions when I'd pulled over at one of the lay-bys to have a five-minute cat nap and woken up eight hours later. Jürgen, our coach at the time, had not been happy.

This Christmas Eve I arrived without any extended stops and, with plenty of piss-taking about how awful I looked, got ready for the race.

The warm-up was ridiculously painful, but the race was brilliant, I think the fact that I couldn't feel anything helped. According to the times, at halfway three of us were dead level, then my liquid carb-loading from the night before kicked in and I won it. It was very rare that I beat Redgrave at anything other than eating, but this was one of those times. The best cure for a hangover is definitely to get up and do some training.

After our second breakfast we did another session and then it was time to head for Wiltshire. I loaded a rowing machine into the back of my tired old white Rover 214, which my brother described as a skip on wheels. My tactic for staying awake in the car was to eat, either four- or five-decker sandwiches of white sliced bread or a white farmhouse loaf from the baker in Henley. Consequently, my car was knee-deep in crumbs and bread bags.

I drove back to Oxford, nipped into the city centre to do my Christmas shopping, got home, threw some clothes in a bag, got back in the car and it didn't start. This wasn't unusual, I'd become quite good at pushing it down the street to jump start it; before long I was on my way.

I was going home for Christmas. I was looking forward to seeing my family. I was looking forward to my training; I needed to get fitter and stronger. I had more trials in the New Year so I had to keep it all going, but I knew that it would be more relaxed and it would just be nice to be at home.

Christmas Day was supposed to be a day off, but I had set my alarm early, I was going to get up and go for a run. Daley Thompson used to speak about Christmas Day being the best day to train, because no one else was training. You could get one over on your opposition.

I woke up and looked out of the curtains. It was an amazing sight. The small garden was white with a thick frost. The car was thick with frost; the roofs of the other terraced houses were thick with frost. I got dressed and slipped downstairs and outside. I decided to run towards Longleat, a stately home a few miles outside the town.

I ran up the empty road in the half light, everything glowing orangey-white under the street lamps. Ten minutes later I was leaving the town behind me. As I ran up the hill past the last houses, small fields opened up on either side, with white glistening hedgerows. Lengths of barbed wire fence were coated white, every blade of grass was white. The dark shape of the Longleat forest was getting closer.

It was all absolutely stunning.

I ran beneath the dark trees, over the brown, broken bracken with it cracking underfoot and occasionally snagging and catching at my feet. I came out of the pine wood and ran up a long walk between the trees. It was now much lighter. The walk was about 20 metres wide, lined with large rhododendron bushes, with the trees crowding in behind.

It was a beautiful run. I ran and just kept running, completely wrapped up in the beauty around me. After about an hour I realised that I'd just been running in one direction, away from my parents' house. I ended up running much, much further than I had planned, but it was worth every step. I had the rest of the day off and it was fantastic.

On Boxing Day morning, again my alarm went off early. I was supposed to do an hour's run and 20 kilometres on the rowing machine, but I lay in bed. Instead of just flicking the switch and getting on with it I asked myself if I wanted to get up and go for a run. I thought about it then rolled over and went back to sleep. I could do it later.

After breakfast I thought about going for a run, but going for a family walk with the dog was more appealing. After lunch I felt too full and I reasoned that I'd been for a run the previous day so I was still all square. After afternoon tea I did manage to drag myself outside, get the rowing machine (known as an 'ergo') out of the carport and do a reasonable session in the gloom of the late afternoon light.

With the ergo moving around on the uneven paving stones I spent the whole session watching the numbers on the digital display working out what percentage I'd done and what I had left to do and how long the 20 kilometres would take me. Sitting on the rowing machine outside was a strange experience. Normally they were in the gym. The carport was an alien, unhelpful environment. With very little enthusiasm I finished the session wondering what I was missing inside the house – rather than daydreaming about the Olympics. I did feel slightly guilty that I hadn't run that morning, but I vowed I'd make up for it the next day. I had a big year ahead.

The following day followed a similar pattern. I turned off my alarm and pulled my annoyingly small single duvet tighter around me and found some good excuses not to go running. The ergo session, 60 minutes at a low intensity, I delayed and delayed – I stupidly didn't use the 'ten-minute rule', which meant telling yourself you only had to do it for ten minutes. That might have got me to get my backside to the ergo sitting in the carport. I thought about my next five kilometre ergo test – but there were too many reasons not to do the session now.

It was easy to justify. "I trained my arse off every day and having a few days off now will let me recover a bit more and I'll come back stronger". I really wanted to go faster and win, but I became pretty good at finding reasons not to start training.

The following day was the same. My alarm went off, but this was my chance to catch up on sleep.

During the seven days I had at home I only managed two runs and two ergo sessions. I should have done about ten sessions. I just couldn't be arsed. My parents' routine wasn't designed around training sessions, so I told myself that finding time was hard. I didn't have anyone else to push me along and I got into the habit of asking myself if I wanted to train rather than just getting on with it.

I wanted to race, I wanted to win, but here in the depths of Wiltshire it was all quite distant. It was different in Henley; everywhere you looked there were rowers trying to beat you, reminding you why you needed to train so hard; it was easy. In Wiltshire, I felt guilty for not doing it, but not guilty enough. It was too easy not to do it. So I didn't.

On the morning of the 2nd January I was back in Henley raring to go.

Now, with everyone around me, I was back to training at full speed.

Motivation: What floats your boat?

Ben: "I was desperate to win, but at times I still needed every motivation strategy to keep me going."

Chapter summary

The way to hell is paved with good intentions. No matter how excited you are now, put some simple strategies in place to keep yourself going tomorrow, and the next day, and the next.

The team's ten strategies for keeping motivated were:

1. Know what floats your boat
2. Believe
3. Make the journey entertaining
4. Get competitive
5. Make yourself hungry
6. Daydream
7. Flick the switch
8. Create measurable milestones
9. Build a motivating environment
10. Use the ten-minute rule

Wearing the gold medal is thrilling; standing on the podium is amazing, having *Hello!* magazine wanting to cover your wedding is glamorous...

But:

- Getting up at 5 a.m. every morning for six years
- Doing painful weight training in a damp, cold boatshed
- Eating 7,000 calories a day
- Getting enough sleep when your mates are out getting pissed
- Being exhausted all day, every day
- Doing the same thing day in day out

needs more than a few moments of fame to keep you focused. How on earth do you keep motivated when the day-in-day-out reality is boring and painful and often scary or difficult, especially when there is absolutely no guarantee that you'll get in the boat, let alone gold at the end of the long hard slog?

Motivation simply means keeping moving in the right direction.

Whether you are trying to lose weight, grow a business or learn a language, motivation is crucial, all too often we give up en route.

- How many diets have you quit?
- How many New Year's resolutions have fallen by the wayside?
- How many times have you said 'if only,' but not taken action?
- How many projects has your organisation shelved due to apathy?
- How many behaviours have you promised to change and not quite managed it?

For most of us motivation is a bit like a badly trained pet Labrador. It shows up and we get all excited about a new idea, but by the time it comes to putting the idea into practice, motivation has sloped off.

Motivation isn't logical. It often ignores things you should do, like floss your teeth or give up smoking, but attaches itself to daft endeavours.

Ben: When I was at university I had plenty of friends' essays I could have easily copied out to blag my degree, but I didn't. Instead I learnt all the words to the film *Highlander* off by heart. For years I told myself that I should learn Italian – my wife is Italian, our kids are pretty well fluent and we holiday there every year. For years each time I came back from holiday I was very motivated to learn Italian, but the motivation waned very quickly and I'd return the following year no better. Thankfully this is now changing and I'm managing to motivate myself much more effectively, it's only taken 18 years.

As a consequence, however worthwhile or exciting your goal is now, make sure you pay attention to getting and keeping motivated – that way you'll recognise those danger signals and won't 'fall off the wagon'.

How to keep motivated

Ben and the crew used a number of methods to keep them going day in day out. None of them worked every time, they needed to choose the right one(s) for each situation.

1. Know what floats your boat
2. Believe
3. Make the journey entertaining
4. Get competitive
5. Make yourself hungry
6. Daydream
7. Flick the switch
8. Create measurable milestones
9. Build a motivating environment
10. Use the ten-minute rule

There is a scale of motivation from 'survival, just get on with it' to 'massively fired up and raring to go'. Whatever our goal is – whether we are a CEO wanting to double our company's turnover, a junior cyclist wanting to win a place in a racing team or an individual thinking of running for the local council – it's unlikely that we will be at the 'massively fired up and raring to go' end of the spectrum all of the time… but can we be there more often? Or closer to that end than the survival end?

When I ran the London Marathon and saw my mum and dad in the crowd it was an amazing high – I felt I could run forever – but, for many of the 26 miles, I just about survived by counting over and over from 1-100 and back again. During the training before the actual race I think I used all of the strategies at some point: e.g. creating weekly measurable milestones to get fitter, simply 'flicking the switch' when it was time to go for a run, daydreaming about handing over a big fat cheque to Cancer Research… and so on.

1. Know what floats your boat

What 'floats your boat'? In other words, what drives you? What's important to you? What does 'a life well spent' mean to you? These potentially trance-inducing, existential questions are ones we all too often swerve. Which is a pity, because they are our strongest sources of motivation for persisting with our goals.

- Why did Ben work for over a decade just to get a snazzy medallion?
- Why do parents stand on freezing cold pitch-sides watching their kids kick a ball?
- Why do nurses stay well beyond the end of their shift, for no extra pay?

Because they are connecting with what's fundamentally *meaningful* to them. Of course Ben didn't just want the snazzy medallion (although it is rather splendid and shiny), he was driven by core values like pride, achievement, being the best he could be. When we connect with the core of what's important to us, we are willing to get up at stupid o'clock, or freeze our backsides off, or put the hours in. Unless our goals align with what 'floats our boat' at a deep level, it is difficult to stay motivated. Our goals become a nagging 'should' and we are likely to get all rebellious and stroppy.

For example, in my early twenties, I smoked. I knew it was stupid, I knew I was killing myself, I knew I 'should' stop, but that wasn't a big enough reason. My core values include things like making a difference, connection with others, fun, creativity. Being a smoker actually aligned *with* most of these! I was 'connected' with mates smoking in the pub, it was fun, it felt cool (I know, I know, sigh…), creative. It was only when I fell in love with a rabid anti-smoker (my now husband) that my values became aligned with *not* smoking – I got much more fun, connection and feeling creative by quitting.

At *Will It Make The Boat Go Faster?* we often run sessions with organisations where we get everyone to explore why they might want to give a monkey's about the company's goals. Not why they 'should' but why they genuinely, honestly might get meaning from working towards them. We start with each individual's drivers – what floats their boat and ask them how the company's goals help them fulfil those values.

At a recent session with a manufacturing company in a uniquely drab, beige hotel conference room, we had one production line team leader talking passionately about how he wanted security for his family. The factory was in a pretty deprived geographical area and for his family to thrive he wanted the company to thrive. He spoke from the heart about wanting to be a role model for his kids, to show them that they could do pretty much anything if they put their mind to it, and that him smashing the company's targets would show them just that. There was barely a dry eye in the room by the time he'd finished.

Perhaps it sounds cheesy reading it here, but my goodness that whole company were genuinely motivated. Can you imagine how different that felt from the standard company conference where the chief exec goes all jazz-hands on stage and tries to convince people how compelling the £x million annual revenue target and most people sit, glassy eyed, trying to look enthused…?

2. Believe

Ben: "There were sessions where we'd come in off the water and it had been so cold that there was ice on the boat, the oars and even our kit and people asked me why on earth was I doing this? It was because I believed that we could win the Gold, I believed in the guys I was with, I believed in the coach – I believed that it was all worthwhile."

If you doubt your goal is possible, or if you're in two minds about how worthwhile it is, then your motivation Labrador will be off at the first whiff of something more interesting to run after – and it won't be seen for dust when things get boring, difficult or scary…

- How many people do you know who chickened out of asking someone out because they didn't believe they were in with a chance?
- How many people do you know who haven't applied for a job they really wanted because they didn't think they'd make the grade?
- Have you ever hit the alarm snooze button rather than go for that run because you believe that missing one run doesn't really matter?
- Have you ever not bothered to engage with a new initiative at work because in your heart of hearts you simply don't believe it will get implemented?

How do you build beliefs? That's what the next chapter is about, so in this chapter we'll look at some more ways to keep motivated:

3. Make the journey entertaining

It's tempting to think that the promise of achieving the goal should be enjoyable enough, but it isn't. For example, you know that you'll enjoy wearing your favourite clothes and looking great when you've achieved a healthy weight – but that feeling is a long way off when you are sitting looking at a chocolate cake that will taste great right now. So how can you make the journey fun? Ben enjoyed the rowing itself and the camaraderie.

Ben: "The enjoyment came from the scenery, the camaraderie, the piss-taking, the feeling of achievement and improvement…"

What might 'an entertaining journey' look like for us in everyday life? Listening to music whilst vacuuming? Watching TV whilst ironing or exercising on the turbo? (NB *not* ironing *whilst on* the turbo.) Having a meeting at work while going for a walk rather than staying stuck in the same old meeting room?

Corporate examples we've seen include: ping pong tables in break out areas, sales teams having bingo competitions where you have to smuggle a certain word into your next sales call and companies who have put funky sofas and refreshing colours around the office to cheer up the physical environment. Why not ask colleagues what would *genuinely* make the journey more entertaining?

4. Get competitive

The desire to win fuelled Ben's motivation massively.

Ben: "I raced Doran, the Romanian stroke, countless times. I first raced him when I was 18. I first beat him when I was 27. He must have thought I was there to make up the numbers, because I'd never beaten him. I was training my arse off just like he was. Similarly, I reckon the German 8+ would have turned up for a Regatta and looked at who was racing and gone, 'US… tricky, Romania… tough, France… easy, Great Britain… piece of piss.' Rowland Barr, the stroke for the Germans, wouldn't have known who I was. I knew exactly who he was. I wanted to beat them so badly, to settle the score to make sure that they finally woke up and took notice of me."

If we're all brutally honest, we are probably more competitive than we'd like to think.

- Do you secretly want your child to be the funniest, cleverest or cutest?
- Do you mow the lawn or wash the car every weekend to be the best on the street?
- Do you play 'my story's better than yours' super trumps in the pub?

Just stand in the queue to board an easyJet plane and mankind's competitive streak is all too apparent.

In Ben's world he needed something competitive to help him get through the endless planning, reviewing and training. In our world a real or notional competition can help us stay motivated despite the boredom, rejection or effort we need to put in to reach our goals. For example, I'm currently working on a goal of better peace of mind, and to that end have an everyday layer goal of meditating for at least ten minutes, at least three days a week. The app I'm using has turned it into a competition where I can invite friends to compete with. I was initially highly sceptical that competitiveness would be appropriate for this kind of zen goal…

But so far it is working brilliantly.

5. Make yourself hungry

Ben: "If we get everything on a plate, perhaps we aren't hungry enough. For more than seven years I supported myself whilst also having to train many hours a day. I worked in a bingo hall; helped out on a farm; cleaned swimming pools; coached the Oxford women's crews. I frequently ran out of money and had to hitch or cycle the twenty-two miles to training and back. The cycle there was OK, but the cycle back after training was a nightmare. All this was happening while friends were getting 'proper jobs' and starting to do well. I really wanted an MG sports car; a car that was cool and actually worked (unlike mine). I saved for seven years, but kept having to raid the piggy bank. My brother decided to get one and six months later he'd bought it."

There were rumours about the Romanian crew – Ben was never sure if they were true, but the rumours made a big impact on him – that if the Romanians won they got a house and their family was looked after and if they lost they didn't. Can you imagine that?

If you are too comfortable then it can be difficult to motivate yourself to change. For those of you old enough to remember life before remote controls, did you ever sit and watch a rubbish TV programme because you couldn't be bothered to get off the sofa and change channels? Only when something truly dreadful came on were you motivated to change. The pain of the status quo can be as motivating as the promise of achieving your goal.

Maybe this means making a commitment or taking an action that makes it uncomfortable not to follow through:

Examples we've seen include:

- Burning boats so it's impossible to go back to the old world – like when I gave away my maternity clothes to force myself to get fit.
- Putting an IKEA flat pack in the hallway so it's less annoying to put the furniture together than climb over the huge box every day.
- Doing the important but scary or unpleasant task first thing in your diary, so you only get 'rewarded' with more enjoyable tasks afterwards.
- Keeping reminders in your inbox and not dismissing them until you've actually done the task.
- Asking a colleague to harangue you until you've finished an unpleasant work task.

Making yourself hungry also adds to the sense of accomplishment.

Ben describes the atrocious gym at Leander fondly:

Ben: "We put the gym together ourselves. It was an old boat bay that we whitewashed and cleaned up. There were holes in the wall where water poured in when it rained. It was so damp that the weights were rusty and the floor covering was rotting. We nicked the carpet from a Henley Regatta tent each year and put it on the floor to stop us skidding around. It was a dump, but we all quite liked it because it was a place to work hard."

6. Daydream

Ben: "When I qualified for the 1992 Olympics a family friend sent me a letter with the following quote attached, it's something that I still think about."

> *"All men dream: but not equally. Those who dream by night in the dusty recesses of their minds wake in the day to find that it was vanity: but the dreamers of the day are dangerous men, for they may act their dream with open eyes, to make it possible."*
>
> *T. E. Lawrence (1888–1935), Seven Pillars of Wisdom*

Daydream about achieving your goal. Imagine it so vividly that it feels real. This has two benefits. Firstly, it's fun, it makes the journey enjoyable. Secondly, it strengthens your desire and belief, it connects your brain emotionally, as well as rationally, to your goal.

Ben: "When I was at school I'd sit in A Level Economics classes, daydreaming about becoming Junior World Champion. Unfortunately neither worked out! The point is I did nothing for Economics, but I trained my arse off to become Junior World Champ. The daydreaming was really important – it got me to train harder than anyone else and sacrifice more than anyone else at school."

How was Ben's helpful daydreaming any different from fantasising about winning the lottery or being a rock star? The frequency and intensity.

Ben: "With the rowing, I dreamt about that a lot. The picture was just always there. While I had a clear picture of standing on the podium there were never any questions and I went out there and trained hard to make it happen. The pictures of other goals (like being able to play the trumpet!) were always faint and distant and consequently I did not practise. And the dreams about winning the lottery are just dreams because other than buying a ticket they don't motivate me to take action to make the dream become a reality."

Maybe you think, "I'm not a dreamer", but have you ever been on holiday before you've got on holiday – i.e. you are longing for it so much that even though you are at work you can almost taste the ice cream and feel the sun on your skin? Or have you ever spent time thinking "I want that dress/phone/car…" and imagined having it? We all daydream whether it's in technicolour pictures or gut feel. Why not relish the daydream of "I want to run this company" or "win that award" or "bring in that customer"?

7. Flick the switch

Sometimes asking, "Do I want to do this?" is the wrong approach. For example, if it's raining outside asking "do I want to go for a run?" the answer may well be "nope, I'd much prefer to surf the internet on the sofa". However, if you've done the work in chapter one and got your layered goals sorted out, then taking action will take you where you want to go, so asking whether you feel like running right now isn't helpful. In other words, sometimes it's best to simply stop faffing and get on with it.

Ben: "We used to talk about 'flicking the switch'. When you put your hands on the boat you focus. You can piss about having breakfast, but when the hands go on the boat it's focus time. Time to make sure you are actually in the boat rather than on the bank. Time to put the extraneous stuff out of your head."

Ben turned up day in day out to training in the same way that plenty of us turn up for work day in day out. We might not leap out of bed overjoyed on a Monday morning, but we just get on with it. Why? Because it's routine and because there will be serious consequences if we don't. In other words we all 'flick the switch'; maybe we just need to start using the strategy in areas where we haven't applied it before. E.g. instead of thinking, "I need to go for a run sometime this week", we could put a specific day and time in our diary to make it part of our routine.

At the company, Will It Make The Boat Go Faster?, we've put in a number of routines so we simply 'flick the switch' on important tasks which we found we were avoiding. We've tried to make them our unthinking, default setting. For example:

- A three-minute, performance review is a standard agenda item at the end of every meeting, so our default setting is to reflect on what's working and what isn't, so we can perform better next time.
- Monthly calendar entries for everyone to knuckle down and do invoicing and expenses – just do it!

Ben: "It was good to think that none of it was negotiable. For example if a friend was getting married you can't say to the others in the crew 'I'm going to skip today and I'll make up the training tomorrow'. If you need nine people in the boat and one doesn't turn up then they have screwed things up for everyone. If we'd been training individually there was no way I would have done it all."

8. Create measurable milestones and rewards

Ben: "Doing 20 kilometres on the rowing machine would take me about 70 minutes. I'd get through it by thinking 'OK, that's 10% done, nearly half way there, 10% to go…'"

Have you ever mentally ticked off the motorway junctions when driving or counted down the days on a calendar? How can you use milestones to help you achieve your goals?

Even when the Sydney Olympics seemed a long way off, the crew always had stepping stone goals that were within touching distance. On the dark days when a four-year slog seemed too long and too difficult the crew could focus on the next rowing machine test or Regatta, which was only days or weeks away.

These milestones were tangible, measurable and transparent to others. The milestones gave the crew a sense of achievement, a sense of moving forward. The fact that they were public appealed to Ben's competitiveness and also focused the mind on the consequences of not performing – you'd be out of the boat.

Sales teams typically have monthly targets. A common parenting hack is to create star charts to reward little Timmy every time he tidies his toys away or washes his hands etc. What about the rest of us? How many times this month will you go for that walk, or pick up your Spanish vocab book or mentor that tricky team member? And what would be a genuine reward when you've taken those small, but crucial steps?

9. Build a motivating environment

Ben's description of skiving training at Christmas sounds all too familiar. Have you ever thought you'll finish off work at home one evening, do some exercise on holiday or read a challenging book on a train journey… only to feel massively unmotivated when the time comes? The environment we're in has a huge impact – it can be conducive or unconducive to what we're trying to achieve. 'Environment' might mean the *physical* environment – the best meeting rooms have all the kit and the flexible seating to make collaboration easy.

My father ran a paper mill. I adored visiting it as a kid. The whole environment was designed to turn pulp into paper as efficiently as possible. Every conveyor belt was in just the right place, every tool put away exactly where it should be – so that no matter if it was 3 p.m. or 3 a.m. everyone could find exactly what they needed to get the job done. The entire environment was geared up to 'make the boat go faster'.

If you visit the England Institute of Sport Boxing centre in Sheffield or the British Sailing base in Weymouth there are inspirational pictures and quotes throughout the buildings. They are designed to create an inspirational environment so the athletes will maximise their performance.

'Environment' might also mean the context and culture. For Ben at home for Christmas, the family environment was totally geared up to relaxing, over-indulging, staying indoors and vegging out. Doing Olympic training must have felt very much at odds – it would have taken massive extra effort to overcome these unconscious barriers.

Creating the right cultural environment boils down to behaviours. We'll talk more about explicitly setting 'team rules' in the 'Teams' chapter. For example, has your workplace got the cultural environment where it's OK, 'the norm' to get praise and recognition? To have honest conversations and challenge each other to make the boat go faster? At home or with friends do you get the piss taken out of you if you set New Year's resolutions? So, do you need to find some sort of support group – be it a slimming club, a running club or a meditation group – that creates the right environment for you to succeed?

10. Use the ten-minute rule

The ten-minute rule is a tried and tested time management technique. If we set ourselves a goal of doing something for just ten minutes we'll probably end up getting further than if we set ourselves a meaty target. For example, say we wanted to learn a language our goal might be to learn vocab for ten minutes today… *but then we'd allow ourselves to stop if we wanted.*

Why does this approach work so well? Because the first bit is often the hardest, i.e. switching off the TV, and opening the vocab book. Once we've sat down with "le singe est dans l'arbre" we often get into it – we are relaxed because we've got permission to stop – and, typically, end up spending more than ten minutes on the task.

Conclusion

In order to achieve a goal that is months or years away we need to motivate ourselves to continue taking action to get there. We also need to work on our motivation to keep doing the everyday habits that make such a big difference to life in general – such as keeping a good work/life balance or maintaining a healthy lifestyle. Even with the most compelling goal, our motivational Labrador can slope off.

The crew's strategies are a menu of options we can choose from to get ourselves up that scale of motivation as much as we can, and keep that motivational Labrador firmly by our side with shining eyes and a glossy coat.

So, we have a goal and we are motivated. What next? The next chapter looks at how to build our beliefs.

CHAPTER 3

BELIEFS

May–June 2000

Beliefs: Whether you believe you can or you can't, you're probably right.

May-June 2000

22–18 weeks before the Olympics

One Monday morning, full of intent and purpose, I cycled towards Hammersmith Bridge and turned right to get into the back of the boathouse. We'd raced at the first of the three World Cup regattas the day before. We had let ourselves down and now we had to put things right. We should have won, but we'd screwed up and we'd handed victory to the Croatians. It was time to make amends.

We'd flown back from Munich the day before and 'Brock' – John Brockway, the guy who drove our boats round the world – had driven the boats through the night to make sure that we wouldn't miss any training. As I pedalled my bike around the corner there was the boat trailer; 16 upturned hulls tied to four horizontal racks.

Our boat was the only black boat on the trailer. The 57ft boat was too long to be transported by trailer in one piece so it had to be split into two sections. The shorter section was about 20ft long. It was on the lowest rack and, as always, the longer section of our boat was on the top rack.

As I cycled along the side of the trailer towards the front it quickly became clear that something had happened. My jaw dropped as I saw what was wrong. The bows of our boat, which had been on the foremost part of the trailer, were missing. About 18 inches of our boat had disappeared!

Our boat was knackered and we didn't have a spare boat. My spirits hit the floor. How were we supposed to make up for the frustration of Munich? Disappointment surged through me.

As I made my way into the boathouse I joined the swelling group of irate crew members around the exhausted but jovial Brock. He was standing brandishing the 'missing' 18 inches of our boat as if to reassure us that everything was fine. I'm not sure how many times he relayed the story that morning, but each time he did he maintained his normal upbeat manner as the atmosphere in the boathouse darkened with gloom and despair.

At about 5 a.m. that morning John had been driving through south east London, on his way from Dover to Hammersmith, when the tow bar on the back of the lorry he was driving had suddenly sheared off. The trailer overtook him and then found a bus shelter to slow itself down. It was lucky that it was early in the morning, because there wasn't much of the bus shelter left by the time our trailer had finished with it.

We didn't have another boat. In fact, as we stood there we realised that we didn't have a boat at all. We were screwed. How could we make the changes and improvements we needed with no boat?

Thank God that we had at least ordered a new boat for the Olympics, but it was due to arrive from the US in a month's time – just after Vienna Regatta. The broken boat was the only boat we had to race in for Vienna in three weeks' time.

As usual Martin gathered us together and reassured us that this wasn't a problem. Shit happens and we just had to deal with it. If we wanted to win we had to be able to deal with any problem that came along. Brock would take the boat to a British boat builder who would glue the bows back on. It would be fine. Not perfect, but fine. When we then got our new boat we would go even faster! We had to focus on the task in hand of improving and we had to get on with it.

There were some things that we could control and some things that we couldn't. We had no control over what had happened to the boat. We couldn't change the fact that our boat was knackered. If we wanted to make up for losing in Munich we had to get control of what we could, and that was how we went about training. The Searle brothers' boat got damaged a few weeks before the 1992 Olympics and it didn't stop them winning so why should this have an impact on us?

Yes what had happened was a shock, but we had really strong beliefs to help us deal with it. We believed that aiming for Gold was important, exciting – and that we absolutely could do it. Even a setback like this wasn't going to shake our belief in ourselves or each other. There was too much evidence to show us that we could do it.

We were desperate to win in Vienna and if we were to do that we needed to get control of everything we could, the rest was bullshit. We had a conversation about what we had to do and we then got on with doing it.

We spent a couple of days on rowing machines and in single sculling boats while the boat was being repaired. Andrew came into the 8+ and Fred was moved out and into a 4. We all wanted to get it right in Vienna, but for the guys on the bow side it was even more desperate, selection was far from over for them. We had a lot of speed that we still needed to find – and we didn't have much time to play with.

As if we didn't have enough to worry about we were running out of money too.

Our funding came from the National Lottery and it made a massive difference. We no longer needed to work part-time to try and fund our full-time rowing, our grants paid for our rent and our food, not much else, but it was brilliant. Lottery money also went to the sport's governing body. This meant that they could pay our coaches, pay for our equipment, pay for our training camps and everything else we needed. Well, almost everything we needed.

Budgets were obviously tight. The plan that Martin had put together included going on more training camps than the rest of the team, it included using more coaches, which is how we had Harry working with us. It allowed us to use Chris, the sports psychologist, more than other crews – to make sure that we were constantly building our beliefs. Martin also got other technical experts to help us.

We needed more money.

The training camps we did before each regatta were in Ely. We tended to stay in an empty, disused house in Cambridge by the river Cam that had mould growing in huge quantities all over the place. As it was right next door to the Cambridge University Boat Club gym, we used the weights room and rowing machines and we used their boathouse 20 miles away in Ely, because it had a very long, straight stretch of water. It was a really cheap camp, but it wasn't free and the bills still had to be paid.

Just before the Olympics we planned to go upmarket and stay in a hotel in the middle of Ely. Most of our training would be on the water, so we would have to do less travelling. We also needed to pay Harry. There was money in the budget for Martin's wages, but there wasn't much for Harry and we needed Harry. We needed some more money, but the coffers were empty and it didn't help that we'd just knackered our boat. But this was important – there was only one thing for it, *we'd* have to go out and find some money.

Sponsorship wasn't really an option; we didn't have anything to offer. We had two more regattas where we could offer someone the opportunity to have their name on the side of the boat, but the first one was less than three weeks away and the second one was less than six weeks away. Then it was the Olympics – with no sponsorship allowed. What's more, so far, we hadn't won anything so why would anyone want to sponsor us? We had no reputation and nothing to offer. There had to be other options.

We were used to looking for ways around problems, having spent all year trying to figure things out and find our holy grail, so why should this be any different?

Normally the holy grail was boat speed, it was how to get off the start faster, it was how to maintain the fastest cruising speed in the world; this time the holy grail was hard cash.

We may not have had much to offer a sponsor, but we did have a compelling story that we were massively excited by and we knew that others would be excited by it as well. We knew some people who had good contacts, and we had strong belief which would drive strong actions… so why shouldn't we achieve this?

Rowley and Fred (who still wasn't sure of his seat) took charge and masterminded it. Rowley had some insurance contacts at Lloyd's of London, he was going to approach them and ask for help, the rest of us would write letters to other contacts we had. Between training sessions we'd search for people's addresses and we'd write to them, if we wanted the training camps and Harry's involvement… we had to make it happen.

In the meantime we were preparing for the Vienna Regatta. We had a lot to look forward to, winning in Vienna (there is another chapter about what happened in Vienna), our fundraising evening and getting our new boat.

As the boat went faster on the water, the fundraising started to take shape. MRM Hancock, an insurance broker, was really interested in our story and agreed to help. The MD had rowed at school and he thought that what we were trying to do reflected what they were trying to do as a company – namely to build a strong team and strive for excellence. They promised to give us some money and host an evening event for us in the Lloyd's building in the City. They'd invite as many of their contacts as possible, we could invite all of our contacts, we'd take our boat into the basement at Lloyd's, have some food and drinks and we'd ask them to empty their pockets.

The day arrived and we all turned up looking as smart as we could in some shirts and ties that Fred had persuaded someone to give us. In bright sunshine we parked our van and boat trailer in front of the Lloyd's building. While some of us went inside to clear all possible obstructions, the rest untied the boat and lifted it off the trailer. When the building services people were ready for us – with a number of suited bystanders wondering what the hell was going on – we picked the boat up and carried it carefully through the glass doors.

It might be knackered already, but it was the only boat we had, so we tiptoed across the lobby area and to the down escalator. Despite being used to handling the boat, it was the first (and only) time I'd been on an escalator with a 40-foot section of rowing boat in my hands. With inches to spare at either end, it was inches from the ceiling above and inches from the handrails of the escalator. We got it in and set it up in the middle of the room. All we needed now was people. Rowley was bricking himself, worried that people wouldn't show up. We were all praying that the evening would work.

They turned up! Soon we had a room with probably 200 people all waiting to hear our story.

We had to build their belief in the same way we'd had to build our own. We spoke to them about rowing, about the fact that it's a sport that delivers results at every Olympics. We told them about why we absolutely believed we could win gold – we were building momentum, we were on a roll, we were world silver medallists, we were about to win our first World Cup regatta, and we were going to keep getting faster.

We told them that we could give them nothing in return for their money except an investment in our dream, but that we hoped that they would get a huge sense of excitement, pride and enjoyment from seeing us win.

From the business leaders we had written to (out-of-the-blue) to contacts we knew from businesses; from Lloyd's brokers to passers-by who threw coins into our bucket as we unloaded our boat… people gave money. From a £5,000 cheque to a handful of coins, the money came in.

We raised £36,000! It was exactly what we needed.

We left Lloyd's amazed that so many people had been inspired to help us. It was incredible that other people believed in us. It was a sign of how much we believed in ourselves that we'd convinced them to contribute. As the cheques rolled in and the total grew, our plans became a reality. We were on a roll; our momentum was building.

Beliefs: Whether you believe you can or you can't, you're probably right.

Ben: "In 2000 I felt calm because I just knew we could do it. I had total certainty and confidence that we were fast. Very fast."

Chapter summary

Self-belief accelerates success. Most people pick up beliefs in a haphazard way, but there are plenty of simple strategies for actively cultivating useful beliefs.

1. Four crucial beliefs:
1a D – Deserved
1b I – Important
1c C – Can do
1d E – Exciting

2. Sources of beliefs
2a Personal memories
2b Role models
2c Metaphors/analogies

3. Strategies for strengthening beliefs
3a Repetition
3b Evidence walls
3c Emotional depth

What impact is uncertainty having in your world?

- Does your sales team have unshakeable confidence that they can hit their targets? Or do they walk into a pitch with a slight hesitation that rubs off on the client?
- Do your managers *know* they can unlock the potential of their teams? Or do they pay lip service to staff development because in their heart of hearts they believe current performance is pretty much as good as it gets?
- Are you confident in your parenting approach, or do you worry that you're getting it wrong?

As Henry Ford reputedly said:

> *"Whether you think you can or whether you think you can't, either way you're probably right."*

Strong belief is vital to achieving our goals, but exactly what should we believe? If we believe we can fly and start jumping off tall buildings we'd be locked up! How was Ben's belief that he could win Gold any different from a deluded fantasy that he could sprout wings and take off? Even if we know what it is reasonable to believe, how on earth do we go about growing a belief? It's not as simple as buying brain compost and belief seeds and growing-your-own.

Ben didn't always have certainty and conviction. He wasn't one of those annoying celebs you see on chat shows who talks about "always knowing since I was five years old…" If you ask Ben about the rowing championships in 1998 (when the crew came seventh) he talks about, "*Forcing* ourselves to *try* and believe."

Ask him about his beliefs before the 2000 Olympics and it's a very different story. His conviction is evident in his body language as he talks. Ben's tone is matter of fact as he says, "We knew we could win." He looks you in the eye; he is relaxed, he's not boasting, he just had total conviction that he'd win Gold.

So what changed between 1998 and 2000?

Firstly, the crew had four clear types of beliefs that helped them to achieve their goal. Secondly, they used three sources to supply those beliefs and, lastly, they used three strategies to strengthen them. We'll look at the four types of beliefs first and then explain the sources and the belief-building methods.

1. What do we need to believe?

Think of four wheels on a bus – each wheel works independently, but they also all have to work together. If the tyres are soft it's much more difficult to control the vehicle. If we're missing a wheel we'd probably come to a shuddering halt.

If our core beliefs are strong – the metaphorical wheels on our vehicle are pumped up properly – we roll easily over small bumps along the way to achieving our goal.

An easy way to remember the four wheels is the mnemonic *DICE*:

- D – Deserved
- I – Important
- C – Can do
- E – Exciting

1a I deserve this

We need to believe we deserve success. We deserve to write that bestseller or get that promotion or close that million-dollar deal. I don't mean in an arrogant way, I mean we need to counter the – surprisingly common – tendency to self-doubt; the unhelpful beliefs that we're not good enough, not worthy, that only 'special' kinds of people get to win gold medals. It's been dubbed 'the Imposter Syndrome' and there's a growing body of research showing how easily that nagging voice in our heads can convince us that we don't really know what we are doing, we don't really deserve to be listened to as an equal or to have that job – and we ought to stay inside our comfort zones. The simple way that Ben pumped up this belief 'tyre' was to strip things back to basics:

Ben: "I never thought I deserved to win at the Olympics. God no, who deserves that? But I did have as much right to win one single race as anyone else, because that's all the Olympic Final was… simply one single race. One single race between our crew and the other guys we'd been racing for years. With everything I'd put in I deserved it as much or more than them. It was just a race."

With that in mind, focus on your goal and write down five reasons why it's totally reasonable that you should achieve it. You don't need to be arrogant, quite the reverse – it's just a book, or a promotion, or a deal. The opportunity is there for everyone else, you've worked hard for it – there, that's two to start your list already!

1b This is important

The goal must be important to us. We're busy, we have a never-ending to-do list, so why do we believe this goal is important enough to get priority over other things jostling in the queue for our attention? There need to be rational, sensible reasons, to make sure we aren't getting carried away in a moment of rashness. Ask yourself:

- Why is this important?
- What positive change will it create – what are the benefits?
- Do the pros outweigh the cons?
- Am I willing to trade time/money/energy to achieve this?

Most times we overload ourselves and try and pursue too many goals at once. To use a daft analogy, it's a bit like going into IKEA and getting carried away in the marketplace. Are all those tea lights and cushions really 'important' enough for us to hand over our hard-earned cash? Are they really 'important' enough to take up the space on our mantlepiece…?

This focus is crucial and gives us the fuel to keep going when things get tough – we are bound to encounter bumps along the way towards our goals. It's at difficult times that it's oh-so-tempting to give up, so make sure that, right at the forefront of your mind, you have superglue-strength reasons why it's important to stick at it.

1c I can do this

You need to believe you can do it. If you don't quite know *how* you'll achieve it, you need to believe that you will, absolutely, figure out a way. Try using the nifty little word, 'yet', as in: "We may not have the whole answer *yet*, but we can and will get there." In future chapters we'll look at more tactical strategies for turning mountains back into molehills, but for now, cultivating that core 'I can' belief will help keep the door open so you can access these bouncebackability methods.

Ben: "In 1998 we knew Jürgen's approach wasn't working for us. There were many possible routes; our job was to find a route that worked for us. The moments when I thought about giving up were the times when I lost my self-belief because I couldn't see a way for things to get better."

It's interesting that the team believed there was more than one route to success. Ben and I often find our clients have got stuck because they think there is only *one* answer. They waste energy hunting for some holy grail, some magic dust – maybe if they copy an *expert* they will get the right answer.

Notice the difference between asking 'can I do this?' and 'how am I going to do this?' Ask yourself the second question and you are much more likely to get useful answers to propel you towards your goal.

1d This is exciting

The goal needs to be enticing, something we are passionate about. There are plenty of things that we may believe to be important, but simply don't *excite* us. Most people would agree that global warming, injustice and poverty are important issues, but not everyone gets fire in their belly about them. It's that fire that creates *action*. Where does that passion come from? What were your answers to the question 'What floats your boat?' in the Motivation chapter, on page 45.

Ben: 'In my training diary I wrote how pursuing gold totally aligned with my values and made me feel passionate – why it absolutely floated my boat. For example…

- *Respect: to gain respect from oarsmen like Steve Redgrave, Matthew Pinsent, Greg Searle*
- *Pride: to show that Britain is/can be good and win*
- *Team: for everyone in the boat and the wider team – to say thank you for all the time and effort people had put in, for the volunteers who deserved to have a damn good story to tell their grandchildren…*
- *Friendship: to make up for every wedding that I'd missed because I had to train – Sally, Sam, Annabel, Neil, Pete, Tiff…*
- *Physical challenge: for every ergo test that hurt like hell*
- *Being as good as I could be: for every mistake, experiment, change – the countless times I'd gone outside my comfort zone…*
- *Family: for my parents and Isabella. I owe it to them for all the pain I've put them through and the unending support they've given me."*

Be honest with yourself! What floats your boat doesn't have to be saintly to be useful. For example, perhaps what really excites you about sticking to getting fit is not the rational health benefits, but the excitement of proving your nagging, disbelieving partner wrong…

Recently, we worked with the 40 most senior directors in a pharmaceutical company. The company was pushing through a big restructure, but progress was slow. We did an 'MOT' on their DICE beliefs about the change. The MOT uncovered plenty of excitement about the change, and a strong feeling that it was an important, worthwhile step. So the 'I' and 'E' of DICE were there, but the 'D' and 'C' were missing. Talking truthfully, many felt that the company processes were such a mess that they didn't really deserve to be at the industry top table. They also struggled to see how on earth they could pull off the change successfully. Once it was clear which 'tyres' needed pumping up, they could get to work…

2. Where to get beliefs from

We've looked at the four 'wheels' on the bus – the four beliefs that will help us reach our goal – that we are *deserving*, that it's *important*, that we *can* achieve success and that it's incredibly *exciting*.

How do we pick up these useful beliefs? We need to consciously hunt for them. Have you ever walked past a friend in the street or missed your bus stop because you weren't concentrating? In the same way, useful facts might be staring us in the face, but unless we *actively* look for them, we can miss them entirely. Ben and the crew made it a deliberate habit to look for reasons why they would succeed.

Ben: "The last training camp in '98 was at Varese. In one of the sessions – out of nowhere! – we did a 1,000 metre sprint at world record pace. In other words if we'd done that over 2,000 metres in a competition, we would have broken the world record. So we knew we could do it, it was a turning point. We hadn't got a clue how we'd done it – we needed to figure that out, but the first thing it did was build our belief in what was possible."

It would have been so easy to dismiss this as a fluke, or to miss the significance, but the crew got into the habit of finding proof that they would win Gold.

There were three places in particular that proved fruitful hunting grounds for useful beliefs: their personal memories, role models and metaphors/analogies.

2a Personal memories

Can you think of a time when you won against the odds or did something you were proud of? When we are struggling to achieve a current goal it massively helps our self-belief to remind ourselves that we have achieved success in the past. For example, Ben remembered an episode from his school days.

Ben: "As a 17-year-old my school coach, Mark Hayter, took a group of us to the under 18's national team trials in Chester. Robin Graham (a guy in my year) and I were in a pair together. I remember watching the top Junior pairs in awe.

To our total astonishment we came second. We were nobodies. But we'd beaten some of the pairs we'd watched with awe. With no experience at this level we could go fast, really fast. What else was possible? Who else could I beat?"

That personal experience was a powerful source of strength years later when the British crew had to beat crews they had never beaten before in order to achieve gold.

What have you achieved in the past that proves you have the capability for success, for learning, for changing, for improving? It's so easy to forget or take for granted the massive achievements you've made in your life:

- Remember starting your first job? Doing your first exam? Managing a budget for the first time? So whatever new challenges you are facing now, surely you can manage them?

- How much better are you now at using a computer or making a presentation than you were when you started out? So surely you'll master the new skills you need to achieve your current goal?
- What tough times have you bounced back from? Difficult relationships have you handled? So surely you can turn around the setbacks you are facing now?

Your past successes are a rich source of belief for your current endeavour.

2b Role models

Who has done what you want to do, or something similar? If they can do it, why can't you? Sometimes it strengthens our beliefs to look at superstars and realise they are human beings just like us. The Oscar-winners, the Chart-toppers or the multi-billion-pound business owners.

Ben: "In 1992 at the Barcelona Olympics the Australians won the Gold Medal in the men's double. Stephen Hawkins and Peter Antonie were the smallest crew by a mile. There is no way that they should have won given their size but they did. They were amazing. They inspired me because our crew wasn't the physically strongest in the world. It helped me realise that we could win Gold through technical brilliance and teamwork."

However, our idols might feel a bit too distant and other-worldly, so look closer to home as well. Who is just ahead of you? What can you learn from them? Which of their strategies can you adapt for yourself?

Ben: "Now, as a business owner, I find it really inspiring and helpful talking to other entrepreneurs who have recently been through what I'm going through currently. Generally, they've had similar issues and challenges and succeeded – so why shouldn't I? And if they've hit bumps in the road, then surely I can steer round them, now that I'm warned and prepared?"

2c Metaphors and analogies

> *"I wandered lonely as a cloud…"*

> *"If music be the food of love, play on; give me surfeit of it…"*

Metaphors and analogies make pretty poetry, but they are also powerful belief-changing tools. They work like cranes in our brains lifting ideas from one mental compartment to another. (See what I did there?! Oh, my sides.) They can, therefore, take an idea our minds have labelled 'scary and challenging' and transfer it to 'easy and doable'.

The crew talked about their journey to the Sydney Olympics as being like a stone rolling downhill, gathering momentum and rolling faster and faster. Easy to picture isn't it? In fact you can almost feel it, can't you? Analogies appeal to the emotional centres in our brain and are easy to remember. Research suggests that the more we remember or visualise something the stronger the neural networks laid down in the brain, which strengthens our belief.

What metaphors or analogies would work to help you get your goal?

- If you are feeling stuck, what would oil your wheels?
- If you are lost, who could guide you forwards?
- If you have a mountain to climb, what are some milestones on the way to aim for?

3. How to strengthen beliefs

The crew found the three sources of useful beliefs – personal memories, role models and metaphors/analogies incredibly powerful, but they didn't stop there. They actively grew and strengthened their beliefs using three key strategies:

3a Repetition

The crew constantly reminded themselves of their useful beliefs in order to strengthen their conviction. For example their psychologist, Chris Shambrook, captured a written list of *reasons why we are going to win*. There's a copy on page 85.

They talked regularly about the reasons: in everyday conversations, before and after training and in sessions with Chris. It became as normal as talking about the weather or the latest sporting results. This dialogue was particularly vital when the pressure got immense:

Ben: "The day before the Olympic final, after an incredibly stressful few hours, we got together and reminded ourselves why we were going to do it. I had tears streaming down my face; I just cared about it so much."

How can you remind yourself of your beliefs? Examples from our clients include:

- Making it a standard agenda item at team meetings.
- Keeping personal journals to write down and revisit reasons.
- Putting visual reminders out – e.g. one client put a (small!)

rock on his desk to remind himself of the rock-solid reasons why he would succeed.

3b Evidence walls

One of the crew's visual reminders was so powerful that it warrants a section in its own right. The crew used a wall in the boatshed to Blu-Tak up *evidence* that they could win. They kept adding to it and adding to it. There were pictures – such as role models Hawkins and Antonie on the podium (the Australian pair who were supposedly too small to win gold). There were graphs and stats – e.g. showing the force/time curves achieved on the rowing machines – showing improvements. There were write ups of performance review, showing key learnings. Imagine the power of all that evidence? Imagine how that bolstered their belief? What would be the equivalent for you?

If it's a personal evidence wall, then perhaps it's a book you carry round or an online photo album. One of my clients has an 'evidence wall' in the notes section on his phone to bolster his beliefs before tough board meetings.

If you work in a team, then perhaps it's a public wall like Ben and the crew. At Will It Make The Boat Go Faster? we have a physical wall in the office plus a WhatsApp group (as folks are often out on the road). We use all the sources we've talked about in the chapter: there are emails from client organisations about the difference we've made to them, examples of big sales we've landed, stories about role models, this week one of the team posted that she'd achieved a PB marathon time at the weekend. Looking at the evidence wall, our company crazy goal doesn't seem crazy any more, it feels absolutely within touching distance.

3c Emotional depth

The second method the crew used to strengthen their beliefs was to fire them up with strong emotion. Not just happy-clappy feelings like excitement and desire, but ones that, on first glance, are seemingly unhelpful like jealousy, anger, the desire to say, "I told you so."

Ben: "When we lost to the Aussies in the 2000 heat we were absolutely furious. I also knew that if they had only beaten us by that small amount when we were rowing really badly then they were in trouble."

Anger is energy. It would have been so easy for Ben and the crew to burn themselves up being angry for giving such a rubbish performance. Instead, they used the anger as a powerful catalyst. Rational reasons aren't enough, if they were we'd all eat our five a day and floss our teeth every night. We must cultivate emotional leverage to turn the hard lumps of rational 'I could' into a burning fire of 'I can'.

Ben: "In 1991 when I first went to Leander Club to train, everyone had just done a bench pull test. You lie on your front on a plank about a metre from the floor and you have to lift a 45kg weight from the floor to the plank. It's a seven minute test. The first six minutes you have to lift the weight every two seconds, in the last minute you can do as many as you want, so long as it is more than every two seconds. The worst result was 40 something lifts. I had a go and managed about 20. I couldn't even keep going for one minute, let alone seven.

I didn't know when the next test was, but I wasn't going to be humiliated in front of Redgrave and everyone else. There were a few people in the club who I knew that I could beat and with that belief came the simple clarity that all I had to do was practise. Every day, for about two years, after training I'd go to the weights room and practise. While everyone else was changing and starting breakfast, I'd practise. Two years later I came second in the test with 50kg, I did 225 lifts."

When have you felt strongly enough about an issue that it's driven you to find a way to resolve it? What emotions are going to motivate you now to keep hunting for those reasons why and keep reinforcing your belief?

Conclusion

Remember that pharmaceutical company we talked about earlier in the chapter. The senior directors who were strong on the 'T' and the 'E, but missing the 'D' and 'C'? For them the 'deserve' bit was sorted out by having a look at role model organisations. They found countless examples of companies who have got their house in order and made a step change in their success (and this was true even in their industry, for some of their competitors), so why couldn't this company? In terms of 'C' they created an evidence wall. They kept adding to it, discussing it, and sharing it with their teams. With all four wheels pumped up properly, they began speeding ahead.

Having properly pumped up tyres is a basic safety requirement for having a car on the road and the same is true for having strong beliefs to achieve our goals. It's easy to think that beliefs are out of our control – we either have self-belief or we don't – but Ben's experience shows that's simply not true.

We have a choice about what we look for and register. Do we choose to look for the reasons we can't? or that we can? It's bizarre how often we seem to argue for our limitations, when a simple bit of focus will give us plenty of evidence that we can achieve our goals.

We can search through our personal memories, look for role models, review metaphors and analogies and thereby create *solid evidence* that we are going to succeed. Add a dash of emotion and a slug of repetition and that's a powerful mixture. Beliefs are the bedrock – without them it's pretty likely that our car will seize up when we hit the first pothole in our journey. It's too risky to leave it to chance. Remember Henry Ford's advice? When you believe that you deserve your goal, that it's important, that you can do it and that it's incredibly exciting – you are probably right.

Building strong beliefs is the positive bit, the other side of the equation is using *bullshit filters* to guard against negative beliefs and that is exactly what the next chapter is all about.

GB OLYMPIC 8+ 2000.

THE HISTORY... THE FOUNDATION BENEATH THE PERFORMANCES AT THE OLYMPICS.

- THE DESIRE AND CREDENTIALS ARE UNQUESTIONABLE.

This crew has the potential to win in Sydney because...

- *THE WHOLE HAS BECOME GREATER THAN THE SUM OF THE PARTS.*

- There are 4 years of trial and improvement behind this crew.
- The momentum behind the crew is still growing... snowballing.
- The crew has the best physiology ever of any British 8+.
- The critical approach to excellence has left no stone unturned.
- The crew has confidence in the support provided... so believe in the processes engaged in.
- Mistakes made have been learnt from and rectified.
- The individual strengths from within the crew have been combined and exploited to the full.
- The crew is ROBUST... which brings a relaxed approach.
- The crew has learnt to be process focused.
- There is a shared belief within the crew... and a confidence in the unit.
- The crew has become increasingly "on the money" technically.
- The crew has developed openness and honesty.
- The crew has become a fun unit to be part of.
- The crew has become physically tough when racing.
- The crew has learnt to row away from the field... and has learnt how to WIN, with a methodical approach to racing.
- The past performances have shown what the crew is capable of in the future.

A summary drawn from the evidence wall, which the crew took to Sydney

CHAPTER 4

BULLSHIT FILTERS

Vienna Regatta

Bullshit Filters: Accept the facts, challenge the negative interpretation.

Vienna Regatta

June 2000. 15 weeks before the Olympics.

The Vienna Regatta course was a few miles from the city centre, a dammed section of the New Danube that ran alongside the Old Danube. It was the second Regatta in the World Cup series, a set of three Regattas with a three-week gap between each of them. Our aims for Vienna were simple: get off the start fast and then get into the rhythm that would give us the fastest middle 1,000 metres in the world.

After the World Rowing Championships in Canada in Sept '99 we'd realised that having the fastest middle 1,000 was all well and good, but you've got to be in it to win it. In an 8+, if you don't get out of the starting blocks fast, you're playing catch up all the way and making it much harder to win. In the review of the World Champs we had discussed whether we should play it safe and stick with our plan of having the fastest middle 1000m which we were pretty sure would give us an Olympic Silver or did we risk it all and change the emphasis to maximise our chance of winning. It had been a short conversation. For the last nine months we'd been working on power and raw speed to give us a faster start and then being able to maintain our devastating rhythm through the next 1,000 metres.

Three weeks before the Vienna Regatta we'd won the heat at Munich Regatta in fine style. We caned it off the start, moved into our rhythm and cruised home. In the final we were rubbish, we'd got carried away by people talking bullshit that we were much better than anyone else and we would win easily and we shoved our heads up our backsides. We let the Croatians take the lead and we could do nothing about it. We were furious. We'd let ourselves, and each other, down. We wouldn't make the same mistake again. Making a mistake was fine; making it twice was unacceptable.

So here we were in Vienna and it was time to put things right; time to show everyone else what we could do – and time to show *ourselves* what we could do. We were going to block out all of the distractions and maintain our focus on what we had to do. Our bullshit filters were going to be fully on.

The water in Vienna felt really different from anywhere else we rowed, but we quickly found our rhythm. The year before had been a fiasco – it took days to work out what to do in the weird-feeling water – but we'd learnt from it. Some of the boys had written notes in their training diaries about what to do and we'd adapted pretty quickly this time around. We were going well.

On Friday, in our heat, the main competition was Romania. They hadn't beaten us since this time last year and that wasn't going to change today.

It was windy. Wind and rowing don't normally go together that well and you couldn't fail to notice that there were a number of massive wind turbines in the area. When your bum is only four inches off the water and the side of your boat is only about six inches from the surface of the water, one-foot waves are a nightmare. They hit the riggers on the side of the boat, shatter into spray which flies down the length of the boat and then what's left of the wave pours in over the side of the boat, making it run lower in the water, meaning that smaller and smaller waves have the same effect.

During the warm-up for the race we got buffeted and soaked. My God it was heavy, slow going, but it was going to be the same for all the teams and we would cope better than everyone else. Today was going to be our day. We were going to leave the start like a scalded cat. We were going to make up for screwing up three weeks before. We had a good warm-up.

Sitting on the start we used our spare T-shirts to mop as much water out of the boat as we could. Even as we sat there more water was lapping over the sides of the boat and filling the foot wells. We mopped and bailed for as long as we could.

The Romanians, in the lane next to us, were laughing about the conditions. While they laughed we focused on what we were doing. We kept our bullshit filters on and focused only on what mattered. Yes there was wind and rain – fact – but we could control our interpretation. The conditions actually meant we had a massive advantage… because we knew we could row in any conditions.

The buzzer sounded and we were off. Accelerating, accelerating, being knocked by a massive wave, accelerating, hitting the next wave, almost stopping, accelerating, the next shudder and flying water, accelerating, flying water. We were bashed and buffeted and pulling away from everyone else. Nothing was going to stop us. We got into a rhythm, hit another wall of water, ground to a halt, accelerated, found a rhythm, and then got knocked out of our stride again.

Water was constantly flying down the boat. We kept disappearing into clouds of spray but we were taking the opposition apart. They had all but given up in the ridiculous conditions. We were going to row our race.

Suddenly a huge wave ripped down the boat. Luka, all 16 ½ stone of him, got knocked off his seat. He was sitting on the runners for his seat and his seat was half off the runners and on top of my feet. He stopped rowing and started scrabbling around behind him to find it. Rowley, the cox, couldn't see what had happened and started screaming at Luka to f***ing well start rowing again!

While Luka was shouting back that he'd lost his seat he knocked it off the runners completely. His seat was on my feet and I couldn't row anyway because I couldn't slide forward. I had to stop and force his seat back on to the runners. Five, six, seven, strokes went by before we got it on, he lifted his bum, landed back on his seat, screamed "I'M BACK" at the top of his voice and took the biggest stroke of his life to make up for the ones he'd missed.

His oar got caught in the water (catching a 'crab'). In other words, because of the boat speed his soaking wet wooden oar handle was ripped out of his hands, the handle flew towards him and he instinctively threw himself back. He was now lying over my feet, the oar was wrenched parallel to the boat, and the boat lurched over to one side. I nearly smacked him with my handle as I came forward for the next stroke. The last time someone caught a crab during a race was when I was about sixteen! I had to stop rowing again. Both Luka and I grabbed his handle and tried to wrench it back round again.

The other boys were trying to get the boat straight and get it moving again. Thank God the Romanians and everyone else had decided that the conditions were ridiculous and weren't really trying. They had taken about three boat lengths out of our lead and were now quite close. We got Luka's oar back in front of him and we joined the rest of the crew, without a shout, but just trying to accelerate, move, find a rhythm, hit a wave, find the rhythm again, hit another wall of water.

We won the race by some distance, we were almost laughing as we crossed the line. The conditions had been a joke. What happened to Luka – well, none of us had ever seen that before – it had been a ridiculous race, but we'd done what we'd had to do, we'd got off the start faster than everyone else, we'd been faster through the middle and we'd won. We went straight to the pontoon. Another 100 metres and we'd have sunk.

That evening in the hotel and the next day we had a number of people telling us different things, how well we'd done and that the final was a foregone conclusion or that the Aussies had looked fantastic and the final would be really tough, it was all bullshit. The only thing that mattered was that we kept our filters on and only listened to the people that we trusted.

Sunday's final came around pretty quickly. We were not going to make the same mistakes as we had in Munich. We were going to perform the way we knew we could.

It was a grey, overcast windy day. The blades of the wind turbines were slicing at the low clouds scudding overhead. There was a steady wind blowing up the course, but nothing like the conditions of the heat. These were perfect conditions for us. In truth, no matter what the weather we would have been saying that it was ideal, because there was no point in moaning about something that we could not control. It was the same for everyone and while other people got bent out of shape by the weather, we would make the most of it.

The warm-up went pretty well. We did most of the bursts in the direction that we were going to race in to get used to the steady wind. The small waves hit the underside of the riggers and checked the boat rather than stopped it. The practice starts were solid and aggressive. We were going to leap out of the start and take the race by the scruff of the neck. This was the Aussies' first European race of the season and we were going to show them who was in charge.

Time to get ready. Everyone was doing their final checks, final quiet words to the people in front and behind them. Six people in front of me preparing to hurl the boat off the start. The cox leaning out, looking down the sides of the boat making sure we were straight and ready. Past him was the pontoon and past the pontoon was the empty nudist colony; the Austrians clearly didn't think it was the right weather to strip off, but it was the right weather for us to get out of the start, and make it happen.

The Starter was calling across the crews. I slid forward, measuring that I was the right distance forward by the position of my elbow against my knee.

"Attention"
"Go"

Accelerate, accelerate, move, move, move, lengthen, lengthen. We picked up the boat and hurled it, picked it up and hurled as if it were an eight-man javelin. We flew out of the start. We got a lead. We drove the boat on, through the wind, through the water. I think we saw red and pulled the boat down the length of the course.

We'd won. The first World Cup race we'd won. The first time this crew had won. The first big international Regatta I'd won in *nine years of trying*. We'd WON.

Arms were in the air. We were shouting, grabbing each other's ankles, slapping each other on the back. We'd won.

We made our way to the medal pontoon. We'd won. We were given our Gold medals. The 2000 Rowing World Cup Gold Medals. We were given the yellow bibs to show that we were the World Cup leaders. We were on a roll. There were some brief interviews on the pontoon, some photos, the BBC were there filming. We'd won.

As we celebrated Louis was taken away for drug testing. After each race one or two people were normally tested. We still had to row back to the normal pontoon where we could get our boat out of the water. We grabbed Tim Foster's dad so he could row back in Louis's seat and we did a mini lap of honour.

Waiting on the pontoon were Martin and Harry. Our celebrations and smiles were met by faces of thunder. Martin and Harry just looked at us. We'd won and all they could do was look at us with faces of parents whose children had just scribbled with marker pens on the newly painted living room walls.

Tim's dad made himself scarce.

"What the f**k do you call that?" Martin demanded.

"We've just won, Martin."

"You've won shit. You beat the Aussies who got off the plane after a 24hr flight four days ago. You act like you've won the Olympics. You've won nothing. How did you perform in that race? How did you perform?"

I was furious. "We've won our first Regatta. We got off the start, dominated the race and won, are we not allowed to celebrate?"

Martin was having none of it. He continued to ask us how we'd performed. We had to admit that we hadn't rowed well. We'd pulled the boat down the lake. We hadn't had our devastating rhythm. We'd ground the win out. We hadn't done what we'd planned to do. We hadn't developed the rhythm the way we trained to do. We'd been short and aggressive. Where was the long, rangy rhythm we'd spent so many months and hundreds of miles working on?

We had to admit that if we rowed like that again it would be the last race we'd win. Showing the Aussies how happy we were also hadn't done us many favours. What made it worse was the photo that appeared in a number of papers the next day of Simon having crossed the finish line, his left arm in the air with a finger raised towards the Aussies. Simon was adamant that it was his index finger but we all knew the Aussies would be cutting it out and putting it on the bedroom walls of their hotels for emotional fuel to strengthen their desire to beat us.

It was a very strange Regatta. It was the first one we'd won. We'd shown that we could win. We'd shown that we could keep our heads when we were in the lead. We'd taken a big step forward from Munich.

The problem was that we'd also left our bullshit filters off. We'd fooled ourselves into thinking that winning the Regatta was important when that was bullshit. What we really wanted was to win the Olympics and if we wanted that we needed to *perform* well. We needed to row our race, our rhythm. At the time I didn't think that Martin went about it in the right way and it really wound me up. Having spoken to him in the years since then I understand that his decision to put a firework under our backsides had been thought-through and measured. He wanted to create an emotional response from us that we could deal with over the coming days and weeks. He pointed out that his job was not to be nice to us and be our friend; it was to make us faster than anyone else in the world.

Bullshit Filters: Accept the facts, challenge the negative interpretation.

Ben: "There'll be plenty of evidence that you can't do it and plenty of people saying you can't do it. You just need some really good bullshit filters."

Chapter summary

Negative comments, negative thoughts and negative interpretations will drain your energy and throw you off course. Use 'bullshit filters' to filter out unhelpful information and focus on what's useful.

Why do we need bullshit filters?

1a Bullshit beliefs create poor performance.

1b Bullshit beliefs make it much harder to build useful beliefs.

How do we build bullshit filters?

2a Don't talk bollocks to Basil.

2b Accept the facts, challenge the negative interpretation.

2c Find a better interpretation.

2d Use bullshit as emotional fuel.

- How many times have you got carried away or blown something out of proportion? "Oh no, I made one spelling mistake; they are going to fire me."
- How many times have you been told, "you can't", "you shouldn't"? "Noone from round here gets that kind of job, don't be daft!"
- How many times have you been labelled? Perhaps your teacher called you lazy or your parents called you clumsy or a classmate called you stupid?

Instead of laughing away our negative thoughts or other people's unhelpful comments and moving on, sometimes, we let them stick and start to accept them as unarguable truths.

We might sort through our bedroom cupboards and think, "Why on earth have I kept that pair of purple socks all these years?", yet we rarely do that with the unhelpful thoughts clogging our heads.

Ben and the crew worked hard to develop bullshit filters – ways of getting rid of the negative thoughts and feelings that would get in the way of reaching Gold. Why was this so important? Why not just stick to building useful beliefs as described in the beliefs chapter?

1. Why do we need bullshit filters?

There were two reasons – firstly because bullshit beliefs create poor performance and secondly because bullshit beliefs make it much harder to build useful beliefs:

1a Bullshit beliefs create poor performance

Ben: "Bullshit thoughts make you feel rubbish. In 1998 we were painfully aware that we only had 24 months. We didn't have the time or the energy to waste on bullshit."

Without getting bogged down in the complexities of neuroscience, research shows that information from our five senses enters the brain a bit like water draining into a river. The river then wends its way through our head and our mind interprets the information. The way we interpret it makes us feel a certain way about it, which, in turn, makes us decide what to do, and then we take some form of action.

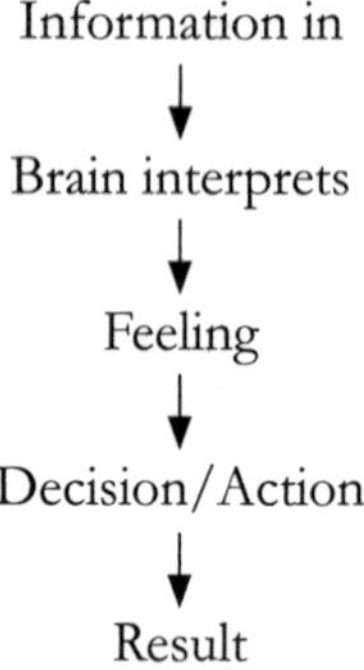

Have you come across the term 'rubbish in, rubbish out'? If you put poor quality meat into a sausage machine you'll get poor quality sausages; it's the same with us. Bullshit information in or bullshit interpretation means bullshit performance. Here are a couple of examples:

	Example one	Example two
Information in	British crew lose to Russia in 1996 Olympics	Your colleagues say "this product is rubbish"
Interpretation	For four years I gave it everything and I'm still not good enough, I still can't beat them	I'm wasting my time trying to sell it
Feeling	Despondent, despairing, embarrassed	Bored and unmotivated
Decision/Action	Give up	Half hearted selling
Result	End of rowing career	No sales, no bonus

1b Bullshit beliefs make it much harder to build useful beliefs

Another reason why bullshit filters are so important is that letting in bullshit makes it much harder to build useful beliefs. You know how a river carves a deep channel, which makes it more difficult to divert the water to follow another direction? In the same way, the more we let information flow along an unhelpful neural pathway the stronger our unhelpful belief gets. We end up forgetting that it's just an opinion, just an interpretation and act as if it is a universal truth. The more we feel certain, the more we become resistant to thinking something different, something useful.

I have a friend who works in a Further Education College which runs adult literacy classes. One of the biggest challenges for the tutors is the negative beliefs the adult students have about their competence. Years and years of being told – or telling themselves – that they are 'stupid' have taken their toll. The students accept this massively unhelpful opinion as fact and struggle to believe that they can learn and improve.

One of our clients, a bank, gave sales targets to their branches for certain insurance products. The staff 'knew' it was an impossible target and there was lots of legitimate chat about how it couldn't be done, backed up with plenty of valid reasons. However! In one branch one employee not only achieved the target, he absolutely smashed it. Intrigued, the managers investigated what he'd done that other people hadn't. It turned out he was new to the bank. He'd not been party to the 'legitimate chat' about 'valid reasons' and assumed it was a totally doable target. He hadn't been exposed to the bullshit input. His 'river' was fresh!

2. How to build bullshit filters

So, if bullshit can have such a huge negative impact, how did the crew create bullshit filters and how can we copy them? Just knowing how the brain works – knowing the flow from information in, interpretation, feeling, action, to result – is really helpful, but there are also four simple strategies we can steal from the Olympic crew's kit bag to build powerful bullshit filters that protect our progress.

The crew's four strategies for building bullshit filters were:

2a. Don't talk bollocks to Basil
2b. Accept the facts, challenge the negative interpretation
2c. Find a better interpretation
2d. Use bullshit as emotional fuel

2a Don't talk bollocks to Basil

This strategy is about – wherever possible – stopping unhelpful information entering your head in the first place. Stopping bullshit from polluting the river, or at least scooping it out as quickly as possible…

The crew kept away from bullshit whenever they could. Lots of bullshit comes from other people so that meant avoiding unhelpful people in the first place or – if that wasn't possible – avoiding certain topics of conversation, or filtering out what they said.

Ben: "When Fred joined the group he brought with him a few Oxford Brookes sayings including 'don't talk bollocks to Basil'. I have absolutely no idea who coined the phrase, but what it meant was don't listen to or share stuff with people you shouldn't be talking to. Focus on people who are of interest to you, people who matter. Focus on who or what will make the boat go faster. Anything else is simply talking bollocks to Basil."

Our loved ones might give well-intentioned, but massively unhelpful, advice when they don't want us to get hurt. Our friends and colleagues might give us unhelpful tips because they don't appreciate our context. For example, Ben was grateful that Steve Redgrave focused solely on his own crew and didn't get involved in other crews:

Ben: "I have massive respect for Steve Redgrave, at Sydney he had four Gold medals and was about to get his fifth, but when it comes to our crew, he didn't think that we could do it and he might as well be my mother's stepmother's grandmother's aunt, quite frankly."

It is usually within your control to stop talking bollocks to Basil, what about when Basil won't stop talking to you? What if your boss/colleague/best mate is a Basil? Ben and the crew were cheek by jowl with 'Basils' right up until the day of the final. It was hard. All they could do was avoid bullshit conversations wherever possible.

Ben: "We shared a flat in the Olympic village with the rowing four; we were good mates. On training camps I'd play cards most nights with Steve and Matt, but I knew that they believed we couldn't do it. There were conversations with my family, and with Isabella, my wife, where I had to filter out what was being said."

Although Ben never explicitly asked people to shut up, many people got the message. He would listen passively, but not comment, change the conversation or walk away at the first opportunity.

Not only might you be weakening your self-belief by talking bollocks to Basil, but in some instances you might be helping your competitors to strengthen theirs. There was one crucial occasion where Ben was *forced* to talk to Basil, and simply worked to reduce the fallout. When Britain lost to Australia in the 2000 Sydney Olympic heats it meant the crew had to face the 'repechage'. The repechage is where the losers from the heats have to race against each other to secure a place in the final – only the first and second place crews go through. Ben and Fred also had to face a press conference.

Ben: "We'd never done a press conference and hadn't had any media training, but we just kept in mind not to talk bollocks to Basil. We didn't dwell on how angry we were – we didn't want the Aussies to know how fired up we were. We certainly didn't explain to the press that the Aussies were in trouble because we'd rowed so badly and they'd only beaten us by a second and a half. We just tried to lull them into a false sense of security by going, 'ooh, the Aussies will be tough' while inwardly going, 'we are going to absolutely nail you'."

That sounds pretty tough, but probably the biggest Basil we need to face is actually not the international media, but ourselves – that nagging internal critic. It sounds daft, but simply recognising the inner critic as a 'Basil' is useful, because all too often, it sounds and feels like some wise Oracle, telling us the unquestionable truth, when it absolutely isn't. Which brings us on to the next strategy…

2b Accept the facts, challenge the negative interpretation

Ben and the crew didn't challenge facts – for example they lost the 1996 repechage in the Atlanta Olympics and they couldn't wave a magic wand and change the stark reality – but they absolutely challenged unhelpful *interpretations* about what had happened. For instance, some people told Ben he had only ever lost and he would continue doing so. He appreciated that this was just an opinion in the same way that when the judges give their feedback on *The X Factor* it's just opinion, when your boss tells you you're not ready for promotion, it's just opinion. When the voice in your head tells you you're not good enough, it's just opinion.

Many of us don't think about the difference between fact and interpretation and that can be dangerous – opinion can all too easily *feel like fact*, because we feel certain about it. We confuse a feeling of certainty with something being true when the two are completely independent. For example, have you ever felt absolutely certain that you left your keys on the table and in fact you have them in your pocket? Have you ever felt absolutely sure that you sent an email when all you ever did was draft it?

How did the crew know when to challenge an interpretation? By asking that core question, 'Will it make the boat go faster?' (i.e. will this interpretation make the boat go faster?). If the answer was 'no' then they'd keep challenging the bullshit until it lost its power.

Unhelpful interpretation	**Challenge**
This means you can't do it	Really? We screwed up *one* race, not every future race
You've never won before, you can't win now	'Never'? I won stuff at school, I just haven't won in the National Team *yet*
You can't turn things around in two years	Says who?! Why not? What would happen if we did?!

The crew spent a lot of time on team discussions – to the point where other crews remarked on it. Challenging negative interpretations was a vital part of that debate. How can you copy this idea in your life – perhaps put it on your weekly team meeting agenda or your personal to- do list? It's very simple and very powerful.

2c Find a better interpretation

As the saying goes, every cloud has a silver lining. The crew believed there was always a useful interpretation; they just had to find it.

Remember the example we used earlier, of the crew losing to the Russians in the 1996 repechage? What might be a different interpretation of that?

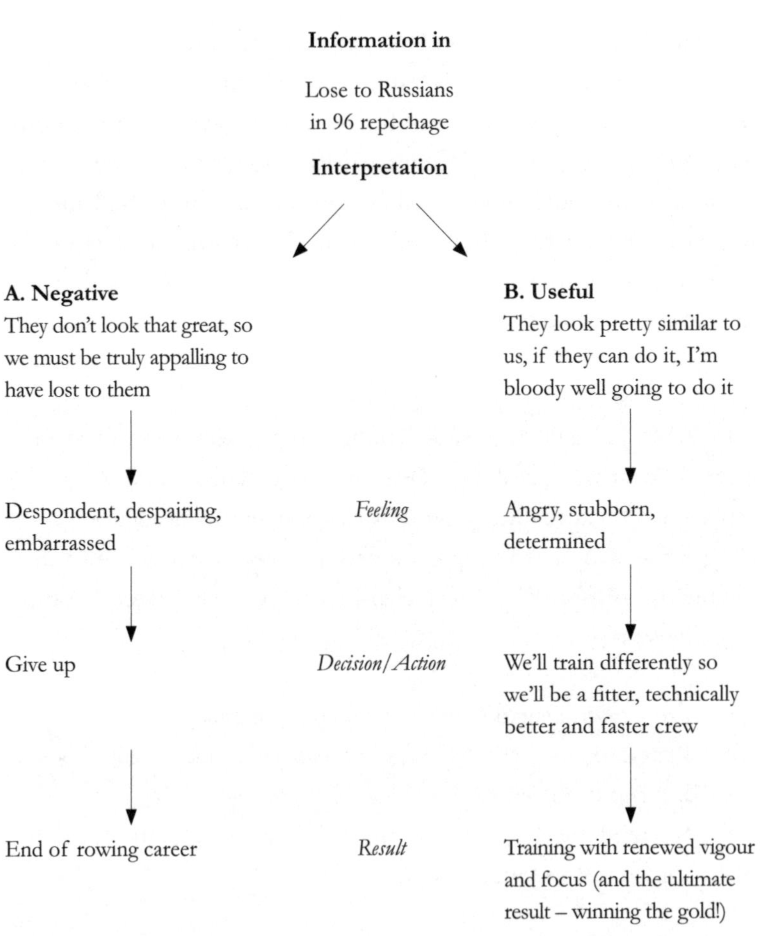

Both interpretations make total sense don't they? It's not that one is right and one is wrong. I'm sure you could think of many other possible interpretations too. But crucially, the interpretations drive *totally different results*. Most people, most of the time, give their brain a free rein around interpretations – they let the 'water' dribble along the path of least resistance. It doesn't mean the thinking is any more logical or any more right, it is just the lazy option.

Conversely, the crew didn't allow negative interpretations to creep in. They remained perfectly rational and logical (well, they tried to!). They were just very careful to *choose useful* interpretations. They actively encouraged water to flow down the *reasons why we are going to win* route and filtered everything else out as bullshit. We need to ask ourselves "how will this make my boat go faster?" or "how can I use this?" to uncover useful interpretations that will propel us forwards.

In 2014 I had a crazy goal of writing and performing a solo stand up show at the Edinburgh Festival Fringe. There were *plenty* of bullshit, unhelpful interpretations clogging up my head and I was confusing fact and interpretations big time. I find it helpful to write this stuff down so I can challenge it more easily. Here's some of the stuff I wrote in my journal:

- I'm a middle-aged woman. That ship has sailed
- I need to pay the bills. I'll lose a stack of money doing this
- I'm not funny enough
- It would mean leaving Al (my husband) to look after the kids for a week and that's unfair

First I challenged what was fact and what was interpretation. Things like "I'm not funny enough" isn't fact, it's opinion. There will always be haters, humour is subjective.

Next I looked for the useful interpretations. Sometimes this neutralised the negativity, for example:

- Yes, I might lose money, so do a budget! Save up for it like you would for a holiday.

Sometimes it uncovered really helpful interpretations. Asking the question, "what could be good about this?" unearthed the following:

- I'm a middle-aged woman. Great! This is actually really useful. It means I know my tribe. I won't be competing with the 3 a.m. student comics. Marketing will be a hell of a lot simpler and my show will be much more authentic.
- Leaving Al for a week. Why not ask him how he feels rather than assuming? It turned out he was fully supportive, and we had a useful conversation about the adventures each of us wanted to do. For example, Al goes on an annual golfing trip with mates and at the time of writing has just completed a charity cycle ride from Bristol to Paris.

2d Use bullshit as emotional fuel

Ben's bloody-mindedness comes up in pretty much every chapter! Here is another example. When people made disparaging comments or doom and gloom predictions Ben would use it to fire his 'I'll show you' motivation.

Ben: "Externally I'd be polite, (I hope!). Internally I'd be going, 'la, la, la, whatever. I am going to damn well show you.' The key was not reacting to them, but instead using it."

One of the crew even kept a special box. He'd write things down which people said that pissed him off. He'd open the box when it came to racing and used the comments to pump himself up. In other words it became more emotional energy to *strengthen* his belief.

How can we make sure this kind of energy drives us forwards rather than chewing us up? Would a box help you, or a journal to write your emotions down? Or perhaps a significant photo pinned on your fridge or kept in your wallet?

Conclusion

We need filters to protect ourselves from unhelpful bullshit and to grow strong, positive beliefs. There are lots of Basils out there. Who are yours? Who will give you unhelpful opinions that get in the way of your goal? Avoid them, or learn to filter out their poor opinions so you can stay on track.

Sometimes the Basils are obvious, but we need to watch out for the subtle ones too – such as friends who don't want us to waste time or to get hurt.

Often we are the worst culprit – 'Basil' is that doubting voice in our own head. Facts are facts, we can't change them, but we absolutely can change our interpretations. When we find an interpretation which isn't useful we need to let it go! When we find a more useful one we'll accelerate more quickly and smoothly towards our goal.

Now we've got the mindset that will help us to achieve our goals, but how do we actually get to work on our goal? The next chapter is called "Making It Happen".

CHAPTER 5

MAKING IT HAPPEN

Henley Royal Regatta

Making It Happen: Today is going to be a good day.

Henley Royal Regatta

Sunday 2nd July 2000, exactly 14 weeks to the Olympic final

This was my fifth attempt at winning 'the Grand'; the Grand Challenge Cup at Henley Royal Regatta. In the previous four attempts I'd lost every race, twice to the French – the ultimate humiliation – once to the Germans in quite a good race and, in 1995, to the US, who were reigning World Champions. That had been a brilliant race, but we'd still lost. This was our chance to put it right, this was my chance to win the Grand Challenge Cup.

We had a straight final against the Aussies who we'd beaten the week before. The Australian Olympic 8+ against the British Olympic 8+; a simple head to head. It was going to be a cracker.

At 2.57 p.m. the Umpire stood up in the long sleek umpire's launch that was temporarily moored to the stakes driven into the middle of the river bed behind us. About ten metres to my right were the Aussies, about four metres past them was the bank, which was crowded with spectators waiting to see the biggest, fastest boats of the rowing world power off the start.

It would take us about ten seconds to get the 950 kilograms of boat and rowers up to a maximum speed of eight metres per second.

Behind me sat Andrew, the bows of our boat and the course that lay ahead. There were no markers dividing the lanes as there were at most regattas, there was nothing to separate our water from the Aussies' water. Henley Royal Regatta isn't like other international regattas. In other regattas you race on lakes, very often man-made, the lanes you race in are marked out with small, round marker buoys and there are no other boats allowed on the lake other than the racing boat and umpires' launches in an effort to keep the water from being churned up.

But this was Henley and Henley is different.

The spectators that crowded the bank next to us at the start stretched away in an unending line, 2,122 metres to the finish line. There are no marker buoys and the river is not shut to non-racing boats. The water was being aggravated by countless motorboats, ranging from the three-metre-long boats for one-hour hire, to the cabin cruisers, which invariably included a boat of Elvis impersonators and a crew of 'Hawaiian dancing girls'. There were also the huge Thames ferries with jazz bands on decks, probably a floating car and goodness knows what else. Most of them would be oblivious to what was happening on the course and, as far as I could make out, their sole job in life was to make sure that the water was crap and lumpy on our racecourse. But this was going to be a good race because we were going to make it a good race, we could either complain about how crap the water was, or we could make it happen. We knew that all that mattered was how well we rowed.

In front of me sat the other six members of the crew, their backs towards me. There was Simon, broad shouldered and tall. Louis, short, by comparison. Luka, dark and hairy. Kieran, Fred and Steve, then Rowley, who was completely out of sight. Behind him was the freshly painted stake-boat (everything at Henley is freshly painted), where a teenager lay holding the stern of our boat in his hands.

The Umpire was standing, telling us that when he saw we were straight and ready he would raise his flag and say, "Are you ready? Go!" He told both countries to get ready. Rowley told Andrew and me to make the last corrections to the line of the boat making sure that we were pointing straight down the course. We slid forward on our seats and got ready.

"Are you ready?"
"Go."

We drove our legs down as hard as we could. Quick on the second stroke, power, quicker on the third; more power. Fourth faster. Fifth faster and longer. Sixth longer with speed, seventh power, eighth power, ninth power; where was the rhythm? We were up to strokes thirteen, fourteen and the Aussies were moving on us, but where was our rhythm?

We fought our way up the course. We should have been fighting them, but we fought ourselves. The Aussies were off; they flew down the track opening up a lead on us with every stroke. With every stroke they moved away. With every stroke we fought each other. We searched and struggled to find a rhythm, but it never came. We trailed across the finish line more than four seconds behind the Australians.

The Aussies were ecstatic, but we had disappointed everyone, it hadn't even been a race. It had just been crap. It was a non-event. It was absolute rubbish. We had rowed so badly it was unbelievable. The basic rhythm that we'd spent the whole of the previous year working on had been completely non-existent. We might have rowed badly in Vienna, but this was utter bollocks. We'd been utterly humiliated.

I was gutted with having lost. This was the fifth race I'd lost in the Grand – my home event – I'd never won one. But I was even more gutted that we'd rowed so badly.

Had our momentum stopped? Were we on a slide into oblivion? Was this the end of our Olympic dream? Were all of these years of work going to end the same way as every other season had for me? We'd been on a roll. We were gathering momentum and we were supposed to be unstoppable.

Our rhythm was the fastest in the world. But what had happened to the rhythm we'd worked so hard on? Was it the crew changes we'd made between Vienna and Henley? We'd brought Fred into the seven seat and Andrew had replaced Bob in the bow seat. I was sure it wasn't that. We had to make sure that the rhythm was always there no matter what, it had to be there otherwise this would be another disastrous year. Why hadn't it shown up? Why were we so inconsistent?

Losing at Henley was one thing, but seeing your Olympic dream slide away was something different. The pressure of racing is one thing, but the pressure of seeing nine years of work go down the pan was a whole different ball game.

In the hours after that defeat, I started to calm down and think more clearly. We were still in control. We needed to remind ourselves just how much was within our power to change. We'd lost one race, but that didn't mean that it was all over, it meant that we had to look at what choices we had and make good decisions about what to do next.

We lost because we rowed badly. Not because we were useless. Not because we were bad rowers. We just had to make it happen next time.

Some people made really 'useful' comments and told us we were 'bottlers', or that we'd been lucky the week before. We could listen to them, or we could keep the faith. We could either keep believing that we could win or we could start listening to the bullshit. I could think about every race I'd lost at Henley and add it all up to show that I could never win, because the past predicts the future, but I knew we were fast, we'd shown it in Munich in the heat, at Vienna in all our races, in so much of our training. The race was just an opportunity to make sure we kept our urgency, to make sure that we stayed on top of our game. That result was just there to make us go faster.

The next morning was Martin's day off, a very rare day off for him, but I still decided to go and see him. I needed to take the first step to putting things right. We had to sort out the rhythm and we had to commit with every ounce of energy we had if we were to win the following week in Lucerne.

Making It Happen:
Today is going to be a good day.

Ben: "My father always said, 'If a thing is worth doing it is worth doing properly.' The trick is getting started in the first place."

Chapter summary

We have an incredible amount of power to make our dreams reality. We need to adopt the mindset that we are simply going to make it happen… and then get off our backsides and get to work. The secret to turning nice ideas into firm action is:

- **W** Open the **W**ardrobe door.
- **R** See the **R**ainbow.
- **I** Choose the **I**guana.
- **T** **T**ake the first step.
- **E** Put some **E**ffort into it.

Have you ever felt daunted by a challenge?

- Maybe you're chasing an ambitious sales target?

- Maybe it's 5 a.m., the kids are screaming and you've got the whole day to get through?
- Maybe you're thinking about studying for a qualification, but scared about the time and work it will take?
- Maybe you wanted to start your own business, but felt utterly overwhelmed?

In 1998 Ben and the crew had bombed out of the World Championships, so wanting to win Olympic Gold within two years was a pretty overwhelming target. Martin told the crew about a Kiwi single sculler called Rob Waddell. Rob had a saying:

"Today is going to be a good day, because I'm going to make it a good day."

There is a lot in that simple sentence:

- I don't have to hang around hoping that someone else will make it a good day and worrying that they might not. *I* can make it a good day.
- I am going to *choose* to make it a good day. No one is forcing me to, it's my active choice.
- I am going to get off my backside and take action to *make* the good day happen.
- I'm going to enjoy it.

In other words things are far less daunting when we realise how much power we personally have to make it happen. We increase our chances of success. We're not beholden to other people, to fate, to the weather. Taking responsibility also feels good. Taking back control puts you back in the driving seat.

Ben and I have done nearly forty years of performance coaching between us and we consistently find that people underestimate how much power they have.

Many years ago, I used to help companies retain their talented women. This included running sessions to help people integrate back into work after maternity leave. I vividly remember one woman in a group who had unconsciously surrendered control of her situation, and lamented:

"Bad things always happen to me. I work long hours and there's nothing I can do about it – it's just the way things are at my firm. My husband doesn't pull his weight, but I guess that's human nature.

I've got a six month old baby who is an awful sleeper. If it was up to me I'd put him in a routine but my husband doesn't like routine so there's nothing I can do about that. There's no one I can call on to help, so maybe I should quit my job as I get overwhelmed with change – that's just the way I am."

Other research backs our findings. For example the psychologist Martin Seligman (and author of great books such as *Authentic Happiness*) did a range of experiments where he trained people into thinking that they had no power.

Seligman subjected two groups of volunteers to loud, unpleasant noises. He set up the test so that group A were able to stop the noise, whereas group B could not. Later he subjected both groups to loud noise that they could turn off if they tried, but group B – the ones who'd had no control in the first experiment – DID NOT EVEN TRY. They assumed they had no power. Does that sound familiar? For example, often at work we get fooled into thinking we have no control because the culture seems to dictate that we *have* to do certain things. In reality, we have plenty of unexplored power if we choose to use it.

How do you make it happen?

The techniques that Ben and the crew used to take control and make it happen can be divided into five categories. I know it's silly, but I remember them by spelling out 'WRITE':

Open the **w**ardrobe door
See the **r**ainbow
Choose the **i**guana
Take the first step
Put some **e**ffort into it

1 W: Open the wardrobe door

A few years ago a colleague, Stephen, had an embarrassing episode that he was generous enough to share with us so we could all have a good laugh at his expense. Stephen had gone on a business trip and managed to wangle a fancy hotel. As the gleaming lift glided up to his floor he got more and more excited about what his room would be like. To his bitter disappointment the room turned out to be small, with a single bed and a tiny television. The next morning, after a poor night's sleep hunched up on the miniscule mattress Stephen opened what he thought was a wardrobe door… but what was in fact the door to the huge, luxury bedroom. It turned out he had been given a family suite and he had spent the night in the children's annexe room in a kiddy bed.

Just waking up and realising that you have more power than you think makes a huge difference. As soon as Stephen opened the door it was simple for him to walk into the lovely bedroom. As soon as you open your mental wardrobe door you can walk in and make things happen.

Waddell's phrase, *Today is going to be a good day because I'm going to make it a good day,* was enough to help the crew wake up and appreciate how much power they had. They found it immediately cheering and helpful.

Sometimes the wardrobe doors are a bit rusty and need a bit of coaxing open. The language you use is a great indicator of whether your doors are open or closed. When you catch yourself using powerless language, challenge yourself to figure out fact from assumption. Take the woman in the group coaching session we mentioned above, for example. The other women in the group gently challenged her:

There's nothing I can do	*Nothing*? C'mon what can you do?
It's up to them [my husband]	Really? Surely it's up to you too? And what can you do to influence your husband anyway?
That's just the way I am	Nonsense! You've just had a baby! You started liking banana pizza, figured out how to work a car seat and started valuing a good night's sleep over a night out – if the last year's taught you anything it's surely that we can all change!

That's just the way things are at my firm	Well how can you convince them it's an awful way of doing it? They're going to lose a talented employee unless you figure out an arrangement together that works for everyone.

It is easier to spot when other people are whinging, but we can take massive offence if other people accuse us of moaning – other people have excuses, we think we have legitimate reasons! Watching our language is an easy way of measuring where we are operating on the spectrum from *powerless* to *powerful.*

The British 8 won gold at Sydney by a margin of 0.8 seconds. When the margin between success and failure is that narrow, it's no wonder they thought long and hard about what they could control.

Ben: "You have to do everything because you don't know what will make the difference."

The list of things the boys decided *were* inside their control included:

Their bodies.	What they ate and drank, how much sleep they got
Their mood.	They could choose the best 'motivation' tool for each situation
Their actions.	They could stick to the 'team rules' they'd agreed such as choosing to ask for feedback
Their beliefs.	They could cultivate useful beliefs and filter out bullshit

Now we can look at that list and throw in objections, perhaps "Well *I* can't control how much sleep I have – I've got young children and the night times are chaos." The point is where are we focusing our attention, energy and effort? On justifying why we *can't* do something, or on looking for a wardrobe door? On harrumphing about "that's just the way it is" or on figuring out how to get some kip?

What percentage of your time do you spend worrying or moaning about things you can't control? What would the impact be if you shifted your focus – even just a small bit – to what *is* in your control?

Our clients report that they feel happier and calmer; they are more effective and efficient when they focus on finding the wardrobe doors.

Ben: "Maybe getting a new boat got us 0.4 seconds, maybe the training camp at Ely won us 0.4 seconds, maybe dominating the lake got us 0.4 seconds…who knows? We absolutely wanted that Gold so we put as much in our power as we could."

2 R: See the rainbow

In the same way that we typically underestimate how much power we have, we also underestimate how many choices we have. Opening the wardrobe door gets us as far as appreciating that we *can* make it happen. Seeing the rainbow is all about the how – it's about appreciating the different routes to get there.

Ben: "Jürgen thought circuit training was the one and only way to do high intensity training, Martin saw a different route – he got us doing much more specific high intensity workouts on the rowing machine. Another example was the last training camp before the Olympics or World Championships. It was the altitude training camp and it was considered crucial, but we did something different – we went to Ely and did really high quality training there – it was the right thing to do for us."

On a leadership programme recently, a Spanish delegate called Carlos said something like:

"No one in our office puts our coffee machine on. It sounds like such a small thing but it annoys me very much. I am the only one who takes personal responsibility for making it happen. But doesn't that make me the idiot?! I end up doing it all myself! They are left not on the hook."

It's easy to fall into the trap of black and white thinking like this, seeing one choice rather than many. Carlos was basically saying: *either* I'm an idiot *or* I don't get coffee. When we look beyond the either/or, the black or white, there is usually a *rainbow* of options.

- Make the coffee, relish the moral high ground and move on.
- Make deliberately awful cups of coffee to make a point.
- Buy yourself your own private coffee machine.
- Ask someone specific to make you a cup of coffee in return for the one you made them yesterday.
- Talk to your colleagues about how you feel and what you want.
- Go round with biscuits and drinks and say you can have one if you promise to sign up to a rota and do it sometime this week.
- Stand by the kitchen and shout at the top of your voice "it's happened again, you are all a bunch of horrible berks…"
- Make a coffee for yourself and ignore everyone else.
- Make the coffee for everyone and get over it!

Ben: "For me it's very much a mood thing. When I'm tired or angry it's easy to get on my high horse and see things as either right or wrong. When I'm calmer it's all shades. Being in the right frame of mind helps you see the technicolour."

There are 50 ways to skin a cat, leave your lover or achieve your specific goal.

3 I: Choose the iguana

Once we can see the rich variety of options we have, the next step is making an *active choice* about which option we're going to take. What's so important about it being an *active* choice? Well, imagine going to a restaurant and looking at the menu and then being told by the maitre d' that you are going to have the pickled iguana whether you like it or not.

How would you feel? What would the impact be when your plate of iguana arrives – even if it's a mouth-watering local delicacy? Compare that with looking at the menu and making an *active choice* about what you are going to have.

We make decisions every second of every day… what we wear, what we eat, how we answer a colleague's question, when to scratch our nose, how to sit, whether to smile at that guy or girl, which TV channel to watch… most decisions are unconscious so we forget that we have active choices.

Ben: "The whole thing was a choice – there were all sorts of bits of training that were a nightmare. So many things were antisocial, unpleasant – having no money, having no guarantees about what happened next, but it was all a choice. I could have given up at any point and gone and done something else, so what was the point of complaining? I could have walked away any day. It's easy to think 'I have to do a two kilometre ergo test or I have to go to my job'; you don't really. Yes, there are consequences to any decision, but we don't have to do anything."

How might this look in our day-to-day lives? Read the following statements and reflect on which one feels more motivating:

- I've been told to do the washing up
- I ought to do the washing up
- I must do the washing up
- I could do the washing up
- I will do the washing up
- I've decided to do the washing up
- I am choosing to do the washing up because…

It's different for different people, but chances are phrases like *I ought to* feel nagging and draining. The rebel inside us is more likely to go "knickers to that, I'm not going to!" Whereas phrases like *I'm choosing to* or *I've decided to* feel better and are more likely to help us focus on the reasons why – perhaps to picture ourselves relaxing in front of the TV with a gleaming kitchen.

Try the list above again – only this time replacing 'washing up' with your own example, something you are struggling to get motivated about… perhaps 'run the team meeting' or 'go to the gym' or 'have *that* conversation'…

Ben: "The sentiment behind it is crucial. For example before a race if someone asked me if we were going to win I'd say 'We'll try' or 'We'll see' because I didn't want to come across as an arrogant twit, but inside I'd be thinking 'absolutely'."

Once again, the crew came back to the question, 'Will it make the boat go faster?' to crystallise their active choices. How do I need to 'choose to be' to make the boat go faster?

Do you find decision-making easy or difficult? Plenty of people find it really hard. Have you ever stood in the supermarket aisle overwhelmed by the choice of 40 different types of bread? And all the while the voice in your head is going, 'Good grief, you idiot it's just bread, how hard can this be, pick one! Pick one!' We end up wasting so much time. Making an active choice saves time and energy, especially when it's a matter of choosing, say, company strategy rather than simply groceries.

If you find yourself getting tied up in knots wondering what the right choice is, then let go of thinking there's only one approach and ask yourself what might be *useful* out of the many possible options to make the boat go faster?

4 T: Take the first step

Ben: "Nothing's ever going to be perfect. In rowing it's a question of how close you can get. You'll never know until you do something."

Have you ever been sunbathing and wanted to get into the swimming pool, but you can't face those first two or three strokes because you know it's going to be cold? You know you'll love it once you are in there, but you keep putting it off and putting it off?

At the risk of stating the blindingly obvious, a crucial part of making it happen is to *do* something – to take some action – and the first step can often seem like the trickiest bit. Maybe it's because when we talk about doing things 'someday' we get a warm fuzzy feeling, but when we talk about doing it 'today' the fear kicks in. We talk more about fear in the 'Risks' chapter, but fear is just a message to do some preparation and think things through. It's not the automatic stop sign that we all too often mistake it for.

The ten-minute rule we mentioned in the Motivation chapter can help us take that initial first step. Committing to give a project ten minutes rather than doing a weighty chunk of it gets the ball rolling. You don't

have to do a triple toe loop dive into the pool; you can gently go down the steps if you prefer; just come in, the water's lovely.

5 E: Put some effort into it

Have you ever gone to a party you didn't really want to go to? Did you turn up in body, but not in spirit? Unless you get into the swing of things once you are there it's going to be a rubbish party, isn't it? In the same way, in order to make it happen, you need not only to act, but to give your actions some oomph, some wellie! Ben came across some extreme examples of this during his quest for gold:

Ben : "In the 1991 World Championships the German eight had to sit down to get their medals. I'm pretty confident they couldn't give more. The British crew however came third and were jumping around with excitement. In the single sculls World Championship in 1994 the German who won went across to the pontoon to get his medal and kept falling over, getting up, falling over; and yet most people after a race get on the pontoon and stand up all right. Jürgen had a cheery saying: 'When all is black; one more'. In other words if you are pushing yourself physically so hard that you are about to black out, surely you can take just one more stroke."

These examples are off-putting because they are *so* extreme, but aren't they also incredibly useful? They remind us what an astonishing store of energy and effort we have to draw on.

We were working with a customer services department recently. They had a history of having loads of great ideas, but never actually implementing them. We took them through the 'WRITE' steps. They loved the 'rainbow of options' bit and came up with a plethora of creative ideas. 'But choosing the iguana' was a breakthrough. They made a collective, public commitment to do just a couple of actions. We then laid down the gauntlet and got them to 'take the first step' there and then. We got quite a few death stares and lots of (valid) argument that they couldn't do anything 'properly' in the workshop session. My unofficial motto when I'm performance coaching is to be constructively irritating, so we kept pushing until everyone had done something, however small. Examples included people putting meetings times in the diary, others doing five minutes of research, someone sending an email asking for advice.

The results? *They got the ball rolling.* They could feel the momentum starting even before they left the session. They'd kicked off actions which were then easier to keep progressing back in the midst of real-world business as usual. When we reconvened a month later they were able to celebrate 'making it happen' – rather than just talking about it.

Conclusion

It's so easy to kid ourselves that we are powerless and to let our hopes and dreams slip from our grasp. We need to open our metaphorical wardrobe door by asking ourselves, 'What *is* in my control? What *can* I do?'

Once we are in control we can start to see the rainbow of options available (remember Carlos and his coffee?) and make an active choice about how to move forwards. The first step can seem the scariest, but if we make it a small move we'll get the ball rolling. Lastly, we can remind ourselves that we have incredible stores of effort and resilience to see us through. These are the ingredients for making it happen.

Often it's hard to make it happen all on our own, we need other people, and the next chapter is all about how to build a high-performing team.

CHAPTER 6

TEAMS

Sarnen Training Camp

Teams: No one does it alone.

Sarnen Training Camp

13 weeks before the Olympics

We were in Sarnen, a small town about 30 minutes' drive from Lucerne, Switzerland. We had been on training camps here before and we liked it. We stayed in the Swiss Rowing Centre, where the rooms were university style; simple, sparse and functional; and the food was good.

The lake was about four kilometres wide and about eight kilometres long, it could get quite rough when the wind picked up, but normally it was fantastic.

We'd lost at Henley the week before and at the end of the week we had the Lucerne Regatta, the last race before the Olympics. Five days into our training and everything had been going pretty well, although we were feeling the pressure. We had to get it right this time. We had a clear goal that we had to achieve, we were running out of races before the Olympics and the final selection of the crew was still undecided.

As far as I was concerned stroke side was set, but the bow side was up for grabs. The bow side was a mess and those guys were under pressure to perform.

We had been working on the basics. We rowed up and down the lake numerous times making sure that every stroke counted because we had a golden rule not to just plough up and down. We were doing our damnedest to cover the distance as *effectively* as possible. We were working on the way our hands moved away from our bodies, the speed that our hands lifted to put the blades in the water, the speed of movement off our feet. We needed to rebuild our rhythm. We needed to eat up the miles as effectively as possible by covering the water in an apparently effortless flow. If we could do it in racing, not only would we be fast, but we'd be using less energy. If we saved energy on the basic rhythm we could put it in when we needed bursts of killer speed.

Lucerne was the last real test before the Games. We had to lay down our authority and show everyone that we were unstoppable. We had to put the Aussies back in their place. Every session we had to get right.

We were covering up to 50 kilometres each day, on the water two or three times most days. Sessions would finish with not only legs and backs exhausted, but also our heads. We were listening to Rowley, Martin and Harry constantly. We were desperately trying to make the changes that they were demanding of us, we'd all bought into the need to keep improving. There would be sessions when Harry would have the megaphone, we'd discuss exactly what it was he was after then he'd critique every stroke with a "No", "no", "no", "no", "yes", "yes", "no", "no", "yes", "no", "no", "no", "no", "yes", "did you feel the difference?", "no", "no", "no", "yes" – for ninety minutes! All of us were desperate to get it right, desperate to get Harry off our backs, desperate to win, desperate to improve.

The camp was going well, but it was mentally and physically knackering. We had work to do to become the single effective unit we needed to be. Chris Shambrook had helped us to develop team rules, which guided how we'd become an outstanding team, and these rules were never far from our minds.

On Monday 7 July it was day number six of the camp and we had 70 days to go to the heat at the Olympics, in my training diary I started counting down the days.

We did a pretty good 20-kilometre row that morning, it was at a constant 20 strokes a minute and we were trying to keep it lively and dynamic and, above all, with that rhythm. It was a lovely sunny morning; the water was brilliantly flat and the 20 kilometres disappeared pretty quickly below the smooth black hull of the boat. I thought it was a good session.

We let the boat glide in the shade of the lime trees that grew on the edge of the lake. Between us and the trees was a gravel path, a small pontoon designed for pairs and fours (where it was a nightmare to get the 8+ in and out of the water) and a few decreasing metres of clear water.

As the distance between us and the pontoon decreased I took my feet out of the shoes, took my socks off, rolled them up and stuck them up the side of my shorts and, ignoring Rowley's commands, Andrew and I guided the boat on to the flip-flop-littered pontoon. As usual Rowley told us to leave getting the boat onto the pontoon to him and as usual we ignored him. When we were on the water rowing I listened to his every word, but when it came to getting the boat off the water we were better off not listening!

After our second breakfast in the accommodation block we did an uneventful session in the weights room, then lunch to pack in the calories we needed to perform, and a long rest. Then it was time for the second outing of the day. Another 20 kilometres at 20 strokes a minute.

At about quarter to four I wandered down to the boathouse, most of the boys were already there, I did less stretching than most, it didn't mean that I was less committed; we all had our own ways of preparing. Louis would have been there for 40 minutes stretching his back and doing his strengthening exercises, he did between an hour and a half and two hours of stretching a day. I did a quick stretch, gathered the oars, carried them all down the gravel path to the pontoon and was back at the boathouse ready to go a few minutes before four.

We gathered on the concrete apron in front of the boathouse in the afternoon sun, I was tired but I was certainly looking forward to another good session.

Martin appeared carrying one of those red-orange metal fuel tanks for outboard engines looking pissed off. He put it down heavily on the smooth concrete beside him. He started being quite reasonable and explained how we had to accelerate the boat better. To show us he put his foot beside the fuel tank and pushed it away across the concrete saying, "That's what you should be doing, but what you are doing is smacking the oars at the water."

He walked up to the fuel tank and kicked it hard with his open flip-floppy-sandal-things. It didn't really move, but must have hurt his toes like hell. His anger suddenly rose up and he started ranting about us lacking commitment and not wanting to win and wasting his time. We needed to pull our fingers out and so on.

You could feel the atmosphere in the group changing as he went on. To start with I was shocked, but as he went on (rightly or wrongly) I assumed that it couldn't be me he was talking about, I don't think that there was much doubt as to my commitment. I had loads of faults, I struggled to get the rhythm, I struggled to sit straight in the boat, I struggled with loads of things, but I didn't struggle with commitment.

I assumed this must just be Martin's way of trying to get a reaction from Simon today. Simon was inconsistent, but it wasn't through a lack of commitment, we were all completely committed and commitment shows up in different people in different ways. Simon, at 6'8", was a fundamental part of the crew and if he was inconsistent it wasn't through lack of commitment it was through… in fact I've no idea what it was through, none of us did, that was one of the problems.

By the time he had finished half the group was really pissed off – some silently, some not so silently. The 20 kilometres I'd been looking forward to were completed, but without much passion, without much dynamism and certainly without much rhythm. It was crap.

By 6 p.m. we were back in front of the boathouse. Eight oarsmen standing heads bowed in sweat-darkened T-shirts and Martin furious. He had another go at us and stormed off saying he was fed up and he'd had enough.

What was all that about? We were supposed to be building momentum. This had definitely stopped it. I just felt depressed. What had just happened?

Louis was livid. Louis is Mr Process, everything he does is well measured and thought through, he doesn't do anything badly and he certainly doesn't lack commitment – ever. Martin's initial bollocking had really pissed him off. He couldn't tolerate being bollocked for something that he hadn't done, and the second bollocking hadn't helped the situation. Martin couldn't treat us all the same; it was a rule that we had to treat each other in the most appropriate way. We were different and he needed to see it.

We locked up the boathouse and we plodded back to the accommodation block. Some were livid, some thoroughly depressed and some not that bothered by what had happened. After showering and changing we went to find some food, but none of us had much to say.

Meanwhile Martin had got as far as Lucerne, 21km down the valley. He had bumped into the team manager, David Tanner, and told him that he'd had enough. Before long David was on his way to see what had happened and try to put the crew back together.

The next day we had just one session and we did it after a very long conversation to pull the crew back together. It was 69 days to the Olympic final, most of us had been together for nearly two years and we were still discussing rules and how we had to work together. There were a number of apologies and we spoke about what we were trying to achieve and what we had to do to achieve it.

We also spoke about how what had happened had to make us faster. We were not the finished article, as a crew we still had a huge amount to learn, we still needed to make a huge amount of progress. The same was true for Martin. He was a brilliant coach, but he wasn't the finished article either. He still needed to learn and progress. As a group we still had to learn how to come together. What had happened had happened and it was just something that had to make us stronger as a unit.

Teams: No one does it alone.

Ben: "In 1998 we were a rubbish team; by 2000 we were a good team. We had to work on the team as much as we worked on the rowing."

Chapter summary

If you want to build a strong team:

- Have a common goal which everyone wants to achieve, relies on everyone in the team to achieve it, and is measurable.
- Agree how to behave around each other and MAKE THIS STICK.

How did the crew become a gold-medal winning team? They had:

1. A common goal which had three features:
1a Mutual desire
1b Mutual reliance
1c Measurability

2. Agreed team behaviours that were:
2a Developed by the crew

2b Specific
2c Constantly discussed
2d Simple
2e Understood and bought into by everyone

3. This chapter also looks at dealing with team challenges
3a What do you do if someone is incompetent?
3b What do you do if people aren't committed?
3c How do you give difficult feedback to each other?
3d How do you get on with team members you don't like?
3e How do you deal with changes in team composition?

Team can be a horrible four-letter word. Have you ever been in a dysfunctional team where productivity grinds to a halt? Even good teams can be hard work at times, team meetings can be duller than being stuck in a traffic jam with a broken stereo and have you ever had to put up with a team idiot?

Ben: "Team working can be a pain in the neck. Very often it's much easier to do your own thing. In a team you often have to stop doing what you want to do to fit in with others. It means having to get on with people you don't particularly like."

So why bother?

Firstly, because a team can achieve amazing things that no one on their own could accomplish – as Wikipedia lovingly puts it, *"No rugby player, no matter how talented, has ever won a game by playing alone."*

However much we might like to, we can't implement that IT system or bring that new product to market singlehandedly. Being part of a team can also be a really good laugh.

Ben: "When you win as a team it's brilliant. I remember watching the single scullers when they won and thinking they looked rather lame going 'whoohay' with no one to celebrate with."

Another advantage of being a team member is that we have a chance of winning even if we're not the absolute best.

Ben: "To win in the pair you each have to be outstanding. To win in an eight you don't individually have to be so good, I wasn't good enough to be in the pair, but in the eight I could still win."

In a team we can learn from others – copy their good habits and profit from their mistakes without having to go through the pain ourselves. We've also got a deeper pool of references and useful interpretations to draw on to strengthen our beliefs and bullshit filters.

How did the crew become a gold-medal winning team?

So what made Ben and the crew into a team as opposed to a collection of individuals? How did they get from being a rubbish team in 1998 to a gold medal winning one in 2000? Their strategies all boil down to two fundamentals:

1. Have a common goal
2. Agree how to behave around each other.

That's it. No magic pixie dust, no conveniently compatible bunch of people, but some simple ingredients that any team, in any organisation, can put in place.

1. A common goal

Ben: "So many people say they are a team, but actually they just work with a bunch of folks, do their own thing and chat!"

We've already had a whole chapter on layered goals. Aren't we just repeating ourselves?! In this chapter we wanted to draw out the need for *mutual alignment* across different people. In addition, your team goal might be exactly the same thing as the crazy goal we talked about in chapter one – it certainly was for Ben and the crew. BUT in a larger organisation they might be different… aligned, that's crucial, but different. A bit like those Russian dolls that fit inside each other. For example, in a company, what is the goal, the point of the leadership team? Or the marketing team? Or a project team?

All too often this isn't clear and conflicting agendas simmer under the surface. For example, we were working with a technology company recently, where the leadership team had all – supposedly! – agreed the company's growth plans and what they as a leadership team needed to do to drive things forward. When they scratched below the surface, however, cracks appeared. The Technology Director wanted to create a perfect solution for each client, the Head of Production wanted simplicity of coding and assembly and the Marketing Director wanted global alignment of brand. Before they could row their boat anywhere, they needed to *genuinely* agree a common team goal.

The goal is what distinguishes a team from a random group of colleagues. The crew found that there were three elements to a really powerful team goal.

1a. Mutual desire
1b. Mutual reliance
1c. Measurability

An easy (albeit desperately cheesy) way to remember the three Ms is to think about a mouth-watering goal; mmm!

1a Mutual desire

Everyone wants the goal – why? Because it will benefit them *personally*. The benefits don't have to be the same for each team member, but it is crucial that everyone needs to achieve this *same goal* in order to get their individual reward.

Ben: "The Gold medal meant different things to different people in the crew: pride, money, proving other people wrong, being the best – but we all wanted one really, really badly."

Sales teams are a classic example of where this rule is often broken. Of course, sales directors want their salespeople to do whatever it takes to improve the company's bottom line, but, so often, individuals are measured on *individual* sales and they don't get any benefit if the *team's* target is hit. We can encourage people to help colleagues with their homework, but it is daft to *expect* them to help if they don't get any benefit out of it.

One man's meat is another man's poison – we need to make sure that everyone really does want to benefit and knows what that benefit looks like. Have you ever had a present you don't really want? Your mum has gone to a lot of trouble to buy you that thermal vest, but it's not quite you? It's all too easy to assume that what motivates us will motivate other people. A simple way of figuring out what floats each person's boat is to ask them. What excites each individual in your team? What constitutes a reward for them?

I remember working with a team at a High Street shopping chain, with the operations team whose goal was to open five stores in four months – something they'd never achieved before. The team was tired and scared, so we spent a bit of time nailing down 'what's in it for me' for each member individually.

It was clear that the *company* would benefit from the stores opening on time, but how would person A in marketing benefit personally? Or person B in Finance? The answers were quite different. For some it was pride and satisfaction, for some it was an easier life – a smooth implementation would mean no working over the weekends, for others it was about hitting performance targets that would help them get promotion. Once everyone was clear on how they'd benefit you could see the gleam in everyone's eyes and the conversation shifted towards *how* to achieve the goal.

I remember another company that had an *Employee of the month* scheme to try and promote team work. One month the Chief Executive's PA won the award. She got a public thank you speech from the boss, a bottle of champagne and her photo posted in reception. She was a quiet, shy person and her supposed reward – that was intended to make her feel special and valued – was her idea of *pure hell.*

1b Mutual reliance

The team is made up of the right people with the right skills, and everyone relies on each other to deliver the goal. There are no spare parts – everyone has a vital role to play. Crucially, everyone knows what is expected of them and of each other.

Ben: "They may not have been in the boat actually pulling the oars, but Shambles, [Chris Shambrook the psychologist], and Harry and Martin, the coaches, were crucial to making the boat go faster."

Have you ever got hacked off because your colleagues don't appreciate how much time it takes to do something?

> I was on a project years ago to set up a call centre. The telecoms guy was breezily asked if he could pop a few more phones in than originally planned and the poor man pretty much spontaneously combusted. None of us had appreciated the complexity involved in setting up more capacity on the system.

It's useful to have team conversations about what each person does and how it helps to achieve the team goal, so everyone has clarity about their contribution and respect for the work involved. What are each person's outputs? What inputs do they need? What does a 'day in the life' look like for each team member – their key activities? This is particularly important in a matrix structure where one individual might be a member of lots of different teams simultaneously.

1c Measurability

Fuzzy goals are when people say things like 'I want to lose weight' or 'I want to get better at presentations'. The textbook coaching response is to ask, 'How will you know when you get there?' Otherwise they are setting off on a running race without a finish line. If you keep on and on losing weight things will get silly and dangerous. On the other hand, 'I want to weigh ten stone' or 'I want to get an average score of at least 8/10 on my presentation feedback forms' are examples of clear destinations.

We've talked about measurability before – remember the chapter on layered goals? Or the bit in the motivation chapter about creating milestones? We'll keep banging the drum about this. If the team goal is measurable then it's super clear to everyone when they've achieved it or progressing towards it. If it isn't obvious, they'll lose momentum.

Sydney 2000 seemed a long way away in 1998, so the crew used milestones along the way – regattas and ergo tests – to keep the goal tangible. What are the concrete outputs that show you and your team that you are on track?

2. Team Rules

At the beginning of this chapter we said there were two things that got Ben and the crew from a rubbish team in 1998 to a great one in 2000 – a common goal and agreed ways of working. So far we've looked at the common goal, so let's turn our attention to the team rules…

Every single team, every group has rules, it's just that nine times out of ten they are unconscious ones that people have drifted into over time, rather than have actively agreed to and they might be massively unhelpful.

Have you ever been on presentation skills training and been recorded on video? Did you watch the video and think, "I had no idea I did that! Look, I keep wiggling my foot!" It is blindingly obvious to the audience, but when we are presenting ourselves we are so involved we simply don't know we are doing it. In a similar vein, if you want to make your boat go faster, don't let unconscious habits control you or your team.

After the disastrous '98 World Championships in Cologne, the crew's sports psychologist encouraged the crew to agree some rules actively. How are we going to make progress to gold as smooth and easy as possible? What is acceptable behaviour and what isn't?

If 'rules' sounds dull or restrictive, then call them team behaviours; team do's and don'ts; team culture; team contract; team armadillos. It doesn't matter what they're called, as long as everyone signs up to agreed ways of working that will make our everyday *boats go faster.*

There were some interesting features of the crew's team rules that we would do well to follow:

2a. They were developed by the crew
2b. They were specific
2c. They were constantly discussed
2d. They were simple
2e. Everyone understood them

2a Developed by the crew

Chris got the crew to develop the rules themselves. Everyone was involved in generating ideas and discussing them. The crew made it their job to know themselves and each other extremely well.

- They knew each other's technical strengths and weaknesses
- They knew their temperament, their bad habits, what made them angry, what motivated them
- They learnt how to flex their approach to get the best out of each individual
- They learnt what rules would maximise performance

The team rules were there to guarantee that everyone behaved in the ways that mattered and if they didn't they'd get pulled up. Have a look at the crew's team rules on page 162. It includes things like:

- Keep the bullshit filters on high
- Limit the amount of talking bollocks to Basil

A lot of the rules would make little or no sense to an outsider, because they are phrased in the crew's language. The rules also reflected the type of personalities involved – a group of lads in their mid-twenties, hence rules such as 'keep the in-crew piss-taking under control.'

Ben: 'I've been lucky enough to work with a senior manager at HSBC who is known for turning around regional areas within the bank. He's taken areas that are the worst performers and helped them get into the top five in the country. One of the first things he does is to get all the managers together and get them to agree what they want to achieve and how to do it. I think he has one rule that he imposes on the managers, which is that you're not allowed to be a 'Mood Hoover', but beyond that, it's up to the managers. There might be 200 managers in the area so he literally gets them all in one room to figure it all out. They consistently decide that they want to be in the top five in their region and they consistently achieve it."

How can you involve all your team members in developing your team rules? By ensuring everyone actively signs up, you're massively increasing the chances of everyone sticking to them.

2b Specific

When you ask Ben what was important to the crew, or what their culture was, he comes up with a long list:

- Learning
- Process
- Openness
- Being tough on themselves and each other
- Performance
- Being driven
- Being passionate
- Continuous Improvement

It's a meaty list and impressive, but how on earth do you measure it or make it stick? You need to go down to the next level of detail and create practical rules that you can apply to everyday situations.

For example, the crew talked time and time again about what *separation* meant. It was a common term in rowing, but it meant slightly different things to different people. The crew needed to get very specific rules about separating different elements of the stroke. This meant they could all get their arms straight then move the body then move the legs – even when they were doing forty strokes a minute.

What happens if we have rules inflicted on us though? What do we do then?

In the '90s my first graduate job was working as a management consultant for Ernst and Young. It was a massive organisation employing 85,000 people globally and we had a set list of corporate goals and values we were expected to follow. My manager got us to discuss what the values meant for us – what was their relevance, how could they help us and inform the way we worked together. It turned an abstract bit of paper on a wall into real-life agreed ways of behaving around each other.

The British rowing eight had team rules in the run up to Sydney and they also generated new, specific rules for the Olympic Games themselves – these are the ones on page 162. They decided the Olympic Village and the Olympic lake at Penrith were both sufficiently different environments from other regattas and training camps to warrant this. Some were practical rules to help with the scale and complexity of the Olympic Village, such as '*Go to the food hall as a crew. Have a set location in the food hall*'. Some were psychological ones to cope with the extraordinary pressure, such as '*Expect the unexpected – you can deal with it.*'

What specific events do you face that would benefit from specific rules?

2c The rules were constantly discussed

Ben: "Don't expect things to be perfect. Demand high standards, but don't beat yourself up or lose hope if the high standards aren't met yet."

When the British Olympic Association moved offices, a working party put together some rules about working in an open-plan office – in the old building people had been used to having their own offices. The list of open-plan rules was pre-framed as a first crack, something that needed to be reviewed. Unfortunately, the rules weren't discussed and reviewed to get buy-in. They were just imposed so they didn't work as well as they could have.

You need to start somewhere, plot your course, look for opportunities to discuss and assess the impact of whatever you've put down as rules, only then can you appreciate whether you are on or off course and take steps to improve.

Ben: "Talk and talk and talk and talk and talk. It is easy to assume that people know what you mean, what you are after and what's acceptable, but they don't – you need to keep checking."

The crew talked endlessly about their rules – on the water, off the water, before, during and after training sessions. Each of these conversations was a team building exercise in itself – the communication made the crew stronger. If a rule wasn't helping them progress towards gold they would throw it away and find one that did.

Each person found some rules easy and some hard – and they were all different, which provided an ideal opportunity to learn from each other and gather support. The constant discussions helped them figure out who was succeeding and what strategies they were using that the others could copy.

Ben: "Rules are a really, really good starting point for building a team. It's not about achieving common ground, it's not about the lowest common denominator, it's all about working towards the best possible outcome."

2d Keep it simple

It seems really obvious to keep it simple, but it's easy to get carried away when developing team rules. It's a bit like impulse shopping… "Ooh, what about being nice to each other, that sounds lovely? Shall we do that too?" Remember that the rules are only there to help us achieve our goal, so stick solely to the essentials. Having too many rules can muddy the water and people get distracted worrying about which rule takes precedence over which others. By revisiting the rules time and time again the crew made them simpler and simpler until they eventually could almost throw away the list of rules and stuck to that one golden question:

"Will it make the boat go faster?"

2e Everyone understood them and bought into them

This feature was a function of the others. In other words the crew understood the rules and bought into them because they were simple, specific and the crew themselves had developed them. 'If it will make the boat go faster then of course I'm up for it.' Because the crew talked about the rules on a daily basis they kept checking that every crew member had the same understanding about what was required. They could calibrate if anyone was lacking buy-in and agree how to strengthen commitment and performance.

3. Dealing with team challenges

We've looked at the common goal and we've looked at the team rules. We'll round off this chapter by looking at team challenges. The most common problem is lack of alignment and that's cured by an MMM goal and some team rules. In fact, when you boil it down, *any* of the challenges below are addressed by an MMM goal and robust team rules!! But let's explore some specific challenges in detail for further clarity.

What might throw a high-performing team out of sync, or prevent a good team from becoming an exceptional one? Here are some examples of typical issues that corporate teams come to us for advice about, and some ideas from the British crew's experience which help to tackle them:

3a. What do you do if someone is incompetent?
3b. What do you do if people aren't committed?
3c. How do you give difficult feedback to each other?
3d. How do you get on with team members you don't like?
3e. How do you deal with changes in team composition?

3a What do you do if someone is incompetent?

The bottom line might be to quit the team ourselves or exit the underperformer. But we need to think before we pull the emergency cord. If it is genuinely a competence issue, then training, coaching and feedback are useful tools, and for these to work we need to get more specific.

Ben: 'Figure out how to help them get better. To say 'they are crap' is a massive generalisation. Work out what they are good and bad at and take it from there."

For example, one of the guys in the crew wasn't great at looking after himself. He ate badly, he got ill, and that had a big impact on team performance. The crew supported and nagged him to sort this out.

I coached someone recently who had a team member who just wasn't delivering. It turned out to be a simple misunderstanding about what 'producing a draft presentation in time for the month end review' meant. The issue wasn't performance, it was lack of clarity about what needed to go in the draft and when it needed to land on his manager's desk.

Ben: "Deal with the behaviour, not the person. Be clear on whether it's important that they are good at the task in question. It might be better to leave them alone and get someone else in the team to do it."

Another avenue worth exploring is whether team members aren't giving the required contribution because they *can't* or because they aren't *motivated* to. If they aren't pulling their weight because they can't be bothered, then start with their commitment:

3b What do you do if people aren't committed?

The term *commitment* is a slippery eel. What exactly does it mean? Have you ever meant to go and buy someone a birthday card, but never quite got round to it? "Family is *really* important to me," we tell ourselves, "I've just been too busy to pop to the shops." Our mum with the card-shaped gap on the mantelpiece doesn't see it quite the same way.

We tend to judge our own commitment levels by our *intentions and feelings*, but we judge other people's commitment levels by their *behaviours.* So, make it a level playing field by formulating team rules which clearly explain what people need to *do* or *say* to prove they have commitment.

Ben: "I was really committed to winning at Barcelona in 1992, but the third time I arrived for morning training still wearing my clothes from a party the night before I nearly had my head taken off by guys who'd been training for four years."

The British eight defined commitment very clearly – it meant turning up to training in a fit state; it meant doing a full chin up in training; it meant not talking bollocks to Basil etc.

If someone doesn't seem sufficiently on board then consider what is driving the lack of commitment.

- Is the problem that it seems like too long a haul? Then the answer might be to put clear milestones in place.
- Is the issue that they can't see a compelling benefit? If so then what would float their boat? Pride? Acknowledgement? Promotion?

Time and again research shows that what interests people to perform above and beyond average performance is not money, but what the psychologist Herzberg called *motivators* – things like recognition, interesting work, feeling part of the 'in' crowd…

Ben did a speech recently for a client who deals in car parts. The Sales Director described it as deeply unglamorous! There's no gold medal, nothing more than a pay cheque, but his aim was for people to be down the pub at the end of a day's work going, "I like my job, it's a bit of a laugh… my boss is a good guy."

3c How do you give difficult feedback to each other?

The crew saw feedback as crucial for raising individuals' awareness to blind spots and for improving teamwork. The team rules gave mutual permission to give and receive it. They found that the more they did it, the easier it got. It's such a rich topic that we've devoted a whole chapter to 'High Performance Conversations', with specific sections both on *asking* for feedback and on 'telling it how you see it'.

3d How do you get on with team members you don't like?

There were plenty of frictions in the eight. Ben tried to punch Andrew; Stevie and Martin didn't always get on, Kieran and Louis had differences, Rowley and Luka didn't speak to each other for a week or so. It is undeniably tough to spend hours a day, week in week out with someone you don't like – especially in a boat that is just two feet wide.

Ben: "When things got fractious, we used 'don't talk bollocks to Basil' (see the Bullshit Filters chapter) on each other. If we need to talk about rowing and making the boat go faster then absolutely talk to me, but not about anything else that's not relevant. Stevie had challenges with Martin, but recognised he was an excellent coach, so he focused on that. When Luka and Rowley had a bust up in the last weeks before the Olympics and didn't speak to each other for days someone or something made them think, 'Is this making the boat go faster? No, so we need to change.'"

When you're in a working environment there's no *rule* that says you must like everyone who is in your team. However, you do need to have respect for their ability to do the job. Likeability and competence are not the same thing.

3e How do you deal with changes in team composition?

The daily conversations which took nothing for granted (remember the constant definition of *separation*) helped new members to understand and buy into the rules very quickly.

Ben: "Assume they – and you – know nothing. Take as much time as necessary to get a common understanding."

When there are changes in the team – or in the project, for that matter – discussion is essential. New team members need to understand where you're up to; what the team 'modus operandi' is, so they follow the same way of working and fit in quicker. A discussion will also help the team to understand the incoming team member and what they bring to the team.

Conclusion

A high-performing team can achieve astonishing results. In order to do that it needs two things:

1. A 'MMM' goal (mutual desire, mutual reliance, measurability) to work towards
2. Agreed team rules which describe what everyone needs to do and say to make the goal a reality.

A compelling goal draws a team irresistibly forwards. It minimises wasted effort and maximises motivation. The team rules make it crystal clear what is acceptable and what is unacceptable behaviour. If the rules are developed by the team members themselves, they create massive buy-in and are more likely to become self-policing. This lessens the chances of emotional slanging matches and increases the chances of grown up conversations which will *make the boat go faster.*

What next? Well, we've touched on it… now let's dive into the detail. The next chapter homes in on 'High Performance Conversations'. These interactions might be between team members, but even the most solitary of endeavours can massively benefit from quality conversations with others…

GB 8+ SYDNEY OLYMPIC GAMES
CODE OF CONDUCT.

VILLAGE CODE.

- Meals – go to the food hall as a crew. Have a set location in the food hall.
- Keep communication between each other "transparent" at all times.
- Take mobile phones to aid communication.
- Punctuality important in the village.
- Limit the amount of talking bollocks to basil.
- Have the bullshit filters working on high.
- Keep the in-crew piss taking under control.
- No "performance" talk to outsiders.
- Chill when we need to.
- Exploit the extraordinary nature of what you are a part of – enjoy the experience.
- Take collective responsibility.

PENRITH CODE.

- Gb kit for training.
- Keep the outings as normal as possible.
- Find out important information regarding the course and training as early as possible.
- Always professional – punctuality important part of this.
- The focus is in our boat.
- Execute the normal routines. Stick to the routines.
- Expect the unexpected… you can deal with it.
- Use the normality of the environment.
- Keep crew feedback high on and off water – keep communicating.

GB8 + Sydney Olympic Games Team Rules

CHAPTER 7

HIGH PERFORMANCE CONVERSATIONS

Sarnen, July 2000

High Performance Conversations: Say what needs to be said and hear what needs to be heard.

Sarnen, July 2000

13 weeks till the Olympics

The Sarnen training camp was coming to an end. It had been an interesting camp! We were longing to get to Lucerne and race. We'd had some incredible sessions where we'd really stepped our rhythm on. Sessions where we'd refined our approach and continued to improve how we were performing and then sessions where we'd pulled ourselves apart. The key had been to keep talking.

We'd all learnt a bit more about being able to have honest, performance-enhancing conversations. It's a journey that I, as an individual, and we, as a crew, had been on for some time. As an 8+ group we had to spend time and energy on how we could improve our performance reviews, how we could give better feedback and how we could be more honest with each other so that we could maintain our momentum.

I think that my feedback journey had started from my insecurity. I needed to know if I was good enough. Did I deserve to be here? Was I good enough? The best way to find out seemed to be to ask a coach so that I would know what to improve. Then I had a chance of deserving to be here. I reflected on the journey that I – and we – had been on:

Reflection 1. Baptism with fire and a need to know how I was doing. October 1991

I was rowing at Leander Club in Henley on Thames. I'd competed at the Under 23 World Championships in August and now the members of the national team were back from their post-World Championships holiday I found myself training with them. It had been my goal but it wasn't what I expected. Jürgen, the head coach, had put me, an inexperienced 19yr old, in a 4- with three men who had won medals at various World Champs. Two had raced at the Olympics, one had raced with Steve Redgrave at a World Champs, they were older, bigger, stronger and more experienced than me. I was *scared* of them all… and that was before we got in a boat. What I found when we started rowing was completely different to anything that I'd experienced before.

I clearly remember a week or two of grey October days. The river in Henley was flowing slowly, there was no wind making the water flat and smooth under low, flat, grey skies. The grass on the banks was still thick and green and the leaves on the trees were becoming crisp as they turned red, gold and brown. In my month old, proudly won, GB Under 23 Rowing Team kit I sat in the middle of the boat with these three other men in a ragtag collection of kit they'd swapped with rowers from around the world and all I could hear was one of them calling me a c*** every few strokes. "F***ing get your oar off the water". "F***ing get your oar down to the water". "F***ing hell you're useless". "What the f*** do I have to row with you for, you c***". It was relentless and I was shit scared of him. Jürgen had told me not to worry about 'Mr F***off' but at the end of the sessions when I asked him for feedback his response had been mixed as well. The first couple of sessions Jürgen said something useful but after three or four days he lost his temper with me, complaining that I was always asking for feedback and I just needed to train.

Over the months and years since then, I had learnt a couple of things. Firstly, my insecurity and desire to get better was really useful, I just needed to ask better questions and normally before the sessions. "Jürgen, I'm working on timing my leg drive better, can you let me know how I get on during the session or after the session?" worked much better than a broad open question at the end of a session. Secondly, I realised that I was pretty good at hearing what people said and finding the useful information in it. I was pretty good at interpreting what I was told to help me improve, I even managed to interpret some useful points from 'Mr F***off's' rants.

Reflection 2. Going deep with Shambles. Hammersmith, January 1999

When had we as a crew really started to focus on having high performance conversations? I think January 1999 might have been the start, and my God it was hard…

Our psychologist, Chris Shambrook (Shambles), had one-to-one sessions with each of us. They lasted between 30 and 60 mins. Most of us had found them pretty uncomfortable knowing what would come next – the group discussion.

Now here we were having the group discussion. There were 16 rowers crowded around the boardroom table in the British Rowing offices. The room was too small for the table and definitely too small for the 18 people in there. The polystyrene ceiling tiles were just about high enough to let Kieran and Simon stand without ducking but we had all had to stoop to get in through the low door frame. Some wore a motley collection of club and national team kit, some in jeans and T-shirts, all sitting uncomfortably in the cheap unholstered chairs. Some fidgeting awkwardly. Some in silent anger. Some sullen and withdrawn and some bored.

Martin and Shambles sat together at the end of the table working hard to maintain some momentum and guide us through the conversation, they had a clear process, but it was hard going for a bunch of 20-to 26-year-old blokes.

This was the first time that we'd done this as a group and the first time that some of the boys had done it all. Shambles had pushed us all hard to be open and honest in the one to ones. He had summarised everything we'd individually said onto four sheets of A4, divided into three sections:

1. What we thought our strengths were.
2. What we needed from others.
3. What others needed from us.

I thought that my strengths were my experience in rowing generally and my Olympic experience, I needed everyone to be driven and motivated, and what they needed from me was for me to be a team player and positive in my criticism and feedback. I was really pissed off. I was sure that I was a team player and I was sure that my feedback was positive and would help people get better.

Shambles kept reiterating why we were doing this. What was most important was boat speed, not ego and there were quite a few bruised egos around the table, including mine. The reason for listening, the reason for learning, the reason for changing had to be very clear: making the boat go faster! Have some time to reflect and digest what we had heard and decide what to do with it was the next critical step.

We had done similar sessions a number of times since then. They'd become more honest and easier each time.

Reflection 3. Nicknames and awareness. Ely, August 1999

We had a week before we left for Canada and the World Championships. Despite having had an increasing number of conversations about how we spoke to each other and gave each other feedback, we clearly didn't get it right all the time.

As with many groups of young men we had lots of nicknames. Everyone had at least two and not many of them were complimentary. But it was fine, we were all fairly tough and thick skinned and it was all just stupid banter. It was fine. However, one of the guys wasn't so thick skinned and really disliked his nickname, in fact, he *hated* all of his nicknames.

We were staying in the Lamb Hotel in the centre of Ely, a real treat compared to the mould-filled house we normally stayed in in Cambridge while training in Ely. The other Team GB rowing crews were in Austria at a high-altitude camp but we had opted to stay in the UK and train at sea level. The camp had been progressing fairly well, we had covered a huge number of miles. We'd just finished our third session of the day, another steady 20km session. We had rowed away from the small city on the hill and into the featureless landscape along the flat endless canal for 10km, before turning to row back towards the city with nothing but flat canal and flat fields and fences behind us. We had finished the post session review and were gathering our kit to walk the five or six minutes back up the hill, the only hill in what seemed like about 50 miles, past the cathedral to the hotel to change before dinner, when Martin called me over.

"Ben, do you remember the conversation in Hammersmith a few days ago about nicknames?"

"Yes Martin."

We'd had a short, to the point conversation where we'd agreed to stop calling one of the boys by any nicknames because he really didn't like it, it was getting him down and it simply didn't make the boat go faster.

"So why are you still doing it?"

I wasn't quite sure what Martin meant. I remembered the conversation and had agreed that I'd do as I was asked. I had promptly stopped, or so I thought. The conversation with Martin continued, and he gave me very clear feedback listing exactly where and when I had used the nickname three times that very afternoon. He didn't need to talk about the impact of my behaviour, I already knew! I was mortified, embarrassed and pissed off for being picked up on this. It had become such a habit I didn't even know I was doing it.

Reflection 4. Food for thought. Brock University, St Catharines, Canada. 14th August 1999

The camp had been going really well. The first race at the World Championships was nine days away. We were staying in student accommodation on the main Brock University campus and rowing 15 miles away at the South Niagara Rowing Club. It was a good piece of water that was a spur of the Welland Ship Canal, which links Lake Erie and Lake Ontario avoiding the Niagara falls. We were continuing to work on various aspects of power and speed of movement, on poise at the back of the stroke, speed of movement and timing at the front end of the stroke and so on. We were also continuing to work on ever increasing levels of openness and honesty.

Harry as ever was an amazing role model, always clear, always calm and never letting anything go that wasn't to his incredibly high standard. That morning Louis had had a conversation with me that he thought it was time for me to stop setting my alarm for 3 a.m. every night so I could call Isabella, my fiancée. I really enjoyed acting as her alarm clock and saying good morning to her. He pointed out that I might go straight back to sleep but he could hear my alarm pretty clearly through the wall and he didn't go back to sleep so quickly. I was disappointed but it was very reasonable of him.

That afternoon we'd had a really good conversation as a crew after we'd done a fast 500-metre piece and faster 250-metre piece about how we needed to be looser and more confident. We'd discussed the reasons why we could be more confident, what might get in the way and how to deal with those thoughts and issues. It had been open, straightforward and simple. A really good conversation. And then that evening I got it completely wrong again!

We were all sitting in a group at a long table in the canteen in the university, I had just started tucking into my supper of a piece of chicken, a pile of potatoes, another pile of veg and some fruit for pudding when Kieran put his tray on the table and sat opposite me. Kieran was not the most healthy person in the group, he seemed to have more than his fair share of coughs and colds and between mouthfuls he told us that he wasn't feeling at his best and he wondered if he was coming down with something.

All six foot eight of Kieran rowed exceptionally well. He sat in the middle of the boat powering it along in the most beautiful rhythm. The World Champs were nine days away and he was tucking into his veg-free, fruit-free meal again complaining that he wasn't feeling great.

The measured, thoughtful feedback of earlier that day disappeared. The thoughtful honesty about what we needed to focus on, what we each needed to improve and take control of vanished. In a sharp acidic voice I asked Kieran what he was eating to help keep him fit and well. Before he finished the first sentence of his reply, I hit him with everything that I'd been dwelling on for some time. That I didn't think that I'd ever seen him eat veg or a piece of fruit and funnily enough he was ill the whole time. I had plenty of evidence to throw at him. It came out in a rage surprising everyone on the table and causing Kieran to storm off without finishing any of his food.

Not only had I let myself down with my reaction but I'd also ensured that Kieran didn't eat any of what he needed for training the following day, or racing eight days after that. Frustration at his poor diet and the pressure of the up-and-coming race had caused me to react incredibly badly. We couldn't afford for that to happen again.

Summary of reflections: Sarnen, July 2000

Sitting in Sarnen I was thankful for all of these occasions when we'd got it right, got it wrong and learnt from it or just been a bit better than before. I felt better prepared to have good conversations on the run up to the Games.

If I had been able to fast forward and show myself how we would handle some of the conversations in the Olympic village in a couple of months' time I would have been even happier with the progress that we had all made.

Fast forward 1. The homework paid off. The Olympic village 12 September 2000

We were sitting in a pretty strange meeting space. The floor was concrete and had car parking spaces painted on to it, three of the walls were the wire mesh you found around tennis courts with brown sacking draped over them to act as screens and the fourth wall was a featureless concrete wall and the ceiling was concrete dissected with a couple of neon lights and a sprinkler system. Eleven of us sat on white plastic garden chairs, full of anticipation, excited, scared and in quiet conversation.

We had arrived in Sydney that afternoon from the Gold Coast training camp, three floors above us was the flat that we all shared with the rest of the men's rowing team, two floors above us was the flat for the women's team, on the ground floor was the coaches' flat and here in the basement, a converted car park, was the Team GB HQ supporting all 350-odd athletes and all of the support staff. Their office was small and compact, vibrant and business like. We were in one of the HQ's meeting rooms. Tomorrow we'd head down to the Olympic Regatta course for the first time for a 12km session and our opening heat of the Olympic Regatta was six days away but this evening we were planning.

There were the nine of us from the crew, Martin and Chris Shambrook. We knew what training we had to do over the coming days, we knew the technical points we had to work on and we didn't spend too much time discussing these points. What we were there to discuss was the team, our behaviour, our approach. A month or so before in Ely we'd discussed and come up with a set of team rules, a 'code of conduct for the Olympic Village' and a separate one for Penrith, The Olympic Lake. These team rules were based on a number of conversations about the environment that we would be going into and how we need to act and behave. Having had our first meal in the ginormous dining hall it was time to ensure that we were happy with the rules and crystal clear on how we needed to behave to maximise our chances of winning.

The measure of how far we'd come as a crew was when Louis turned to one of the other boys and very directly asked him to continue to give him feedback and support, to talk to him about rowing but for the 12 days until the final, if it wasn't about rowing, could he just not talk to him. The response was a calm 'sure'. We would be living together in the same flat, we would be together for almost every waking hour but both knew that they wound each other up so it was just a simple request with a simple response to give us all the best chance of achieving what we all wanted.

It hadn't always been that simple! But two years of practice, two years of honest, difficult feedback conversation had paid off. All of the practice had made it easier to be open, easier to be honest and easier to converse in a way to make the boat go faster.

Fast forward 2. The Olympic opening ceremony. The Olympic village 12 September 2000

The room was the same as two evenings previous. Sacking on three of the walls and concrete on the fourth, the floor and the ceiling. The Olympic opening ceremony was the topic for tonight. It was three days away.

This was the third proper conversation about it. The first had been in the Lamb Hotel in Ely a month before. It had been a straightforward conversation, I was the only person in the crew including Martin who had been to an Olympics before and I had told the crew what it was like to march in an opening ceremony.

For the 1992 Barcelona opening ceremony the British Rowing team along with every other rowing team in the world had boarded a fleet of buses for the 45-minute journey from the rowing village to the stadium area in Barcelona. We had made our way to the gymnastics venue where the 169 countries competing were shown to the seat allocated to them. There was a sea of colour with different national teams' outfits. There were waves of excitement and a constant flow of thousands of conversations that filled the hall. We sat in our allotted seats and ate our packed dinners desperate to know what was happening in the main stadium a few hundred metres away but the huge screens above the gymnastics mats stayed blank.

Eventually the name of a country appeared on the screens and that nation would stand and make its way out of the arena. It was an age before Great Britain appeared on the screens. We pushed and shoved to get out of the arena and join the back of a very, very slow queue where we were arranged into two groups, the women at the front and the men at the back. There was talk about marching in step but it was pretty obvious that that was never going to work.

As the queue approached the tunnel into the stadium the excitement grew and grew and grew. I was there with my mates from the rowing team, we were wearing dark blue suits with the Olympic rings just under the Union Jack on our breast pockets. We wore Olympic ties and our hats had the Olympic rings on them. As we stepped out of the tunnel into the Olympic stadium we would be representing our country at the Olympic Games. It was incredible. It was a dream come true. It seemed to take for ever to get through the tunnel into the bright lights of the stadium.

The noise, the atmosphere, the energy. It was incredible. I'd never experienced anything like it before. It really was incredible.

And then the speeches. And then the wait. And then the shuffle towards the buses. And then the total confusion trying to find buses going to the right places. And then the bus journey home. And then the queue getting back into the rowing Village. Six-hundred-odd people queuing for one security guard to scan every pass. And then bed. Exhausted.

Atlanta had been different. Every bit as exciting but instead of the slow queue to the stadium it was an 800m sprint. A member of the Polish team had a heart attack and died on that run, our cox Gary Herbert was almost trampled to death as he fell in the stampede. It was also a hot night and we'd drunk huge amounts of water in an effort to stay hydrated but once in the stadium there was nowhere to go. There were no loos so gradually the empty water bottles were refilled by desperate athletes. I'm not sure what the women did! It had been a huge amount of fun but exhausting. I tried to talk about both sides of the experience evenly.

A few weeks later we had more of a group conversation about it. I tried to remain impartial just giving the facts that I could. Tonight, however was decision time. We now knew how far the stadium was from the Village, a few hundred metres. We knew the probable timings of leaving the Village and returning to the Village, they were between 5 and 6 hours apart. We knew the return time to the Village, about midnight. The question was would we go or not?

It ended up with 7 in favour of not going, 1 in favour of going and 1 abstaining. The person who wanted to go was disappointed but he understood. We had discussed it and the group had decided. It had been a very simple and straightforward conversation thanks to all of the effort that we had put in over the previous two years being able to say whatever needed to be said and hear whatever needed to be heard to make the boat go faster.

High Performance Conversations: Say what needs to be said and hear what needs to be heard.

Ben: "If you see something that's not as good as it could be and choose not to discuss it, you're helping us lose."

Chapter summary

Life is infinitely easier when you can:

- Say whatever needs to be said – confident that it will be listened to without offence being taken
- Hear whatever you need to hear, without getting bent out of shape
- Have conversations that don't go round in circles, but are pretty much guaranteed to lead to clarity, decision and action

A key ingredient of the crew's success as a team was their commitment to three types of 'High Performance Conversations'.

1. **Ask for feedback**
2. **Tell it how you see it**

3. Make a decision

The strategies for having these conversations are:

1. **Ask for feedback**
    a. Be helpful to your neurons
    b. Choose a useful source
    c. Make it a regular habit
    d. Keep probing
    e. Digest
    f. Act

2. **Tell it how you see it**
    a. Have a useful intention
    b. Break the surface tension
    c. Tailor your approach to suit your audience
    d. Be a lover and a fighter
    e. Cut to the chase
    f. Communicate facts as facts and interpretations as interpretations
    g. Spell out the consequences
    h. Commit to next steps

3. **Make a decision**
    a. Have a clear purpose
    b. Have a process
    c. Have team rules specifically around communication

If a conversation will make your boat go faster, have it. If it won't, don't. There, shortest chapter in the book. Done.

Sounds utterly obvious, but this is very far from the norm. All too often, we communicate to achieve an objective which – if we are ruthlessly honest – isn't very laudable. It's about making ourselves look good, proving ourselves right or letting ourselves off the hook. For example,

- When we seek feedback, are we really looking for performance improvements, or are we actually looking for *reassurance* that we don't need to change?
- When we talk to our colleague Pavel about Bob's annoying behaviour, are we *really* wanting to improve team dynamics, or are we hoping Pavel will agree that Bob is an idiot, and we keep the moral high ground?

On the other hand, we often avoid conversations we know we probably should have, because we don't want to rock the boat or sour a relationship. And yet we know that open, honest conversations are so powerful. Whenever I'm working with a group and ask them how they need to behave around each other I can guarantee that 'open and honest conversations' will always come up. It's no surprise that they are a constant theme through Ben's story. The crew's honest conversations enabled them to agree actions to improve their physical strength, technical skills… to do all the things which ultimately made their boat go faster.

So, what were the crew's secrets for having high performance conversations?

This is a *massive* topic, easily a book or three in its own right, so we're only going to focus on three types of high performance conversations which were pivotal in the crew's journey to gold and which time and again we see making a step change for our clients.

1. **Ask for feedback**. How to gather fresh perspectives from different viewpoints which you can choose to act on (or not!) to up your game.
2. **Tell it how you see it**. Voicing – perhaps uncomfortable, unsolicited, or controversial – insights, feelings and views – because they might create opportunities for performance improvement.
3. **Make decisions**. How to have team conversations that yield clarity, progress, decisions and *action*, as opposed to groupthink, pointless argument or waffle.

For any of these conversations to be 'high performance' ones, as opposed to idle tittle tattle, the absolute key is that they have a WHY, i.e. what is your goal for having a conversation? How will it benefit:

- You, personally?
- The other individual(s) in the conversation?
- The wider context – e.g. the family you are members of or the organisation or company you are all working in?

These three elements are a bit like the legs on a three-legged milking stool. If the conversation only helps one 'leg', you'll end up with a wobbly seat that is likely to collapse under the weight of the topic. For example, I can harangue the kids to put their dirty clothes in the laundry bin rather than strew them like confetti around the house, but unless it will benefit them in some way, why should they bother? And will it really benefit the 'family unit', or am I just serving my own tidiness-freak agenda?

We'll keep going on about the milking stool throughout this chapter.

Let's look at each conversation in turn:

1. The first type of high performance conversation: Ask for feedback

When I first met Ben, I quickly discovered that he is a feedback junkie. He is always asking for feedback. This was startlingly different from my default setting. I used to wait patiently for my annual appraisal, hoping for a pat on the head, fooling myself that in the meantime no news from my boss was good news. Ben had just retired from rowing and started running workshops with corporate groups, so I assumed his feedback-addiction was his way of mastering a new skill. Nope; he does it with everything, new and old. My first reaction was urgh! Why seek out unpleasant feedback? Ben had a long list of reasons:

Why ask for feedback?

- It stemmed from his belief in better, his quest for momentum and improvement. He knows that other people can see things that we can't.
- It gives us more data, more choices. We don't have to blindly follow what people say. Ben treats feedback purely as information, an input.
- We might actually get some! The majority of our clients say their organisations have eerie feedback silence. Asking for it puts us more in control of the timing, volume, content, tone.
- We get to be really specific – to home in on what we'd actually like to know, rather than get an unwanted avalanche of stuff we know already.
- We can set it up in advance: it's far more useful to have a colleague primed to look out for – say – our questioning skills in a meeting, or a teammate primed to assess our passing skills in a hockey match, than wait 3 months for an appraisal.

- It sets a powerful tone; it shows that we know there's no limit on better and we want to improve. If you are leader it will encourage others not just that it's safe to give *you* feedback, but it may well encourage more feedback generally.

Ben: 'Feedback is really valuable. Why would you not want to know something that might make the boat go faster? If you see something wrong in a session at the start of the day tell me now so I can make the sessions the best they can be as quickly as possible."

So, how do we go about asking for feedback? And, by the way, all of these steps are useful for dealing with unsolicited feedback too.

1a Be helpful to your neurons

We should give our poor neurons a break. It's easier to build on existing skills and strategies than to stop and do something completely different – or try and transform our entire personality overnight. The crew had a balanced set of feedback and review questions, which we'll go into in more detail in the next chapter:

- Where am I performing well?
- Where could I perform better?
- What suggestions do you have for another time?

1b Choose a useful source

We typically ask the same, safe people for feedback – whose view haven't we heard and might provide a really useful perspective?

Ben: 'Harry, coaching from the riverbank, could feedback on loads of things we simply couldn't see in the boat. But sometimes we'd get our psychologist, Shambles, into the launch. He knew nothing about technical rowing, but his different perspective was really interesting. What's the point of finding out things you already know? You want to make your boat go faster."

1c Make it a regular habit

Ben: "There weren't really any massive things we had feedback on, because we did it continually, so the issues never grew that big."

The crews used their famous team debrief sessions to give each other feedback. Building in a recognised time and place for feedback is a useful way of making it a team habit. Kate Richardson-Walsh, GB hockey gold-medallist and team captain calls this 'stamping on fires early'.

1d Keep probing

What's easier to answer:

- 'Have you got any feedback for me?' or 'How did my questions come across in that meeting?'
- 'Am I playing well?' or 'Which passes were most effective in that game and what made them good?'

Stick to information they know about: your behaviour (what you did and said) and how it landed (how your behaviour made them think, feel and act). If you are getting blancmange summaries, then keep digging to get more clarity: "when specifically? How specifically? What specifically…?"

1e Digest

Ben: "As a crew we would listen, say thank you (sometimes!), digest it, then decide what to do with it. Perhaps a huge change, perhaps a tiny one, perhaps nothing at all – but the point was that by asking for feedback we had better information than we would if we hadn't bothered."

Mull it over – and this might take a bit of time if it's not what we were expecting, or if we've been told something difficult. Feedback bends us out of shape when we confuse it for facts about our very identity. We need to remember it's simply opinion about our behaviour. Use the techniques in the bullshit filters chapter to accept the facts, challenge the negative interpretation and find better ones.

Ben: "Feedback is just information. Whatever the other person's intention, however poorly they express themselves, it might just be the information which will help you win."

I coached a senior lady in a well-known financial institution which will remain nameless. She told me her manager had given her feedback that she "was crap". I smugly pointed out that this was her *interpretation*, and asked her what the manager had *actually said* to warrant her interpretation and to confuse his feedback about a behaviour with a fact about her identity.

"No Harriet, he said – in a meeting, in front of colleagues – 'you are crap at your job'."

Ah, OK, not quite what I'd expected. But, on reflection, we realised the issue was *still* that she was confusing his feedback with a fact about her identity. Was the situation painful? Absolutely! But did the feedback and her reaction to it contain some useful information? Yes, for example:

- She was assuming this meant her career was doomed, but actually he did this kind of unhelpful outburst to everyone, she wasn't being singled out.
- She'd assumed she wasn't delivering the right things, but on reflection she realised he just wasn't reading her update emails, because he was overwhelmed and stressed.
- As a result, she started focusing less on beating herself up and more on how to communicate to an extremely tricksy manager, how to strengthen her network of sponsors, how to feedback to him how his behaviour was landing... and how to plan her next career step...

1f Act

Make a decision... and take action. If it's a conscious decision to ignore the feedback, fine, but unless this is the case, the information is pointless if we don't act on it. At the very least thank folks for their feedback; even better, let them know what you are going to do as a result and co-opt them as an ally to support you. For example, we've got friends staying at the moment and the father has recruited his daughter as 'caffeine and biscuit' monitor, which is so much easier than relying on his own willpower alone. Similarly, I've got a CEO client at the moment who has told the whole senior leadership team he's working on being more collaborative and has asked them to keep calling it out when he is – and isn't.

2. The second type of high performance conversation: Tell it how you see it

Being able to tell it how you see it is a hugely valuable skill. How often do we avoid a conversation because we can't see a way of doing it without causing offence? Or we don't feel we have the authority to raise a concern? Sometimes, telling it how you see it is simply the mirror image of 'ask for feedback', but sometimes it's much bigger than that. In the aviation and medical industries, junior staff are trained to voice their concerns in any forum – because there are irrevocable consequences of flying with no fuel or amputating the wrong leg.

Telling it how you see it doesn't mean throwing *unthinking* brutal honesty at people, if the message isn't going to land well, how on earth is that helpful? The Mr F*** Off character Ben refers to was *not* telling it how he saw it. He was being a counter-productive bully, terrifying and demotivating a new crewmate. 'Telling it how you see it' does mean saying whatever needs to be said (no skirting around the issue and no mindlessly agreeing to something just because our boss said it). But, it also means doing everything we can to make sure that whatever needs to be said will be truly heard and accepted. There's no magic wand here, real-life conversations are messy and complicated, but there are a few tips to tell it how you see it elegantly and effectively.

2a Have a useful intention

What do we want people to think, feel and ultimately do as a result of calling something out? Perhaps we simply want to clear the air, or nip something in the bud, or perhaps there's a really specific action we want to happen, but crucially, does the outcome pass the '3-legged milking stool' test? I.e. does it genuinely benefit you, the other person(s) and the wider context? If it's simply to offload anger on to others, or to look good… then perhaps we should reach for the camomile tea instead of having a conversation. Ben and the crew's team rules did much of the heavy lifting here. The rules actively encouraged them to 'tell it how you see it.'

Ben: "The rules meant we knew that the intention behind conversations was to make the boat go faster, not to piss people off. When someone was having a difficult conversation with me, I knew whatever they were telling me it was because they wanted to help us to win."

2b Break the surface tension

As rowers put an oar in the water, the oar needs to break the surface tension. Novices make big splashes, because their strokes are mistimed and actually slow the boat down, but world class rowers slice so cleanly, with immaculate timing and precision, so you can barely see it. Similarly, there are ways to start a conversation which will make it easier to segue from 'hi, how are you?' to 'by the way you need to wear deodorant' or 'I think our company strategy is completely wrong'. Tips include:

- *State* your intention, e.g. 'my intention is to clear the air so we can work better together' or 'my intention is to call out a risk that might cause us all lots of pain further down the line', or 'This feels incredibly awkward, but I think you need to know this because I know you want to improve.'
- If we're worried about how we'll come across, we can voice this, 'I'm worried I'm going to come across as arsey, I'm just passionate about this.' Or 'this might come out scrambled, but right now I just need to vomit out the problem'.
- If we think they might have an objection, we can handle this

up front: 'You might be thinking, how much is this going to cost? and yes it will cost a shedload, so let me explain why it's worth it.'

- Acknowledge your contribution to where things are at. 'I wish I'd called this out before, I've let it fester, sorry' or 'I don't think I've given you enough of my time to get up to speed on this. I promise to ringfence time from now on.'

2c Tailor your approach to suit your audience

You know those family stories that get acted out and repeated every Christmas and they're not very funny but everyone laughs anyway? I'm going to inflict one on you now. Great Uncle Alick, on holiday in France, wanted some honey to go with his breakfast croissants, but couldn't remember the word for it. The waitress spoke no English, so Alick started miming being a bee and asked for 'confiture de bzzzzzzz'. Mission accomplished.

How can we tailor our message so we are talking 'in their language'? Do they talk in quick bullet points or in detail? Do they talk about needing 'a clear picture' or 'being on the same wave length'? We each give clues about how we want to be communicated with. Use those as cues to flex your message so it lands. Even better, ask them! If you are working with someone for any period of time it can be gold dust to ask how best to give feedback.

Ben: 'In our crew, people had different preferences and needs when receiving feedback. One of the boys was happy with blunt words of one syllable, he wanted there to be no room for him to misunderstand the message. Another guy was pretty sensitive. We had to find the right time and place to give him feedback. We had to think about how to phrase what we had to say and include lots of pleases and thank yous, we had to work hard to ensure that he was going to take the information on board rather than get upset. He was a delicate flower."

2d Be a lover AND a fighter

How often do we avoid giving praise because we don't want to be patronising? Even though research indicates we need appreciation for what we are already doing more than we need pointers for change?! How often do we simply say thank you, showcase what's going well, or positively reinforce an improvement? Even when we're giving feedback on things we want to change, it can be useful to build this in addition to flagging what's positive. For example, using the structure of 'I like' and 'I prefer' is super simple, for example:

'I like it when you give me deadlines that are longer than a week' and

'I'd prefer it if you asked my opinion before raising the issues with our manager.'

2e Cut to the chase

In our efforts to be polite, we can often dance around handbags and become totally vague and unhelpful. We need to be clear about what exactly we're on about. For example:

Is it a one off? They were 30 minutes late to the meeting and you want to stamp on that potential fire early – or is it a pattern? They've been late the last 23 times and thereby wasted hours of other people's time? Or is it a pattern that's become so entrenched that we now need to talk about something much bigger – we've asked them umpteen times to be punctual to meetings and they never do, so now the topic we need to talk about is how we work together, how we restore trust, or their career progression chances…

The next few tips could all sit under the banner of 'clarity', but we've divided them up for ease:

2f Communicate facts as facts and interpretations as interpretations

We've talked a lot about this in the beliefs and bullshit filters chapters: facts are facts, noone can mess with facts. 'You were 30 minutes late to the meeting', 'We've lost the past 6 games', 'I'm feeling scared', 'there are no clean pants in your chest of drawers'. Everything else is down to interpretation. When we mindread, or tell stories, and present them as a fact… well, that's how wars start. Instead, we need to make the separation super clear: e.g.

- 'you were 30 minutes late to the meeting [fact] and that's coming across as disrespectful [interpretation]'.
- 'we've lost the last 6 games [fact] and my take on that is: if we don't radically change our approach, we'll never win [interpretation]'.
- 'I'm feeling scared [fact], so please can you slow down and leave a bigger gap to the car in front [my interpretation of what needs to happen for me to feel safe]'.
- 'there are no clean pants in your chest of drawers [fact] and I'm feeling like the laundry slave to Little Lord Fauntleroy [that's a fact as well isn't it?… Gah… it's also an interpretation…]'.

2g Spell out the consequences

Who gives a monkey's??!! Why should the other people take heed of our pearls of wisdom? Maybe it's clear from the way we've spelled out our intentions, but maybe it's worth spelling out the benefits of taking action and the horrors of inaction for them, in their world.

2h Commit to next steps

If we throw a grenade then run away, we're not improving anyone's performance. What's next? What are we asking for e.g.: 'Can you commit to arriving when the meeting starts?' or 'can we both have a mull and chat this through tomorrow?'

3. The third high performance conversation: Make a decision

Picture the scene. A bunch of people have got together to discuss a topic. It could be any group and any topic… how often to mow the communal garden, what the business strategy is for the next three years, what the team's training plan should be for the next few weeks…

But the caricature is pretty similar: Things start off well, but then people have different ideas and start to play 'my idea is better than yours' top trumps. The snarky one in the group (there is always one) starts to derail things; the excitable one takes you off on a tangent, the impatient one gets a bit ranty, and that shuts up the quiet, reflective ones, and then you run out of time.

How did eight hulking great, adrenaline- and testosterone-fuelled lads, plus a slightly less hulking great cox, and their entourage, have high performance discussions which led to sensible decisions and action?

This is a vast topic, but here are a few key tips from the crew.

3a Have a clear purpose

Yup, the three-legged milking stool is back again, like that Slade track topping the charts every Christmas. What are you trying to achieve from the conversation and how will that benefit the individuals in the conversation, the team as a whole and the wider organisation or group? Unless we have that, it's just a natter.

Ben: "We committed to talking about what was most important. When discussions went off track, we'd remind ourselves what the point of the discussion was and refocus on that – boat speed."

3b Have a process

'Process' might sound a bit over-engineered, but the joy of even a super simple process is that it can do so much heavy lifting for us. It's a bit like going to a restaurant and knowing if it's self-service or table-service. If we don't know the process it can be incredibly frustrating. A simple process for making group decisions might be, for example:

1. **O**pen: generate ideas, increase knowledge, raise awareness
2. **A**nalyse: consider pros and cons, evaluate risks, quantify
3. **P**rioritise: narrow options down, come to a decision and commit to action

These deliciously create the acronym OAP, which makes me endlessly happy. Remember if you don't have an OAP process you might become an OAP before anything actually gets done. Oh my sides…

Each one of these steps could have a technique to support it if needed:

- Open: individual brainstorming
- Analyse: timeboxed taking it in turns to consider pros and cons
- Prioritise: voting to decide what to take forward

If you know discussions are super important and might get heated, or where there are different agendas or big egos involved, it pays well to agree the decision-making process *up front*, otherwise things can unravel in the heat of battle…

3c Have Team Rules specifically around communication

In the Teams chapter we talked about team rules. These were the commitments the whole crew signed up to so they could get the best out of each other and drive towards their crazy goal. A lot of them were about communication:

Ben: "We had rules about being 'ego free' and making 'appropriate compromises'. It wasn't acceptable for me to hang on to my idea just because it was mine, we all needed to prioritise based on what would make the boat go faster. Compromise probably didn't always mean meeting someone else halfway, because often that's just a rubbish fudge. Compromise might mean going for your idea 100%, or someone else's 100% – and crucially sticking to that. Not slagging you off afterwards or saying yes and not following through."

Before you embark on a discussion when decisions are needed, what are your rules of engagement?

If you work in an organisation, how much of your time do you spend in meetings? How effective are those meetings?! Meeting etiquette sounds a bit Jane Austen 'The first born should be seated to the right of the host and the whiteboard notes done in calligraphy' but it's proved a game changer for us with internal meetings at *Will It Make The Boat Go Faster?* we use the following prompts:

Purpose What's the meeting aiming to achieve? E.g. is it to inform people about what's happening? Discuss ideas? Make a decision?

Prework What thinking/reading do we need to do beforehand?

Process What's the approach for each meeting step? This includes who is doing what. There's always a timekeeper and someone recording actions. Whoever is facilitating is expected to use the appropriate techniques for each – whether that's brainstorming for Opening, root cause analysis for Analysing, voting for Prioritising and so on.

A particular word on prioritising: Most groups seem to default to wanting consensus, which is great in terms of buy-in, but can be awful in terms of groupthink and in terms of the amount of time it takes. What is appropriate for your context? One of my personal favourite go-to-processes with senior teams is to ensure that everyone can at least *live with* the decision, and whoever is ultimately accountable has the final say. Even if individuals are not swinging from the rafters in jubilation, they *must* be able to support it outside of the room.

Performance review (i.e. a review at the end of the meeting to see how well it went, using the crew's three performance review questions)

Post meeting catch up A scheduled catch up to hold people to account. Have we all done what we committed to? The actions noted in the meeting should have timings and 'ARCI' allocated. (Have you come across the acronym RACI? We've turned it into

ARCI (pronounced 'arsey' because we are that hilarious and also to make the point that unless we are clear on roles things can get very arsey) where A is accountable: the person who has the final decision and ultimate ownership of a topic or action; R is responsible – the person who will actually do a particular action step; C is consulted, i.e. someone whose input is sought *before* a decision is made and I is informed, as in someone who doesn't have an input prior to a decision/action, but absolutely needs to know what has happened or been agreed.

Conclusion

We've only focused on a few core strategies in this chapter for a massive topic. The strategies apply to any kind of communication – a text, an email, a formal-sit-down-meeting, but we've stuck to 'conversations' as they are the most visceral, powerful mechanisms for getting factual and emotional 'stuff' out of one person's head and into others'.

To make our boats go faster we sometimes need to sharpen the 'why?' behind existing conversations. For example, we'll look in the next chapter, Performance vs Results, how Ben and the crew debriefed every training session. These regular chats only really became high performance conversations from about Oct 1998 onwards because they started to have a clear *point*: to reap as much performance improvement as possible out of each and every session. That's in sharp contrast to those tedious team catch ups we've all suffered, you know the ones, where everyone fills everyone else in on what they've done that week? What's the point?! If they are tedious, chances are there's no clear purpose and they won't be high performance conversations.

Sometimes we get boat speed by *initiating* a conversation. Saying things we've been skirting around or avoiding. Remember Ben referring to crewmates falling out? Eventually they realised it wasn't making the boat go faster if they continued to ignore each other.

In summary, the crew weren't driven by whether it was comfortable or easy to have a conversation, they were driven by whether it would make the boat go faster or not. They did everything they could to ensure that whatever needed to be said was said, whatever needed to be heard was heard… and that conversations always culminated in decision and action.

What's the next chapter about? How a high-performing team, or individual, can focus their attention day in day out to maximise their chances of winning. A strategy called a 'performance vs results' approach…

CHAPTER 8

PERFORMANCE VS RESULTS

Lucerne Regatta

Performance vs Results: Get curious about the recipe.

Lucerne Regatta

10.30 on Thursday 9th July. 12½ weeks before the Olympics

After the last session of an effective training camp in Sarnen we got to work. The oars were stowed in the boat trailer; the riggers unbolted from the sides of the boat, Kieran's shoes were removed so we could get at the bolts that hold the two halves of the boat together. Before long the boat was in two pieces and lashed onto the trailer with the oars, riggers and trestles in the box below it.

The last week or so of training had been really effective because we'd become much clearer on things we needed to do to get the results we wanted – we were getting better at figuring out the recipe both technically to move the boat and as a team to ensure open conversations and fast learning and keeping our attention on the key ingredients.

That afternoon we were paddling with intent on the Rotsee. The Rotsee is a small, natural lake about two kilometres from the picture-postcard Lake Lucerne. It's in the bottom of a small green Swiss valley: the sides of the valley rise steeply, but not very high, from the edge of the 2,200 metres long lake. On the boathouse side of the lake there are some houses in the trees, the other side is more open, a railway line runs along the length of the lake through steep buttercup-filled meadows where cow bells dong. The lake is exactly the same size and shape as a man-made rowing lake, but it is natural and beautiful.

We were here for the last race; the last test before the Olympics. We were here to beat the Aussies – and everyone else.

Our heat was on Friday and it was good. We focused on the simple things that we needed to do to create a rhythm. We won, and more importantly, we won because we'd performed well. We beat a US crew into second. It wasn't their proper crew, but we stuffed them by six seconds. It was a good display of what everyone else was going to have to live with if they were to beat us.

Saturday morning we did a short session that was full of positive intent.

Again it was good.

We spent the rest of the day at the hotel before paddling again that evening. We were staying in the Grand Hotel in Lucerne, the same place we always stayed. It was grand, or had been grand. The rooms were now a little tired but still nice; big with high ceilings, but the high ceiling didn't help pass the day. From ten in the morning until four in the afternoon we were cooped up in our rooms watching crap euro-TV and not understanding a word.

This was one of the worst things about racing, having to wait until you can get out there and do what you've been training for. At regattas we usually trained early and late on the days we weren't racing. We spent the rest of the day excited, scared and nervous, but, predominantly, bored. This was back in the dark ages, before mobiles, Wi-Fi and time-filler nonsense on YouTube. That day was no different, all we had to look forward to was a meeting towards the end of the afternoon (in Luka and Louis's room) before we got the bus down to the lake for our evening paddle.

We still had 15 minutes to go before the meeting, but I was feeling restless so I thought I'd go next door a bit early. I couldn't be bothered to walk out of my door, down the corridor to Louis' room next door so I leaned out of the large sash window and saw their window was wide open, it was only about eight feet away so I climbed out of the window, walked along the 18 inch wide ledge that ran along the outside of the building and started to climb in through their window, thinking it was very funny.

Martin was sitting in a chair in their room looking at the window as I climbed in. I didn't know what to do with myself. Did I climb back out and come back in using the door and pretend it had never happened or did I just finish climbing through the window and find somewhere to sit? Martin went bright red, but stayed pretty calm. The rest of the boys were silently killing themselves laughing, Martin gave me an incredibly cold look with his pale blue eyes.

"Which floor are we on Ben?" he asked.
"Um… the fifth floor, Martin."
"You dickhead!"
You really couldn't blame him for losing the plot with us sometimes.

After a good conversation, clarifying what performance ingredients we needed to work on, so we could win the following day, we got on the bus and went down to the lake. As we got the boat off the rack and carried it down to one of the pontoons the heavens opened.

The temperature suddenly dropped about five degrees and it pissed it down, but a little more water wasn't going to stop us.

The lake was quite busy and we started to stamp our authority on it. Every time we boated at a regatta we wanted to dominate the lake, ignoring everyone else, just doing what we had to do and letting them watch us.

Today something wasn't quite right, it wasn't flowing. Louis asked to stop where we were for a couple of minutes so he could stretch his back, but even after that it still wasn't right. We had to go in.

The drop in temperature and rain had stiffened his back and he didn't seem in great shape. He was sure he'd be all right the next day, but he needed to warm his back muscles up and stretch it out. We headed back to the hotel in an apprehensive state. We had about 20 hours until the final. A final we needed to win.

Everyone was here, with the exception of the proper US crew. We had to show them our supremacy and leave them in the final weeks of preparation knowing that we were too fast for them.

I went to bed that night thinking about Louis' back but knowing that I had no control so I shouldn't be worried. Instead I needed to be fully fired up about taking revenge on the Aussies for humiliating us at Henley two weeks before. I slept well; I always did. I dreamed about the race, as always.

We had an early first breakfast the next morning so we could have a warm-up row and be off the lake before racing started. Louis had been up some time stretching. Halfway around the first lap of the lake we had to stop. Louis' back had gone. We stopped where we were, we cut across all the lanes explaining the situation to an irate safety official that we knew what we were doing was illegal and could get us a false start but we had to get Louis off the water.

Louis needed to be physically helped out of the boat.

Plan B.

We didn't have a plan B. Our reserves were in England and we had no one to sub in. Martin sent us back to the hotel telling us not to worry about it. He would sort it out. It was out of our control, we were to forget it. We had a race to win and we had to think about the rhythm that we needed and the intent that we needed to attack it with. We should be back down at the lake an hour and a half before the race.

Nine is quite a big group, it's quite hard to control nine people and you constantly have to count to make sure that everyone is there. Suddenly eight felt like very few. We were very aware as we got the bus back into the town and to our hotel that we were one short. I'd never prepared to race before without a complete crew. I wanted to think about the race, but I was too aware of the fact that we didn't have a crew.

At our early lunch Martin joined us and firmly told me to get a grip when I expressed my concerns. He was right, that was his problem. My problem was focusing my attention on the things that would make the boat go faster, making sure that I was going to lay down every drop of energy I had in the best rhythm that I could row.

At 3 p.m. we were back by the lake, in a small curtained cubicle that served as the British team's luggage storage area, physio area and warm-up and stretching area. I did my little bit of stretching, I spent some time running through the race in my head, picturing each stroke, trying to feel the rhythm, trying to feel the movement and the power we'd need. I also spent some time visiting the toilets. Each time I went they were filthier and more disgusting and the queues got slightly shorter as the men's fours went out to race and then the men's pairs and then some of the eights started to boat. We still had no sub.

We went over to where our boat was on trestles. It had been checked to make sure everything was tight. Martin explained we had two choices. James Cracknell or Greg Searle.

They both rowed very differently from us. Their technique and rhythm was different from ours. They were both better athletes than any of us, but they rowed differently and the key to gold would be using our own recipe for success.

Greg had raced earlier in the day and was hanging around eager to be asked to sub in. Martin ignored him. He would still have a lot of energy and power and he would tear us apart from the inside if we used him. The other option was James Cracknell. He was paddling back from the finish line as we spoke. Like Greg he was an amazing athlete, but he was knackered. He had just raced in the four and lost. The first race they had lost for years.

He would be too knackered to fight us and he'd have to fit in to our approach.

December 1999, Sierra Nevada, Spain. Jurgen giving me feedback on an ergo session.

April 2000, Sarnen, Switzerland. Simon and me struggling to keep up with Fred and Steve Williams in Sarnen, Switzerland.

June 2000, Vienna Regatta. Crossing the line for our first win.

June 2000, Vienna Regatta. Our first gold medals, before our bollocking. From right to left Steve, Luka, me, Kieran, Simon, Andrew, Rowley, front row, Bob and Louis.

Spring 2000. Steve Ingham monitoring physiological tests

July 2000, Henley Royal Regatta.
The Australians winning at Henley, Britain is no where to be seen.

July 2000, Lucerne Regatta. Training in the rain before Louis did his back in.

July 2000, Lucerne Regatta. We've just won (GB in the black boat) but are too tired to celebrate.

July 2000, Lucerne Regatta. We've recovered to receive our World Cup winners vests. Rowley is off the to the left, Steve, Fred, Kieran, Luka, James Cracknell, Simon, me, Andrew.

August 2000. Martin at his desk in Ely.

August 2000. Physiological testing on training camp in Ely.

September 2000, the Hinze damn, Australia.
Posing with the Olympic Torch. The crew, minus Rowley, and a couple of the volunteers who looked after us at the lake.

20th September 2000. Blasting off the start in the Rep.

24th September 2000. Andrew crossing the line.

24th September 2000. Posing for the press with Harry on the left and Martin on the right.

24th September 2000. "The Olympic Champions are Great Britain."

24th September 2000. Celebrating what we'd dreamed of for so long.

We put the boat on the water. Where was James? All the other crews had boated and were warming up. Where was James? The other crews in the warm-up area were churning the water as they did their practice bursts and starts.

The four appeared, heads down. They slowly rowed into one of the other pontoons. Martin and Jürgen went to meet them. They both crouched beside James. He looked over towards us, got out of the four, said something to Steve, Matt and Tim and did a good job of looking up for another race.

"We rowed so badly I couldn't put any work in. I'm still fresh," he said as he lowered his bum on to Louis's seat. We immediately pushed off the pontoon and paddled along the warm-up area. Time was tight and we only managed a couple of bursts and a start. I could definitely feel James. He was trying to pull the rigger off the boat every stroke he was pulling so hard. This was rowing with intent. All our focus was back on the job in hand.

The start at Lucerne couldn't have been more different from the start at Henley. There were no cheering crowds, no freshly painted posts, no river traffic, just a green valley, cow bells and five other countries that we needed to beat.

We flew out of the start. We got a rhythm and it was working. The recipe was working. We were performing brilliantly. We took the race by the scruff of the neck and we didn't let go.

We got a lead and we maintained it, we had nearly three quarters of a length. We tried to increase it at halfway, it didn't work, but we maintained our lead. This was power and aggression. The rhythm was solid, but we were laying it down too.

500 metres to go and the wheels started to fall off. We kept laying it down. Stroke after agonising stroke we put down as much power as we could in the strong rhythm we'd worked so hard on. The field was moving back on us.

400 metres to go and they were closing.

300 metres to go and Rowley was calling for more. He was demanding more.

200 metres to go. They kept coming back and we kept laying down whatever we had.

100 metres to go; the last 15 strokes. More power; we needed more power.

Ten more strokes; the Aussies were closing.

Five more and we'd done it. 0.3 seconds ahead of the Aussies!

We'd won.

James had been brilliant. He admitted later that he had been completely knackered at the end of the fours race. He'd given it everything he had in the four yet he'd been able to get in our boat and lie through his teeth to tell us what we needed to hear. He thought he'd contributed for the first 1,000m of our race and then been pretty useless as he completely ran out of steam.

But he'd done enough. We'd all done enough. We didn't have the total domination that we were after, but we'd won. We'd got the result we wanted in difficult circumstances, but most importantly we'd performed well. We'd used the best recipe, a recipe we could repeat. This was no fluke. We had raced without the strongest person in the crew; we'd turned over our crushing defeat from two weeks before at Henley. We'd had a disastrous last 20 hours before the final, but we'd bounced back. We'd shown that we could win.

We had 12 weeks to the Olympics and a lot of work to do, but the momentum was there. We would keep building.

Performance vs Results: Get curious about the recipe

Ben: "If you want to win, you need to forget about winning."

Chapter summary

Your best chance of getting great results is to stop focusing on results! Start focusing on the performance that will get you great results… and success will take care of itself.

How do you do this?

1. Get curious about the recipe
2. Focus your attention
3. Review performance

Results are what it's all about. They are, by definition, what we want, what we get paid to deliver: Maybe you have work targets you must deliver or deadlines and budgets to meet? Maybe you've got a sporting personal best to achieve or maybe you are hunting for a new house or new job? Whatever the result we want, surely there are some secrets to steal from the British rowing 8+, because delivering a result, winning was their whole purpose.

Ben: "Don't focus on the result; focus on the performance that will get you the result."

The words 'performance' and 'results' are often used interchangeably, but in the sporting world they are seen as very different. The distinction brings huge clarity. A simple analogy is that the result is the cake, the performance is the recipe and ingredients. The result is the end product, e.g. a gold medal, the performance is how you get there: the mixture of attitude, method, tools, environment, teamwork and so on, that creates the result.

The crew's coach, Martin, introduced this idea of being performance-driven from his background in engineering. Martin reasoned that the crew were not going to win gold by concentrating really hard on winning gold. For years Ben and the crew had tried simply working harder and harder and it hadn't worked. Instead, Martin knew they would win by concentrating really hard on figuring out the best methods, by executing perfect strokes with a devastating rhythm and power, by developing a strong mindset and a strong team.

By following Martin's logic we not only increase our chances of winning, we learn faster too. We might get lucky and win without concentrating on our performance, but a successful outcome is just a fluke unless we know how we made it happen. When we know how we did it, we can repeat it and improve on it. The reverse is true for failures. If we can figure out how we failed, we can avoid making the same errors again.

Focusing on the performance and the result will happen may seem like a statement of the blindingly obvious, but we do the opposite a lot, so it's worth talking about.

Have you ever got so caught up trying to close a sale that you hurry your discussions and talk about your product/service rather than listening to the client? And yet in our heart of hearts we know that if we build rapport, understand the customer's drivers and present real benefits to them, the sale will take care of itself.

When you're trying to get the kids to school on time in the morning. Do you find yourself saying "hurry up, hurry up" for the umpteenth time and still screeching to the school gates in a Formula One fluster? We're repeating activities that we know don't work.

So how did Martin help the team to become more focused on their performance and how can we use this lens to make our lives easier?

The crew's performance-obsessed approach divides into three sections:

1. Get curious about the recipe
2. Focus your attention
3. Review performance

1. Get curious about the recipe

- What gets you one result rather than another?
- What are the variables that might be having an impact?

Most people are oblivious to the causes that get them their results. Simply by waking up and *wondering*, you are one step ahead of the competition.

For example, I'm not going to appear on *MasterChef* anytime soon – in fact when my eldest son was just a toddler he famously announced:

"Daddy cooks stuff and puts it in the fridge and then Mummy puts it in the microwave until it goes ping."

But because Delia went to the trouble of analysing and writing down the ingredients and the recipe for making a cake, even I can benefit from her curiosity and make half decent cupcakes for an annoyingly perceptive three-year-old.

Martin got curious about what the British rowing 8+ should be focused on. He looked at other teams and analysed their performance. He talked to the crew, he used his intuition, all to try and figure out what might be the key ingredients and recipe for excellent rowing.

Ben: "Most sports are about rhythm and timing and in a repetitive sport like rowing, rhythm is king. Martin devoted a whole year to getting a rhythm that was more economical and faster than anyone else's."

What might this step look like in our world?

Take the goal of getting the kids to school on time; if we focused on the performance, rather than the result, what might be some of the important variables to look at? I remember when the kids were small it was things like type of breakfast, location of clothing, my attitude.

- Rice Krispies could be lingered over one grain at a time, but Shreddies were a bit speedier.
- Getting really cross and demanding my children put clothes on took ages, but asking Fireman Jack to put his special protective uniform on was much quicker.

After a bit of musing, I had some 'recipes' I could work on to increase the chances of getting to school on time – as opposed to getting more and more frustrated by just wishing for the goal really hard.

How about a work-related example? What are the recipe and ingredients for a productive meeting? The list would include: having the right attendees, a clear purpose, pre-work, agenda, punctuality, location, people committing to good listening... We saw in the last chapter that we've worked hard on this at Will It Make The Boat Go Faster? with internal meetings. If any of us are invited to a meeting and it doesn't have key ingredients in place it's our duty to call it out – because it's slowing the boat down if we have unproductive meetings.

The great thing about getting curious about the recipe is that you can always get as granular as appropriate. Perhaps for everyday meetings it's enough just to make sure those core ingredients are in place. But sometimes you want to find every tiny thing that might help. Ben and the crew got incredibly detailed about how to put the oar in the water for every stroke because they were looking for every millisecond saving they could. In the same way, because we often facilitate high-stakes, crazy goal workshops for the leadership team at a client, we've got geekily curious about how to use Post-it notes, room layout and movement to draw conversations out or resolve disagreements.

2. Focus your attention

There's a weird truth about focusing our attention: as long as we're purely focusing our attention and not judging or beating ourselves up, then *just being aware of a key variable raises our performance.*

Ben: "When Rowley was coxing us he was constantly reminding us to focus on specific things like moving our hands or getting our weight on our feet. He usually didn't need to tell us to make a change – once we'd focused our attention on the variable the change would just happen."

Try it out yourself! For the things that don't get sorted out automatically, focusing your attention gives you a crystal clear understanding of what to improve.

I was sceptical of this when I first came across the idea. Surely just focusing your attention wouldn't be sufficient? I was mentoring a colleague at the time, a management trainer who wanted to get better feedback from his delegates. He figured out that a key ingredient was the quality of the questions he asked the group during a session. Before we did any training on how to ask better questions he simply focused his attention on the questions he asked in his next session. The quality of the questions dramatically improved – as did the feedback scores. To my surprise, just raising his awareness to an important variable was enough to improve his performance noticeably.

Every three to five weeks the crew would have planning meetings to agree what specific element they would focus on for the next few weeks. This then translated into agreed learning goals for every single daily training session.

Ben: 'Martin made sure each session had a point, it wasn't just about getting the mileage done."

This was pretty revolutionary... Not the idea, but the fact that the crew actually did it! So often we tend to work harder, working longer days – rather than really looking at the how. It's easy to say 'we should work smarter not harder', but do we actually do it?

Ben: "I remember a particular day's training back in perhaps 97, before Martin was involved in the team. It was the first session back after Christmas and there were just four of us there. We didn't think about what we wanted to learn, we just blundered on in. We took the quad out because it is the fastest boat and so we could get the training over and done with most quickly. We had a weights session and then we went for a run which involved me getting pushed in the river for an unscheduled swim. The sole goal was to complete the training as quickly and easily as possible and everything we did was based on that rather than finding boat speed. Consequently, I'm not sure that we achieved anything."

How might 'focusing attention' look in our world? Say we wanted to improve our team meetings. We've already got curious about the recipe and think that the key ingredients are clarity of agenda, timekeeping, and good listening. We then need to set some learning goals for the next team meeting. For example, we agree that we're going to focus our attention on listening in the next session whilst we are progressing through the agenda.

Ben and the crew had Martin there during both training sessions and races to help them keep focused. For example, if the training session was on the ergo, Martin would be all over the crew picking apart every bit of what was happening. He'd get them to focus on the noise the fan was making, or how they were pushing off their feet, or the angle of their body as they pulled.

In the corporate world, managers and peers can play a big part. For example, in a sales team, does the manager judge his or her team purely on sales results, or on how well they are performing on the individual ingredients of the process? How can peers remind each other to keep focused? For instance, we've witnessed colleagues using code words in client meetings to remind each other what to focus on. Even those who work alone can write notes to themselves, set the alarm on their phone or put reminders in their calendar to refocus.

Ben: "It was very easy to get distracted. For example, Harry was passionate and would get wrapped up in the moment. He'd go off on a tangent in the middle of a training session, so we had to keep focused on the pre-agreed training goals for that day. You get what you focus on. You don't have to work harder; it's not through doing more hours, it is by being more focused within those hours."

3. Review Performance

While other crews were only measuring success in terms of results – the number of regattas won – Ben and his crew were reviewing their performance as well as results. Were they figuring out a world class recipe? How well were they following – and improving – this recipe? Were they building a performance which would give them the best possible chance of getting a gold medal?

Ben: "Before the World Championships in 1998 we'd have just stood around before a training session asking, 'All right?' 'Yeah.' That was pretty much the sum total of our thought process. It was a real turning point when Martin made us realise that a result is in the past as soon as it's happened. The result doesn't matter, but understanding the performance that got you there does."

After every training session, the crew would remind themselves of what they'd agreed to focus on at the start of the session and then analyse their performance. The analysis can be summed up in three super simple questions:

1. Where did we perform well?
2. Where could we have performed better?
3. What will we do (differently) next time?

The first question helped the crew build on what was going well: What recipes worked? What ingredients made a positive impact? This not only helped improve their performance, but it also built their belief – answers often went straight onto the boathouse evidence wall.

The second question identified opportunities for improvement: What recipes or ingredients didn't work, or weren't as good as they could have been? What got in the way? Slowed us down?

The last question made sure the review wasn't just hot air – it forced them to commit to *action*. What do we need to repeat because it seems to be working? What do we need to ditch? What ingredient shall we focus our attention on next time? What shall we experiment with?

Imagine the impact of asking those three questions regularly in your world – let's say I called you in a month's time. How many helpful recipes might you have built in that short time? How much time/effort would you have saved? How much closer would you be to your goal? We can help our boats go a heck of a lot faster if we know that Shreddies are easier for a toddler to eat than Rice Krispies, that having a timekeeper in team meetings helps us focus on what's important just as the crew learnt that maintaining the hand speed when the oar came out of the water helped the boat to glide much better…

Performance reviews don't have to be big, unwieldy affairs – quite the opposite. Examples we've seen include:

- Teams using a timer to ringfence just 3 minutes at the end of weekly meetings to review performance in that meeting
- Leaders taking a few minutes (e.g. on the train home each night) to keep a performance review journal
- Managers using the questions in 1–1s
- Teachers using the questions with their pupils at the end of a lesson or project
- Parents using the questions to understand how to deal with their teenagers more effectively the next day

The crew were infamous for the amount of time they spent off the water, discussing things. There were plenty of Basils, taking the mick out of them for not being on the water doing 'proper training', but the crew simply put their bullshit filters on and kept asking these vital questions. Martin also encouraged the 8+ to keep personal performance review journals and most did in some shape or form.

Ben: "Some of the boys had fantastic review journals. They recorded what they ate, how they felt, what they wore, and the impact that had on their results. Our experience at Vienna in 2000 owed a lot to these journals. Back in 1999 it had taken us two whole days to get used to the weird water conditions in Vienna, but in 2000 we could refer to our 1999 journals and remind ourselves about what had worked and which bits of our normal recipe we'd had to change. It took us only two sessions to achieve race pace in 2000. There are a couple of benefits of writing things down. The first one is that you can remember things over a long time period. The second is that when things are written down it's easier to spot patterns – they leap off the page at you."

Research also suggests that writing things down seems to involve more parts of our brain – stimulating our learning and memory more than purely thinking things through.

You might be reading this thinking, "this all sounds fine and dandy, but how can I assess if I've performed well or not?!" It's certainly true that the crew had plenty of fancy statistics they could look at. In our lives there are hopefully concrete measures you can use. BUT, whatever your context, don't let any difficulty in measuring stop you from reviewing performance. It's better to go for some kind of proxy – like a one to ten scale, or those un-smiley/smiley-face customer satisfaction buttons you often get after airport security these days. The crew kept it simple and often relied on asking "what does it feel like?"

Ben: "For the five and a half minutes of an Olympic final, we couldn't rely on the coach's feedback or data from machines. We had to put everything into the rowing itself. So we had to get really good at measuring our performance ourselves, in the moment."

Imagine you are giving a corporate presentation. How can you measure your performance? Feedback forms at the end of the session are one measure of success and can help improve the process for next time. But what about being able to measure during the session if you are on or off track, to drive better performance now. What might be some evidence? Nodding heads? Questions asked? Eyelids open?

How it worked for the team

It took Martin a while to convince the team to focus on performance, but by 1999 they'd signed up to it and the first real test of whether the approach worked was at the first 1999 regatta in Hazewinkel, Belgium. Even then, Ben found it really difficult to let go of measuring success in terms of winning.

Ben: "We spent ages in our planning meeting discussing what our focus for Hazewinkel should be. I was adamant it should be 'get a medal', other boys wanted 'row a rhythm' and eventually we went for that. We would focus our attention purely on rowing an effective rhythm, purely on our performance. Of course, we all wanted a medal, but we'd give ourselves the best chance of one if we focused all our effort and energy on the performance – on the rhythm. During the race we were totally absorbed in our performance – we rowed a really good rhythm and we could feel it. We were so focused on it that some of the boys were totally unaware we'd won a silver medal!"

Conclusion

Focus on performance and success will take care of itself. All too often we get bent out of shape trying to reach a result – get to a meeting on time, close a sale, get great feedback – and lose sight of what we need to do in order to achieve that result – ask directions, build rapport, present a compelling case.

Our attention is an incredibly powerful tool. When we focus our attention on a key variable (and remember this doesn't mean beating ourselves up!) then our performance automatically improves and we identify what further support we need. A win is in the past as soon as it has happened, so we need to review our performance. How well do we know the recipe and ingredients for success? How well are we executing them? When we do this, we massively increase our chances of winning consistently on an ongoing basis.

Once you've mastered a recipe, the next question is: can you still bake that cake when your stress levels are sky high? We've all seen soggy bottoms on *The Great British Bake Off*, or crumpled souffles on *MasterChef*, so the next chapter is devoted to Performance Under Pressure…

CHAPTER 9

PERFORMANCE UNDER PRESSURE

The Lamb Hotel, Ely

Performance Under Pressure: Cultivate your Goldilocks zone

The Lamb Hotel, Ely

7 Aug, 2000, 42 days to the Olympics.

We had driven from London to the small cathedral city of Ely that morning. We'd done three solid training sessions, the first in the 8+, the second on rowing machines and the third in the weights room. It had been a good day and now we were in the private meeting room in the Lamb Hotel, our base for the next ten days, discussing the journey ahead. Most evenings we were going to meet to discuss different elements of the preparation, whether it be the Olympic opening ceremony, the Gold Coast training camp that would follow on from this camp in Ely, our evidence wall and beliefs or different elements of dealing with the Olympic environment.

This evening we were talking about performing in the pressurised environment that we were in. We had 42 days until the Olympic Games started. There were twelve rowers, the reserve four crew were with us, one cox, two coaches, and one or two physiologists or psychologists. We had ten days in Ely, a couple of days at home then we'd be off to Australia to the Gold Coast then the Olympic village itself. We had 42 days to deal with the mounting pressure of getting it right every day. Ensuring that we were learning faster than anyone else every day. Living together, training together, eating together and knowing that we had the race of our lives just around the corner. Knowing that to get it right at the Games we'd have to deal with all of the challenges that went with it, the Olympic village, the dining hall, the other competitors… and each other!

This evening was about reflecting on where we'd performed really well under pressure so we knew what to replicate and where we'd made a mess of it so we could avoid the same mistakes again. The example that came to mind most quickly for me was four months previously. We'd been in Sarnen on training camp before Final Trials. It had been tough. The pressure of day-to-day performance had got the better of me and I'd had to turn that around so that I could deliver the right results at the Final Trials and greatly increase my chance of being selected for the 8+.

Here's what had happened back then…

Sarnen, Switzerland, April 2000

I was sitting on the edge of my bunk in three layers of sopping wet kit, my elbows on my knees, my head in my hands. I stared at my bare feet as the slow drip, drip of water from my hair and kit formed a puddle on the wooden floorboards. This was it. This was as far as I was going to get. I'd done so much good work. I'd got so many good results but it was going to come to nothing.

It had been a *disastrous* session. Final Trials were ten days away. They were the most important trials in the whole four-year run up, because they'd be crucial to decide who got selected for the crew to race in the Olympics… and they were going to be a massive waste of time.

My pair with Simon was rubbish. We had been the slowest of the six pairs in the group for the second time that day. The constant pressure of having to perform every day, every session, with this massive test just around the corner was really getting to me. I was a mess. I was knackered, cold, wet and too depressed to bother getting out of my freezing kit as the water soaked into the duvet and mattress which was sagging on the steel framed bunk bed. It was over, or at least it would be in ten days' time.

Andrew Lindsay and Louis Attrill, Fred Scarlett and Steve Williams, Bobby Thatcher and Steve Trapmore, Kieran West and Luka Grubor, Toby Garbitt and Rich Dunn had all beaten us that morning. There were eight seats in the boat and at the moment Simon and I were ranked 11 and 12. Every single session, every single day we needed to be improving, we needed to be learning and we weren't. It was relentless. Two, three or four times a day – every day – we had to perform. It had been like this pretty much constantly for the last eight months and we had another five months of this constant drip… drip… dripping of pressure to deal with. We spent all day, every day, thinking, planning and scheming how to do it. There was no getting away from it. There was no let up. In the third and final session of the previous day's training we'd had a flicker of hope – we'd been the second fastest pair… but this morning we were rubbish again. The other boys were improving and we were so inconsistent it was killing me. I felt as though not only my hopes and dreams were being crushed but I was being physically broken as well.

I couldn't bear it.

To make things even more miserable, the conditions had been really poor. A cold wind blowing thunder clouds and icy rain had chased us up the lake; it had been a race to get off the water before the thunderstorm struck us. The wind had whipped the lake into short, sharp waves that broke over the bows of the boat and splashed on the bottom of the riggers on either side. The spray and rain had quickly soaked through the multiple layers we were wearing. In a faster pair I wouldn't have minded, I would have almost been happy about the conditions because it would be making us physically and mentally tougher. But in this pair, going as badly as we were, under the pressure to get it right, I hated the conditions and they wore me down. I was tired and depressed. I hadn't slept particularly well and couldn't work out what to do.

We had arrived in Sarnen a week before. We were staying at the Swiss national training centre again but it seemed to be deserted. It was a functional training centre just outside a small village. The dining room served adequate food, the two person rooms with their bunk beds were functional, the weights room in the basement, a nuclear bunker – obligatory in all Swiss buildings of a certain age – was functional. The lake, stunningly beautiful in summer, was very changeable as it was spring. There had been days where the perfect blue sky formed a perfect arch touching the snow-covered mountains to our left and the rolling green and white hills to our right as we stood looking down the length of the lake. On other days low, angry clouds rolled over the lake obscuring the mountains and hiding the hills, emptying their contents of icy rain or slushy snow on the surface of the lake and of course on us if we were in the way.

What was really strange was that we weren't there as a crew or even as a wider team. This was unlike every other training camp in our 12-month cycle. When we went to Ely before a World Cup regatta we took an eight and a four and we operated as two crews *within* the eights team. When we went to Seville as part of the eights group, we'd be rowing in pairs, fours and the eight and we'd do the same – race against each other in pairs, or fours, but still operating as a team, a unit. When we went to Sera Nevada for land training altitude camps with the rest of the rowing team, we would compete against each other on the rowing machines or in the weights room but we were still the eights group, we stuck together and we were a team.

But because this was preparation for Final Trials, this was different. We had been put into pairs a few weeks before and at the Trials – at the National Water Sports Centre in Nottingham – we would race each other for our places at the Olympics. While the trials didn't mean the top boats would automatically go to the Olympics and others wouldn't (they were part of a longer selection process that wouldn't be finalised for another three months) they were very, very, very important. They weren't just testing speed, they were designed to see how we coped with 'peak' pressurised situations. They simulated a high-pressure racing environment as much as possible so that we could practise performing under the intense stress of the Olympics. And that meant that this camp was different.

We were all part of the eights group but we didn't act like it and it didn't feel like it. We had the same coaches, we were doing the same training towards the same long-term goal, but the short-term goal had taken over. We were just a bunch of pairs racing each other, jockeying for position, trying to stamp our authority on the other pairs, trying to let them know that they could never beat us. We operated as pairs. We ate at the same time but we didn't share many conversations. There was no communal area in the training centre which exacerbated things, the only place to hang out between sessions were our bedrooms with our pair partner.

When the crews were announced at a full team meeting, Simon had asked in front of everyone if he could row with someone else… a good start! Louis and Andrew were together (Andrew having taken a year out of the national team the year before to complete his studies had managed to get back in the group). Louis was Mr Consistent, the strongest in the crew. His place on stroke side was certain. Bobby Thatcher and Steve Trapmore were both really good boat movers. Steve was physically the weakest in the group but made boats move really fast, his place in the eight was pretty well guaranteed as the stroke man, the guy who would set the rhythm. Kieran and Luca were having a hard time. They were pretty inconsistent, but Kieran was a fantastic rower and he was certain to be in the six seat on stroke side.

That left one seat on my side of the boat. We had to be faster than the remaining pairs: Fred and Steve Williams, two Oxford Brookes University boys, who had rowed together for years, Steve was very strong and wanted my seat. Toby Garbitt and Rick Dunn were also in the frame, Rick had rowed in the eight a couple of years before, was an awesome racer and was also gunning for my seat.

In our room, Simon and I were uncomfortable. We were both feeling under pressure and really stressed. Simon had raced at the World Champs the year before in a pair and come fifth. He was clearly good, he was an easy going 6'8" Adonis, as my fiancée worryingly liked to point out. We got on well together, we liked each other and in some sessions we were really fast but it was the inconsistency that was driving me crazy.

With the stress getting to me it was easy to blame Simon. I thought that I was generally pretty consistent, I clearly had good days and bad days, we all did, but my performances were pretty predictable so if it wasn't me it must be him! I didn't want to blame people, it wasn't helpful, but if there were two of us in the boat and it wasn't me it had to be him! We'd spoken about it but it was still up and down. What was I supposed to do? I'd spoken to Harry and Martin asking for help, asking for ideas but still it was up and down. Normally I would have spoken to Louis or Bobby or Fred or Steve but because of the pressure and the competition between us I didn't. It was just Simon and me. The support network had gone, we just weren't a team at the moment. It was Simon and me in the boat, Simon and me in the room, Simon and me at meals. It was just Simon and me!

Three days earlier, the weather had been beautiful. The first session of the day had been a long, painful 16-kilometre session with Louis and Andrew finishing a full five minutes ahead of us as we bounced around in the wash, trying to hang on to the tail-end-Charlies. The second session was supposed to be a light, technical session, Harry asked us to row into the middle of the perfectly flat picture-postcard lake and stop. He then got us to do a technical exercise that involved one of us in the pair sitting still while the other person rowed us around in a huge circle with Harry critiquing every move that was made. A pair is not the widest boat in the world and it's a precarious exercise to do. The boat isn't designed to move like that and you really have to concentrate if you want to stay dry. When our turn came to be critiqued Harry manoeuvred his inflatable launch a couple of metres from our boat and in his soft Kiwi voice he carefully explained what he wanted, then talked us through the exercise stroke by stroke.

Not only did we have the stress of doing a bloody hard exercise in the middle of a freezing lake, having had a rubbish session an hour before, but we were also doing it under the all-seeing eyes of one of the best coaches in the world. Harry missed nothing and when you were in his sights he was ruthlessly exacting. It was a great opportunity to have one-to-one support, to improve, to work on our weaknesses, if you could deal with the stress of the situation. Talking to Simon about this years later, he vividly remembers being terrified during this whole session – thinking about the fact that the water was bloody cold, we were a mile from the closest land and he didn't think that we could swim that far before freezing to death when we fell in!!!

As Simon came out of the bathroom, I managed to drag myself off what was now a very wet bed, realising it was actually Simon's bed, I apologised and went to have a shower. We had two more days here before flying home, we'd then have five days in London before travelling up to Nottingham to race. I just had to get a grip for these last few days here.

I knew in my heart that when I got home and could eat what I wanted to, I'd think more clearly. I knew that when I got home I wouldn't be woken up by a church bell clanging every 30 minutes all through the night. I also knew that in the last six days we'd done 224kms and a number of brutal weights sessions. It had been a big week and I was physically on my knees which doubtless meant that mentally I was also on my knees. I just had to go back to focusing on what I could control and let Simon take care of what he could control. I knew that when we got it right we were fast and that Simon was very, very good at getting it right when he needed to.

Final Trials. Wednesday 12th April 2000

At 7.05 p.m. at the National Water Sports Centre in Nottingham, Simon and I lined up against the fastest five pairs in the country. Two of the pairs would end up in the four-man boat, two would make the pair, the rest of us would battle it out for the eight. We had cruised through the heat, had a good semi-final and here we were in the final. We hadn't gone as fast as we thought we could yet, but we were getting there. Since returning from Sarnen we'd managed to get our act together. We'd slept well, which made such a difference. The volume of training had gone down and with a little more energy I could think far more clearly. I was able to put the previous weeks into a bit of context. Yes, it had been incredibly hard, we'd done a huge volume of work and it hadn't been plain sailing but knowing that we could manage those incredibly intense weeks would make future weeks easier.

I had rediscovered my support network at home and being able to talk it all through with people not directly involved had made a huge difference. I reframed what had happened and what we were doing into a more useful context, a context that would help me achieve what I wanted. It had made it easier to think clearly about what we could do, about the improvements that we were making, about what was possible rather than just the wallowing in the troughs. All these techniques were critical – it was critical that we managed the day-to-day drip, drip pressure now because on top of that we'd moved to the high-stakes peak pressure events like these Final Trials… like the Olympic Games themselves.

Sitting there with Simon behind me we were absolutely ready. We'd led Redgrave and Pincent for most of the semi-final that morning. Their nine years' experience of rowing together had paid off in the end, as we'd got tired, but only in the end, and that made them seem beatable. What we'd spent the day thinking about was the basic routines ahead of us. We were clearly racing for our seats at the Olympics, but we'd forced that out of our minds. What was important now was getting the first stroke right, then the next, then the next. If my first stroke was long, explosive and finished properly, then that would enable us to move cleanly on to the second stroke which would be shorter and more explosive and when we finished that patiently we could move on to the third stroke and so on. The first minute was going to be absolutely flat out, we were going to have to take about 45 strokes, but in order to do that we needed to be patient and not rush. That's what we needed to focus on rather than the gravity of the event. It took discipline to focus like this – on what we needed to do, how we needed to perform. Sitting on the start line I controlled my breathing, I'd also been very aware of my posture and energy before getting in the boat. I'd worked to control my focus all day and that's what I was doing as we waited for the race to start. That's why we were ready. That's why the levels of pressure, of excitement and adrenaline were right.

At 7.10 p.m. in the growing dusk we were off. The water was flat ahead of us, the conditions were perfect and we used our height to our full advantage, rowing long, powerful, patient strokes. We were racing for our place in Team GB, but we were focusing on one stroke at a time. Tim Foster and James Cracknel got an early lead and hung on to it all the way. Greg Searle and Ed Coode finished 2nd, Redgrave and Pincent 3rd, Louis and Andrew 4th with Simon and me fighting and chasing them all the way to the line. It wasn't as good as we'd wanted it to be… but it was the best row we'd had. When it really mattered Simon and I had managed the pressure so we could do what we needed to do.

The Lamb Hotel Ely 7th Aug 2000. 42 days to the Olympics

Sitting in Ely reflecting on this four months later there were some critical points that jumped out at me:

When I'd been sitting, soaking Simon's bed in Sarnen, I had known many of the ingredients I needed to manage the situation – to manage the pressure that I'd been under – but I still hadn't been able to *do* them. My performance on that camp hadn't been as good as it should have been. I hadn't made good enough decisions and I had reacted badly to the environment and to Simon making the situation worse. I now knew that sleep was crucial, I knew that eating properly was crucial and I knew that being able to talk problems through was crucial.

Over the next 42 days we would be at home for about five of those days. We'd be staying in different hotel rooms, eating different food and the drip, drip of pressure would continue to gradually mount until we got to race. What's more, for the first 30 or so of those 42 days we'd be doing a huge volume of training, physically we'd be on our knees. We had to find routines to ensure that we could sleep properly. We had to be able to eat properly and we had to keep talking. We had to be able and willing to share how we were feeling, what was working and what wasn't. Having the ability to step back and recognise what was stressing us out, to manage our perceptions so we were choosing what we were doing, to see the challenges and face them objectively would be incredibly important.

The lessons were important but what was also important was knowing that we'd been through it before. We'd been in this environment for two years, there were times we hadn't got it right and we let the pressure get to us but there were also plenty of times that we'd managed it well, where we had managed to maintain our performance.

Those 42 days would take us to the week of racing. That would be 'easy'! At Final Trials I'd shown that I had the discipline to focus on the right things. In the three regattas since the trials there had been ups and downs. When Louis dropped out at Lucerne I hadn't done an amazing job but I'd managed the pressure well enough. I knew what we had to do and with the boys around me I knew that I could do it. I reflected that although I hadn't done everything perfectly, I'd got on top of the drip, drip constant pressure and I'd been able to step up and deal with peak pressure.

And I would do it again… when the big day came.

Performance Under Pressure: Cultivate your Goldilocks zone

Ben: "Pressure can be your friend or your enemy, the key is knowing how to optimise it."

Chapter summary

Life is stressful. Some pressure is motivating, but too much damages our performance. Finding your Goldilocks zone, where the pressure is 'juuuuust right' helps us get the best results.
There are three steps to cultivating your Goldilocks zone:

1. Understand: understand how pressure works for humans.
2. Personalise: appreciate our personal versions of this:
    a. Our physiological indicators
    b. Our performance and results
    c. Our stressors

3. Manage: use a range of strategies to keep the pressure at useful levels:
    a. Manage our reaction to the stressor...
    b. Normalise the stressor: practising peak pressure events

c. Take away the stressor
d. Keep well
e. Breathing
f. Visualisation
g. Routine
h. Moral support

Sometimes we face a peak pressure event: an exam, a house move, an Olympic final…

In 2018 I took my third solo stand up show to the Edinburgh Fringe. I'd practised hard. I was proud of the material. The preview gigs had gone brilliantly. The first few nights nearly sold out and although there's always plenty more to work on, I was really happy with my performance. Then, on a Wednesday night, one of the pre-sold tickets was marked "Press". An important reviewer was coming.

This is a big deal. A good review can set off a glorious, virtuous circle. A bad one can stop a run in its tracks. As I walked out on stage I felt under immense pressure to perform…

… and I choked… pure and simple…

I let the pressure get to me. I turned out a mediocre, wooden performance and I got a – completely deserved – mediocre review. Not only was my performance on the night sub-standard, there are ongoing consequences: the review is published forever in cyberspace for every potential comedy booker or keynote buyer to see.

Sometimes the pressure builds up bit by bit, like the drip, drip, drip of water until a dam bursts…

> A friend of mine is a GP at a busy practice (drip), it was the middle of flu season (drip), her husband was working away (drip), she was scrabbling to get her two sons out of the door to school on time one morning (drip), when her teenager started complaining of a sore throat (drip). She got him a spoonful of medicine but overfilled it (drip), so asked him to come over to her rather than her going to him. He complained that he was way too ill to move (drip), and so what did my hugely competent, emotionally intelligent friend do? She threw the spoonful of medicine across the kitchen and pebble-dashed the walls and both children with sticky gloop.

When have you buckled under the pressure? Perhaps it was a 'peak' event: you turned into a rabbit in headlights in a senior meeting? Screwed up an important conversation and damaged a relationship? Perhaps it was the drip, drip, drip of overwhelming workload, demanding kids and you totally lost it when the train was late to get to a client meeting?

What can we learn from someone who's performed at an Olympic final, the ultimate crucible of pressure? Who has managed to pull it out of the bag at precisely 10.30 a.m. on 24th September 2000? But who also withstood the drip, drip, drip pressure of years of tough physical challenge and ongoing uncertainty about whether he'd even be selected for the crew?

We can summarise Ben and the crew's strategies for performing under pressure as a three-stage process:

1. **Understand**: First, we need to understand what's going on in our brains and bodies, and why.
2. **Personalise**: Next, we need to raise our awareness to our personal, optimum pressure levels.
3. **Manage**: Lastly, we can use a huge range of strategies for handling the pressure and performing when it really matters.

Definitions

Before we dive in, let's define a few terms. Words often get bandied about interchangeably on this topic, which I find incredibly confusing. (As confusing as whenever anyone in my house refers vaguely to 'Tom'. If you don't specify whether you're talking about 'Al's best mate Tom', 'son Tom', 'colleague Tom' or 'son Tom's mate who is also called Tom' you end up buying a wildly inappropriate birthday present…)

If you squeeze a fizzy drink can you are putting pressure on it. If you squeeze hard enough you can bend the metal out of shape. All we mean by 'pressure', in this chapter, is that feeling of being squeezed and potentially bent out of shape.

We'll use the term 'stressor' to refer to whatever it is that is creating the pressure. The hand that crushes the can, the billion people watching you row in an Olympic final, the boss eyeballing you as you are pitching to a major client…

OK, so here's the crew's three-stage process to performing under pressure.

1. Understand

Ben: "I can't remember if it was Shambles or Brian who gave us a graph showing the relationship between pressure and performance. It was a bell curve shape– which means your performance actually goes up to start with, when you feel under a bit of pressure. After a certain point, your performance plateaus. When even more pressure is piled on, your performance plummets."

In other words, there is a 'Goldilocks zone' with pressure – you don't want too much, but you also don't want none at all. Have you ever messed up because you've been too blasé? Without a bit of adrenaline pumping you've had a lacklustre day? Pressure works like caffeine – without a morning cuppa many of us are sluggish. One cup and we are firing on all cylinders, but too many cups can create disaster. (From personal experience, I don't recommend more than three flat whites in twenty minutes before attending a job interview… I wasn't hired, but at least I wasn't arrested.)

Ben: "A bit of pressure is great, but when we didn't deal with immense pressure we went slower. Puking in the bushes on the way to the Olympic lake was fine. Retching whilst on the start line in the 1997 World Championships was not fine."

Why are we built like that? The following is a massively simplified explanation of evolutionary psychology:

In caveman days, food was scarce and it was very useful to conserve energy. If you've ever watched a survival show like *The Island* you'll know they spend a lot of time resting because they are too exhausted to do anything else. It was therefore useful for our cavemen ancestors to have 'do nothing' as their default setting. However, it was also useful for them to get a hormonal kick up the backside occasionally, to summon the energy to hunt for food when the tribe was hungry or go to the trouble of fashioning a tool for the hunt. It was also useful to feel a bit of pressure when others in the tribe weren't getting on with them. To be kicked out of the caveman gang would be a death sentence, hence our great-great-grandfolks evolved to feel under a bit of pressure to people-please.

It was also massively helpful for our ancestors to get a huge hormonal helping hand when they faced a life-or-death, there's-a-bear-heading-towards-us situation. Their hearts beat faster and blood flowed to their muscles to prepare them to run like the wind. Hormones suppressed pain to enable them to fight. Non-urgent systems like digestion got shut down. Their brains' focus became hyper alert and narrowed in on the source of the threat. Everything became geared up to 'fight, flight, or freeze'. 99% of species who've ever lived on this planet have died out. We haven't yet. This system has served us incredibly well.

But…

We've evolved rather like an old building where bits have been added on over the years. Imagine an old cottage with Victorian plumbing in the bathroom, a 1960s conservatory and a modern kitchen. Humans have fundamentally the same design as in caveman days, with new brain regions tacked on top. These new bits help us to think conceptually, imagine things which aren't real, make sophisticated plans for the future, ruminate on the past and so on.

The old, survival-obsessed brain still runs the show, while now the newer, imaginative brain is feeding it with *imagined* threats, and the old brain can't tell the difference. The result? We get the same physiological reaction from confronting a high-stakes meeting as we would from confronting a grizzly bear, but the desire to run away and hide is no longer helpful. Even worse, we get the same physiological reaction from just *thinking* about a high-stakes meeting we've got in two weeks' time, or just *thinking* about that high-stakes meeting we cocked up two weeks' ago. Our caveman ancestors would have calmed down once the grizzly bear had scarpered, whereas we continue to worry. They would also have got rid of the myriad chemicals coursing through their bodies, through physical activity, but we stay sitting at our desks, stewing in a toxic soup of cortisol and adrenaline.

Understanding what's going on can be very helpful to performing under pressure. Hopefully we can be more appreciative when our inner cavemen take over. It helps us to remember that if it wasn't for them, we probably wouldn't be here in the first place. This awareness alone can calm us down and improve our performance.

But there are further steps we can take. The next step is…

2. Personalise

The general bell curve effect is true for everyone, but the rest is personal: our stressors are different and the way we feel pressure and behave as a result also varies. In the 'Performance vs Results' chapter we talked about how Ben and the crew got very, very clear on the ingredients and recipe (performance) that would bake them the 'cake' (results) they were after. Why? So they could repeat what was working and tweak what wasn't to get better and better results. Pressure is simply one ingredient in your recipe for success just as vanilla extract is an ingredient in a Victoria sponge. Get curious about *your* recipe – how much vanilla essence/pressure do you need before it becomes overpowering? There are a number of clues:

2a Our physiological indicators

These days we all have much easier access to the types of physiological measurement that back in 2000 only world class athletes like Ben and the crew did. There are apps that monitor how well you sleep, DIY kits that measure cortisol levels and blood pressure. In our coaching sessions at Will It Make The Boat Go Faster? we use special heart rate monitors that measure something called HRV – how the heart is resting between each beat – which is a key indicator of pressure.

If your organisation expects people to pull all-nighters, go to four different time zones in a week, and run marathons at the weekend, then cold hard data can show that worshipping hero behaviours is actually barking up the wrong tree. It is damaging performance, not enhancing it.

2b Our performance and results

Do we really need fancy statistics?! Isn't it obvious if we are firing on all cylinders and performing brilliantly – or if we are under too much pressure and performing terribly? Sadly, we often ignore or misattribute telltale warning signals. Knowing how pressure shows up for you emotionally can be immensely helpful – like a warning light on a mental dashboard before it impacts your results too much. Maybe your go-to feeling is overwhelm? fear? anger?

Ben: "I don't think I was a particularly angry young man, but this book has plenty of stories about me having arguments, feeling aggressive… because I'm writing about times of massive stress and when I'm under pressure it can come out as anger."

For example, I was coaching a Chief Executive recently who was feeling unbelievably irritated with a colleague. As he talked through the tiny, inconsequential things the guy had done, he began to realise his irritation was completely out of proportion to what was going on. He was massively under pressure in the face of a joint venture negotiation. The feeling of irritation was the red-light indicator on his mental dashboard that he needed to manage the pressure of the negotiation, rather than snipe at a poor random colleague.

2c Our stressors

What triggers you? For example, I am very happily adrenalised on stage in front of hundreds of people, but I tip into panic if you give me a spreadsheet or put me near a cliff face (don't ever get me to do maths whilst abseiling). How about you? If you look back over the last month, what put you under too much pressure? Or what events are you worried about over the next month? When we get to know our stressors we can proactively manage them.

Drip-drip-drip stressors can be more challenging to identify – on their own they are so tiny that we dismiss them as inconsequential. The pressure creeps up on us unawares, and either gradually impacts our performance, or builds to a point where we suddenly flip and get a massive performance hit, *seemingly* from nowhere. Even worse we're more likely to beat ourselves up – thus piling on the pressure even more – because we've lost it over something seemingly trivial.

What are the niggles that pile on the pressure for you? If you are aware, you can deal with them before you find yourself scrubbing junior paracetamol solution off the walls. Here are a few examples as thought-provokers…

- **Bandwidth**: having too many balls to juggle, too many things to keep in our heads…
- **Other people**: the kids' daily bickering, our flatmate's dirty washing up, our colleagues' little irritating habits, niggling criticisms from our manager… day in day out.
- **Interruptions**: the 'ping' of another notification, the 'can I just have a minute?' request…
- **Lack of sleep**: one night's bad sleep is hard, but weeks or months of it puts us under immense pressure.
- **Isolation**: we tend to think of loneliness as a problem for the elderly, but there's an increasing body of research to show that things like too much working in isolation (e.g. at home), over-reliance on social media, the breakdown of traditional community structures all take their toll.
- **Poor diet**: whether it's low iron levels creating low energy, low magnesium levels creating low mood, insufficient hydration driving poor concentration, or junk food yo-yoing our sugar levels, diet has huge impact on our ability to perform under pressure.
- **Our own expectations**: that the world 'should' be a certain way – trains should always run on time, computers should never crash – or that we 'must' be a certain way.
- …

So… now we understand our caveman brain, we know our own optimal pressure levels… the last piece of the jigsaw is using strategies to actively manage our pressure levels so we can perform when it counts. Here are some techniques Ben and the crew found useful:

3. Manage

3a Manage your reaction to the stressor

The company, Will It Make The Boat Go Faster?, was running a leadership development programme recently. As part of it we did a session on inspiring your team. We asked the participants what made them feel under pressure when presenting to others. One delegate said she felt really stressed with an audience she didn't know, another said he hated audiences he did know. They then almost had an argument, justifying their stress:

"If they know you, they want you to do well."

"No! if they know you and you mess it up, it will haunt you every time you see them! And strangers will be cold to you."

"No way! Strangers come with no baggage…"

"…"

Their debate demonstrates that it's not the stressor which creates the pressure, it's the *meaning we give it*: our perceptions and generalisations.

Ben: "There was no threat to my survival in the Olympic final, no bears chasing me, so why was I so stressed? What was the perception I was giving it? That it was my last chance, that we 'should' do well. That I'd be letting everyone down if I didn't."

If we manage our *perception* – the stories we tell ourselves about the stressor – hey presto! the pressure goes down. When we get caught up in a chain of panic, we simply need to change the perception at the earliest point we can. For example, Ben describes being sick the morning of the Olympic final. If he were a Zen Master, perhaps he could have managed his perception of the race so well that he felt totally calm and didn't vomit in the first place. Instead, although he did feel pressured enough to vomit, he managed to stop going up the bell curve there, and manage his perception of being sick so he could get back into his pressure Goldilocks zone. He told himself that throwing up showed that he was up for it, he drew on the support of the crew – remember? They took the piss out of him for being pregnant!

Sometimes this is as simple as telling yourself to STOP when your caveman brain is on overdrive, or having a catch-all mantra that blocks out the negativity.

'I can handle it'
'This will pass'
'I'll look back and laugh'

In essence, all of the strategies below are simply different ways of managing your perceptions, of giving your caveman brain a reassuring hug.

3b Normalise the stressor: practising peak pressure events

Sometimes, the more you practise dealing with a peak stressor, the more your brain learns it can handle it and the less pressure you feel. (This only works if you are actively managing your perceptions, rather than repeating negativity.)

Ben: "Lots of teams build this kind of practice into their training. For example we had plenty of trials, which were designed to simulate race conditions and normalise them. Before Rio the GB weightlifting team realised they weren't used to performing in front of large crowds, so to normalise it they went onto the pitch of (I think a rugby league) match at half time. Rumour has it that the Korean Archers filled a stadium full of people booing to normalise being in front of a negative crowd before heading to the Olympics!"

3c Take away the stressor

Hmmm, we hesitated to put this – we were worried it will sound like we're recommending you give up on your dreams and play it safe. There is something about reflecting on *unnecessary* stressors *and* about *pacing* though. For example, athletes are becoming increasingly aware of *appropriate levels* of physical pressure during training. A friend of mine manages a professional football team and during training sessions the players wear heart monitors and GPS trackers so they can monitor how much effort they are putting in. Sometimes this results in telling a player to stop faffing and put some more effort in, but sometimes it's to stop them putting themselves under too much pressure and training too hard. How does this apply to our world?

- I've banned my husband from watching me do stand up. He's an unnecessary stressor
- We planned in more down time when my son started senior school
- Ben colour codes his diary so he manages his bandwidth

- Ben and I delegate to accountants and bookkeepers wherever possible. Perhaps we'll choose in the future that this is skill we want to work to improve, but right now we are consciously choosing to remove numerical activities we find super stressful.

What's the equivalent for you?

3d Keep well

You remember the fizzy drinks can we talked about at the start of the chapter? How putting physical pressure on it could bend it? Imagine how much easier it would be to squash a can which was already dented, or rusty? In the same way, our base layer of sleep, nutrition and fitness will impact how much pressure we can handle. There is a growing body of evidence about…

- Fresh air and sunlight. It's not just an old wives' tale. Going outside regulates your circadian rhythms.
- Sleep. It's not a luxury – too little sleep is terrible news. Sleep is when our brains do essential work – memory filing, emotional regulation and physical repair.
- Diet. Have you heard the expression 'hangry'? – where hunger makes you angry? Our food intake impacts us in the short term (a terrifying study showed judges in court giving harsher sentences prior to lunch!) and in the longer term – for example, vitamin deficiency impacts our mood, stamina, even our decision-making abilities.

It's funny how much of this stuff we know, but don't seem to care about. It reminds me of the attitude to smoking back in the 1980s. People knew it was killing them but didn't seem to truly *get* it. I bet my grandkids will be goggle-eyed in horror when they hear about me being expected to pull all-nighters at work in my twenties in the same way that I am aghast hearing about relatives not wearing seatbelts or drink driving back in the 1970s.

3e Breathing

Ben: "We were taught breathing techniques to get enough oxygen to our muscles – but we were also taught how to control our breath to stay calm and keep our heart rate down. I found it one of the quickest ways to de-stress."

There is a nascent body of research that controlled, slow breathing might be an effective way of optimising HRV (the 'heart rate variability' mentioned above, which is an indicator of stress). There are plenty of apps out to help us get our number of breaths-per-minute down, without turning puce in the process. In a nutshell, the trick is to breathe deep from your belly – as opposed to high-chested, shallow breathing. Focus on a slow, relaxed out-breath, and then the in-breath almost takes care of itself.

3f Visualisation

We talked in the Motivation chapter about the power of visualisation to energise and keep going. It can also really help to remain calm under pressure.

Ben: "We were given visualisation tapes before Barcelona, but as soon as I lay down and heard the soothing voice saying 'picture yourself walking down steps towards a beach' I'd fall fast asleep. I tried doing them standing up, but they still didn't work because I was so physically knackered. What did work for me was picturing the rhythm I wanted to row – when I visualised that it helped to block out the stress and I felt great."

There are many, many ways to visualise. I stupidly dismissed visualisation for years – I felt it wasn't my bag. My 'aha!' was realising that I think more in speech than pictures, so I use guided visualisation where they talk me through the exercise step by step. There are loads of guided sessions out there, so if, like me, you are initially sceptical, experiment with different types and see what works for you.

3g Routine

What Ben describes as 'just do your routine' back then, sounds amusingly similar to what we call mindfulness today:

Ben: "All I had to do on race day was get up, have breakfast, get to the lake, take one stroke, then another and another."

He endeavoured to strip away all the negative mental chatter and focus his awareness simply on taking one action after another action, after another. New parents are encouraged to give their young children a bedtime routine to help them relax before sleep – insomniacs are advised to do the same. I have helped coachees develop routines for before 'big' meetings, or presentations. When would following a set routine help you focus purely on the task in hand rather than worrying?

But we don't even need a pre-set routine. Simply following one action then the next and the next, will help us to perform under pressure. That's why so many mindfulness techniques focus on the breath – because the in-breath and out-breath will simply keep on happening. Or we can switch the 'internal radio' in our head away from telling horror stories by replacing them with factual commentary: "I am walking up the steps, I am walking to the lectern, I am picking up the clicker, I am smiling at the audience, I am saying the first line of my presentation…"

3h Moral support

Ben: "In 1992 the rest of the team were older than me, better than me. They were scary. I was trying hard to earn a seat at the table. In 2000 I felt under immense pressure, but there were people I could talk to – to Martin, to crewmates. When one of the crew had a kind of panic attack the night before the Olympic Final, some of us sat down with him and read through a printout of our evidence wall together to calm him down."

What's the difference between helpful moral support, and peer pressure?! Only you can figure that out for your situation. The distinction is probably to do with who specifically, how specifically and in what context. Get curious.

Conclusion

We all face *drip, drip, drip* as well as *peak events* of pressure. The stressors might be different, but the effects are the same. A bit of pressure can energise us, but too much pressure can massively impact our performance. Simply knowing that our old caveman brain is trying its best can be calming. Knowing our personal, signature stressors and reactions helps us nip the impact in the bud. Finally there's a wealth of strategies to manage our stress proactively, to perform under pressure and get the results we want, when it matters most.

What are your optimum pressure levels? What are the signs that you have moved beyond the optimum bit of the bell curve and that too much pressure is impacting your results? What are your key strategies for managing the pressure so that you thrive in your Goldilocks zone?

Now we've looked at how to perform under pressure, the next question is: What do we need to do to make stellar performance *sustainable*? The next chapter is all about building momentum.

CHAPTER 10
MOMENTUM

The Gold Coast

Momentum: Win the race one stroke at a time.

The Gold Coast

Sept 2000, less than three weeks before the Olympics

You could feel the excitement as we strained to see out of the windows while the plane made the final descent in toward Brisbane Airport. We flew in over Brisbane harbour, nothing particularly remarkable to see; an industrial area, a reasonable size bridge, and then we were on the ground. We had arrived for another training camp, but this wasn't a normal training camp. This was the final preparation camp before the Olympics. Despite the length of the flight everyone was wide awake and full of excited tension.

We had a little over two weeks before the Olympic Regatta started. We had to keep the improvement curve going, we had to get every last iota of speed that we could.

As we approached immigration the usual comment went around as we completed the immigration forms – business or pleasure? We're here to do the business and it's going to be a pleasure!

We left Brisbane and went south toward the Gold Coast. The British Olympic Association had spent the last few years preparing the hotel to be Team GB's final preparation camp. A camp that most of the different sports could use to acclimatise, get used to the time difference and put the last touches to their preparation. The rowing team had just arrived, one of the biggest teams, 15 men plus 4 reserves and 8 women, plus coaches, medics, team managers, and physiologists.

That afternoon we made our way to the Hinze Dam which was about a 20-minute drive inland, up into the hills. When we arrived the water was flat and it looked perfect. We pulled up into the nearly deserted barbequers' car park and were met by a number of locals who had been responsible for erecting the boathouse (a corrugated iron roof held up by a well-made frame of 2x2s and 4x4s to keep the boats out of the sun). They'd also laid out the 2,000 metres line of buoys that marked out the course that we'd train on.

They seemed delighted to meet us and we all introduced ourselves. They were keen to tell us how pleased they were to have us all and that they hoped we'd be happy with the facilities they'd created. There was a policeman on constant duty and a number of other people would be there to make sure we had everything we wanted. From what we could see it looked simple and perfect for what we had to do – focus on the job in hand and make our boat go faster.

It was good to be back with the rest of the team. We'd spent the previous three weeks in the Lamb Hotel in Ely, while the rest of the men's team had been doing high-altitude training at one of the most spectacular rowing venues; Silvretta in Austria.

We hadn't gone to Silvretta for two reasons. Firstly, the lake was too short. We would have had to do lots of turns, which, in an 8+, just takes too long; your heart rate drops and you get too much rest. The other problem with Silvretta was that we would have been under the eye of Jürgen, the chief coach, and we would have had to fit into his programme.

Jürgen had an incredible track record: coaching crews to win gold medals in '72, '76, '80, '88, '92, '96, 2000, '04, '08, '12, '16. There is no other coach in any sport anywhere in the world to have that record. Unfortunately his magic hadn't worked for us; for the seven years I'd been under his programme I'd lost every race. We had moved away from his system to find our own way of doing things. We had to find a system that was right for us, not designed for a four or pair, not designed for Redgrave, but designed for us, the 8+. We had to believe that we could do it, we had to build our own culture and a key part of that was not going to Silvretta with the rest of the team.

We were now here on the Gold Coast back in the bosom of the team. The camp would be run under Jürgen's instructions according to his programme and we'd join in. Well, we'd join in bits of it and then quietly go off and do our own thing when it suited us best! We were going to stick to our programme and our way of thinking. We weren't going to make a big song and dance; we'd just get on with our thing as we'd been doing for nearly two years and our momentum would continue to build.

The camp progressed well. We'd row away from the buoyed course, row away from everyone else, up one of the long fingers that protruded from the main part of the lake. The further we were away from the dam, the narrower the finger became, the windier it was and the shallower it got until the tops of long dead trees reaching up from the bottom of the now flooded valley began to show above the murky waters. As we disappeared up a finger, Martin or Harry, in the coaching launch, would critique our rhythm, the speed of our hands, the separation of our hands from our bodies, the speed that the blades entered the water and countless other points. We focused on the detail and we strived to make the changes into daily habits.

We had sessions where we skimmed across the surface of the lake with an incredible boat speed. Harry told us that none of us appreciated how fast we were, and we had to keep looking for more, because we would be able to surprise even ourselves with our speed.

We had other sessions that were slow, with countless technical drills breaking down what we had to do into the smallest bite-sized chunks. We'd stop the boat and Harry's victim for the day would have to row the boat by himself in a huge circle as everyone else waited for him to reach the standard required. He encouraged us to experiment to find different ways of achieving the movement that we were after.

There were other sessions at low stroke rates where we covered long distances, measured by how many litres of sweat Fred was pouring into the bottom of the boat.

Then there would be sessions where everything seemed to fall apart, where the rhythm wouldn't be quite right, the pressure would get to us and crew members, or Harry or Martin, would despair that we weren't on track, the whole week had been sub-standard, and we'd be told that we were going to have to do something drastic. This was where the team rules came in and the rest of us would remind them of the previous sessions, of how we could do it, that we were good enough. This was so important and worthwhile we had to keep plugging away; we had to keep believing that we could be better, we were on a roll and we would keep building momentum.

The sessions when we did join the other British crews were the race pieces. All the crews from the men's and women's teams would come together and do the same sessions, maybe a 1,500m, and 1,000m race piece or a 2,000m race or a 1,000m and two 500m pieces.

The idea of these sessions was that they'd be competitive. They'd show how fast all the different crews were going. Jürgen had set a gold medal time for each crew, a time that was a little faster than the World Record, a time that, given fast conditions, you would almost be guaranteed a win if you achieved. If you could do 100% over 2,000m, you would be Olympic champion. Over 500m you would be aiming to go quite a lot faster than 100%.

The idea was that the percentage time would let you know if you were on track. Invariably, people played the percentage game, comparing their percentages to other crews in the team, which seemed like a good thing to do. Being able to say that you've got the highest percentage time in the team supposedly meant you were the fastest boat and you had the best chance of winning. The Redgrave 4- normally had the highest percentage times, and it would reconfirm to them that they were on track to win. But what if you weren't near the top of the percentage list? How did that leave you going into the Games?

This wasn't our concern. Our habit had become to focus on our performance and we had to continue with that habit. We wanted to use the race pieces to work on different things, different technical elements of the rowing stroke. Maybe one day we'd just be working on our hand speed, because if we improved that we'd go faster. We may not be the fastest on that piece, but that wasn't what we were preparing for. We'd spent two years becoming more and more performance-driven rather than just results-driven and we wanted to use the pieces to continue to improve, rather than just race the other crews in the team.

Before flying out to Australia we'd had a few conversations about this. We were going to have to be strong and have our bullshit filters on. We were going to have to keep the faith that what we were doing was right. We had to have a rock-solid belief in ourselves and each other.

The only people who mattered were the nine of us in the boat, Martin, Harry, Chris and 'Hotbuns' (Steve Ingham) the physiologist. We would all tell it how we saw it; we'd be honest and keep focusing on the things that mattered.

On the 6th September we were going to do our first set of race pace pieces; two 1,000 metre pieces, going off the start, finding race pace then sprinting home.

Everyone would be comparing times, apart from us. Our first piece wasn't great, we told it how we saw it, we were rowing a bit short and it was a bit stabby, but it was OK.

The second piece we experimented with a couple of changes, it was much better, not brilliant, but much better; we hadn't made the same mistake twice. It was clear that on the next piece we would have to move our backs faster. After the session we had a good conversation highlighting what had worked well and exactly what we had to do next.

The next day was quite similar, we did two 500m pieces, supposedly flat out. What we wanted to do though was work on getting the rhythm at our normal race pace, making a step on from the day before, continuing the momentum. We had two cracking pieces and the debrief afterwards was a really upbeat conversation about how to take it on to the next level.

While we were really happy about our performance other crews, who were fighting it out to win the percentage game, were wondering what was wrong with us. Our times were slow, but we were happy, it was similar to the previous day. The talk would start about how we had lost the plot and were going to lose again because we were happy with rubbish percentages! It was time for bullshit filters and belief that we had the right performance and that our momentum would continue to build. We had to stick to our plan and not worry about what other people thought of us. We needed to control the controllables. If we focused on getting the ingredients and recipe better, if we kept strengthening our beliefs, then our momentum would continue and we'd get the result we wanted.

Momentum: Win the race one stroke at a time.

Ben: "If you did today what we did back in 2000 you would absolutely lose. It would no longer be good enough. But if you followed our logic of always improving, always building momentum, you'd do extremely well."

Chapter summary

Small changes made on a daily basis multiply into massive improvements in results.

How to build momentum

1. Believe in better.
2. Win the race one stroke at a time.
3. Experiment.
4. Don't make the same mistake twice.
5. Create daily habits.

It sounds sexy to make big, bold changes that get dramatic results. Have you read articles about people who've quit the rat race, moved to France and started rearing pigs? Have you had that moment's daydream that you need to do something crazy to find your joie de vivre? And maybe you do! But there's also a lot to be said for making small changes every day to create big dividends in the long term.

Ben is a big, big fan of making tiny improvements on a daily basis. In fact, Ben is an *evangelist* about what the crew called *building momentum.* The first time we discussed the idea of a chapter on it, the conversation lasted for two hours before either of us looked at our watches.

How do kids learn? Parents don't expect their kids to crawl one day and suddenly start walking the next, or come back from school going, "Mummy I learnt to read today." It takes lots of little changes, with trial and error along the way. Imagine trying to lose weight by shifting a couple of stone overnight, yet we've all seen the before and after pictures of people who have dropped a dramatic number of dress sizes by shedding a pound at a time.

Ben: "In the 1998 World Championships we came a soul-crushing 7th. In an environment where you either win or lose, having spent the previous 12 months dreaming of a gold medal, spending every waking moment and most nights dreaming about winning… only to lose again… imagine what that felt like … so we made some big changes: we changed our working day from 8–3 to 8–11 then 4–7; we stopped doing circuit training (a cornerstone of the previous training programme); we changed strategy; we stopped using the chief coach's training programme and made our own programme.

But

We had the same coach, the same sports psychologist, the same pool of people to choose from, the same physiologist and we had this mammoth goal ahead of us. How do you eat an elephant? One spoonful at a time. How do you win a race?

One stroke at a time. One session at a time. One day at a time. Continuous improvement was going to be crucial. Small improvements day by day added together week by week, month by month, always building momentum."

Maybe you need to make some dramatic changes to achieve your goals and the chapters on change and risk cover useful strategies for that. But whether you need big change or you don't, building momentum one oar stroke at a time will multiply your returns like compound interest on an investment.

How to build momentum

We can divide up the crew's approach into five strategies:

1. Believe in better
2. Win the race one stroke at a time
3. Experiment
4. Don't make the same mistake twice
5. Create daily habits

1. Believe in better

No matter how good their performance, the team always believed they could do better. In recent years, the term 'growth mindset' has become common parlance (backed up by lots of research) and that's exactly what the crew had on the run up to Sydney. When I quizzed Ben on how they knew they could always improve, a few things emerged.

Firstly, the crew just seemed to have a kind of blind faith that there had to be a better way – similar to inventors who have a conviction that things can be improved. Remember a couple of decades ago most of us were using vacuum cleaners with bags quite happily? We might have grumbled a bit about emptying the bag (and when my teenage brother vacuumed up a burning coal Mum grumbled quite a lot about emptying a flaming bag), but it was good enough wasn't it?

Not for a West Country upstart called James Dyson, who had faith that there just had to be a better way and invented the bag-less vacuum that maintained its quality of suction.

For decades plane operators gave us seat numbers and meals on trays and charged us a fortune until Stelios Haji-Ioannou believed there had to be a better way and created easyJet. Can you imagine telling someone in the early 1980s that you could fly to another country for a few euros? They would have laughed in our face!

As well as having this blind faith the crew also focused on past experience of poor performance to prove they had untapped potential:

Ben: "After the World Championships every year you might have a three-week holiday. After three weeks it is ridiculous how much worse you are – how much fitness and strength you've lost, but at the end of the first month's training – where it felt like the coach had tried to kill you – you could see a definite improvement in your ergo scores. We got better; week by week it happened, so surely we could get a heck of a lot better over the course of two years?"

- Have you ever found it's taken a few days to get back into work after a holiday?

- Do you find you have good days and bad days?
- Have you ever acquired a new skill?
- Do you know one of the millions of silver surfers out there (pensioners who have learnt how to use the internet)?
- So isn't it fair to say there's ample proof that we all have untapped potential?

Lastly, the crew focused on examples of great performances as evidence that they had more to give. For example, do you remember that training session in Varese in 1998 which we mentioned in the Beliefs chapter? The crew did a 1,000-metre sprint at world record pace.

Is 1,000 metres a lot different from the official race distance of 2,000 metres?

Yes.

Isn't a practice session a lot different from an Olympics?

Yes.

So surely one fluke doesn't prove anything?

No, but it proved they had potential, and in terms of building momentum, the crew saw this session in Varese as a bit like the first push on a big rock they needed to get rolling. Enough little pushes, multiplied over time, would get them success.

2. Win the race one stroke at a time

David Brailsford (the famous head of British Cycling for many years and then Team Sky and Ineos supremo) calls the approach 'the aggregation of marginal gains'. Brailsford's philosophy is that if everyone – from the bike designers to the nutritionists to the athletes themselves – got 1% better, then the overall effect is phenomenal. That might be building a wheel that is 1% more aerodynamic or a meal plan that gives 1% better nutrition.

For Ben and the crew this meant analysing their performance, – getting curious about the smallest details of their recipe – such as how they separated the specific movement of arms and body during each stroke, how they could ask for feedback more succinctly, or how they built more solid beliefs.

Ben: "When we are crap at one thing, to try and go immediately to brilliant isn't that helpful. Let's focus on being slightly less crap!! Or if we're already good at something, you can always find room for improvement when you look at the details."

As the saying goes, look after the pennies and the pounds will look after themselves.

Imagine you are a manager and your goal is to build a strong team. What might be some easy 'single rowing strokes' you could take, which would help you achieve this? It might be a one-off meeting to make sure everyone's clear on the team's deliverables. It might mean having regular conversations, understanding everyone's motivations or saying thank you. On their own they are small things that are easy to dismiss as trivial, but put together they would make a huge difference.

3. Experiment

Martin introduced the crew to the story of Thomas Edison, who invented a workable filament for the electric light bulb. He was dealing with new technology, a new marketplace, competing with other inventors such as Graham Bell. That sparked the team's interest. They had such a short time frame before the 2000 Olympics. They didn't know what to do or how to do it. There was no historical precedent, no game plan to follow – so they followed Edison's example and experimented.

Experimenting wasn't willy-nilly trial and error. They could eliminate some of the guesswork because they'd got so curious about the recipe. At the very least they would *actively* decide which ingredients to play around with.

Allegedly, Edison conducted over three thousand experiments. He didn't get lucky on day one, but by focusing on the small things, trying different approaches and identifying what worked and what didn't work he got there. The key learning the crew took from this was about Edison's *mindset*. Edison appreciated that if he tried something and it didn't work *it was still progress to be celebrated*:

Ben: "When we tried something and it made the boat go faster, that was brilliant. Of course, it was a pain in the backside when we tried something and it didn't work, but we had to snap out of it and remind each other that we were still a step closer, at worst we'd crossed something off the list of things to try and we could move on to trying the next thing so that was great, we'd learnt something valuable. Edison's example of 3,000 experiments is pretty extreme – it sounds like one hell of a slog, but we'd trained hard for years and lost! Surely Edison's approach is far easier than doing the same thing again and again and being gutted?"

Edison might never have found a workable filament, or someone might have beaten him to it. But if he hadn't tried, if he hadn't continually improved he would have guaranteed himself failure and been gutted for life.

It reminds me of something my mother said when I submitted my first ever article to be published. After my third or fourth rejection letter I was getting pretty dispirited and she said,

"I heard JK Rowling got 26 rejections for Harry Potter before it got accepted, so well done you, four down, another 22 to go and you'll be there!"

What about in the corporate world, where people might not be as supportive as my mother? It's all very well experimenting to find the best sales approach, but if you screw up a sales meeting and lose a deal in the process, there are big ramifications.

Ben: "Coming from the sporting world into the corporate world I found it amazing that people don't seem to practise. People just go to the real thing straight off. In the boat we spent 99.9% of our time practising in a safe environment. Clearly you can't do that percentage in the corporate world, but if you spent 5% of your time practising wouldn't that increase your conversion rate more than 5%?"

In the sporting world there are clear training sessions where you can play around and experiment without dire consequences. In the corporate world the distinction between practice and 'the real thing' can be more blurred. For example, even a junior salesperson going to their first client meeting wants to win the work, but how could you nevertheless create practice space in your organisation?

Some examples from our clients include:

- Peer feedback: asking a colleague to read through your email before you send it, your proposal before you submit it, your meeting agenda before you run it.
- Dress rehearsals. For example practising a presentation in front of others before presenting it to the Board or doing a role play before an important client meeting
- Team discussions. Building in time in regular team meetings to discuss what if…? scenarios, so people can practise their response in advance.

There's a wider cultural issue too – how much do we allow ourselves, our peers and our team members to make the mistakes that are so much a part of learning?

As a number of sportspeople have been attributed with saying, "The more I practise, the luckier I get."

4. Don't make the same mistake twice

It's funny how the world values experience, but rarely questions what's in that experience. Remember how the team used Thomas Edison as a role model? Edison reputedly claimed never to have made the same mistake twice. That inspired the eight. They had 24 months, not a minute more. They couldn't afford the luxury of repeating the same errors. This mindset, this intention, electrified many of the approaches we've looked at in other chapters. For example, remember the performance reviews we looked at in the Performance vs Results chapter?

- Where did I perform well?
- Where could I have performed better?
- What will I do (differently) next time?

Imagine asking those questions with the underlying intention of never making the same mistake twice. It brought a razor-sharp clarity to the crew's discussions.

Ben: "Sometimes we learnt the wrong things and went up blind alleys. Sometimes we made the same mistake twice and that was bloody irritating, but if we kept it simple, kept asking 'What's working? What do we need to change?' we got ourselves back on track and minimised the annoyance. Sometimes we didn't know what to do or how to do it. If there was something we wanted to improve and we couldn't figure out an element to experiment with that was hard, but the solution was to rely on the coach and each other for advice and feedback and to keep experimenting."

How did the crew know whether to change something or keep plugging away with the same strategy to give it time to work?

Ben: "That's an incredibly tough call. What's the difference between a genius with determination and grit who perseveres and a complete idiot who is banging their head against the wall? Alexandra Burke lost The X Factor one year and won it a couple of years later and we applaud her. Then we laugh at other contestants for kidding themselves because they are hopeless. I guess it all comes back to evidence and performance reviews. Many people had written me off by the end of 1998, but that experience in Varese of going at world record pace was solid evidence on my evidence wall that I could still do it if I kept getting curious about the recipe. We'd make a change and it might not work first time, so we'd assess it in our performance reviews – is the change not working or not working 'yet'?"

5. Create daily habits

Have you ever had your car break down and had to push it to get it started again? The first push is the hardest, but once you've got it moving, the pushing is much easier. Or do you remember practising hill starts when you learnt to drive? Driving up a hill with the accelerator on is relatively easy, but once you've stopped, getting going again involves such fancy stuff with the handbrake that it warrants its own section in the driving test.

As the crew pursued the Olympic Dream – and as we pursue our own goal – it is incredibly helpful to create regular habits which drive us forward. By habits, I simply mean activities we do automatically – like brushing our teeth. Habits are incredibly powerful – when our 'default setting' routines are geared up to achieving our crazy goal, we don't have to think, progress just happens.

For the crew this meant having *daily* weights sessions to build their muscles and *daily* stretching to build their flexibility as automatic parts of their routine. And having habits didn't mean unthinkingly sticking to the status quo, because they had performance reviews as an automatic habit *every* day after *every* session to build the team and figure out how they could improve. If you want proof of how strong a habit this was, get this… they even had a performance review after the Olympic Final (after which they'd never row as a crew again) because it was just too weird not to!!

Imagine you are that manager we spoke about in the section above, wanting to build your team. You've decided that a crucial 'rowing stroke' is communications with the team, so you make a New Year's Resolution to walk the floor and chat to people at least once a day. But it's Monday, you had a heavy weekend. One day missed is going to make no difference. You'll do it tomorrow. Except tomorrow you have that offsite meeting – but, hey, floor-walking is just a small thing, it's not a big deal, there's always Wednesday. But then on Wednesday you've got loads of work to catch up on because you were at that offsite on Tuesday.

Three months later you are kicking yourself as your demoralised, dysfunctional team makes some huge screw up. Insignificant bad habits have a significant impact over time. Annoyingly, you can't make up for missing the daily habit by making a one-off extra effort. You can't fool the dentist by flossing for eight hours the day before your appointment.

So, how do you create a new habit? The easiest way is to tag it on to an existing one. If you want to floss your teeth every day, it's easiest to do it whenever you clean your teeth. If you need to do those neck exercises the physio gave you, perhaps you could do them at every red traffic light when driving, or while you are waiting for the kettle to boil. Another tactic is to have a specific time. E.g. when I'm working from home, I set an alarm on my phone for every couple of hours, to prompt me to get up and moving, rather than sitting endlessly at my desk.

It's also useful to think about a reward to embed a new habit. Remember the story of Pavlov and his dogs? Pavlov rang a bell and then brought the dogs food. The dogs soon learnt that the bell meant food so they started wagging their tails and salivating purely on the sound of the bell? In the same way, recent research shows that after a few repetitions we get a dopamine release from our brain's reward system as soon as we start the habit – we don't have to actually wait for the reward to feel good. A reward can be as simple as a 'habit tracker' where you record every time you've done the habit – a bit like a star chart. A lot of apps use this idea and reward you with 'streaks' for regular action.

Conclusion

It would have been so easy for the 1998 crew to jack in the rowing dream. There were certainly plenty of people advising them to set a realistic target like being 6th next time, or 5th, but the crew believed that they could always do things better and committed to give open and honest feedback about what was working and what needed to change. The crew took the scary, 'undoable' challenge and created simple daily habits and daily experiments to build momentum.

What does this mean for us? Before we sell the house and become a French pig farmer, we should reflect on our massive untapped potential – believe in better. Value small changes – remember that tiny improvements multiplied day by day, turn crawling into walking, limited vocabulary into fluent French, a chaotic office into a well organised workflow. Find a way to make experimentation safe and acceptable.

In the space of just two years the crew went from being 7th place, nine seconds too slow, to being the best in the world and Olympic Champions. Just imagine what incredible momentum we can build in our lives and make our boats go faster.

Building momentum is crucial, but what happens when we need to make *radical* changes? The next chapter focuses on how to deal with big change…

CHAPTER 11

CHANGE

The Olympic Heat

Change: Celebrate discomfort.

The Olympic Heat

18th Sept 2000

We were here, at the Olympics at last…

I remember very little of the heat or what happened that morning before we raced. I remember feeling tired and trying to push that thought as far from my mind as possible. I can't even remember who else was in our heat; I just remember that it was us and the Aussies. I do remember the end of the race and what happened next.

I crossed the line furious. The Aussies had beaten us off the start and led us the whole way. It was incredible. It was wrong. It was bollocks. I was furious, absolutely furious. They'd beaten us by half a length. But only half a length. We hadn't deserved to beat anyone we'd rowed so badly. We'd let ourselves, each other and everyone else who supported us down. I was livid. Our only hope of getting to the final now was to race in the repechage with the other fastest losers in two days' time.

Under a hot midday Australian sun we sat in the boat in silence for a couple of minutes trying to comprehend what had happened and trying to regain our breath. We sat pretty still and silent other than rasping breaths and heaving shoulders, with a heavy atmosphere over us.

I pulled my T-shirt out of the storage area below my seat and put it on to cover my shoulders as they had already started to burn in the ten minutes since I'd taken it off. We waited for one of the launches to come over to us and throw us bottles of water. We drank them and in a flat voice Rowley told us to spin the boat around. In an ominous silence we did as he asked. Once we were pointing back up the lake, without asking whether we were ready, he gave us a command and we rowed back up the lake to warm down. Rowley said very little and in silence we rowed up the lake for 1,500 metres before turning to row back to the boathouse.

The 3,000 metre warm-down was angry, sullen and silent; it didn't have the purpose that we were supposed to row with. We were too angry – and tired.

For the second time this season the Aussies had beaten us, but again this had nothing to do with the Aussies, it was us; we'd under-performed, we'd been rubbish. I was most angry about the fact that we'd let ourselves down. We'd been diabolical. God help the Aussies that they'd only beaten us by half a length when we'd been so awful.

Even as we'd crossed the line I knew that we were better than that and that we were better than them. I knew what good rowing felt like and that hadn't been good rowing. Next time we'd row well and we'd have them.

As the boat slid across the last few metres of water to the pontoon a scarlet Martin walked onto the pontoon to grab the end of an oar and pull us in. Not a word was said. With the very minimum of commands from Rowley we got the boat out of the water, put it on its rack, pulled the white cotton cover over the black hull of our boat to protect it from the sun and in silence walked over to where Harry and Martin stood.

I'm afraid I remember nothing of what Martin said. Whatever he said was spat at us with all the anger and passion he possessed. I don't remember much of what Harry – calm, mild-mannered Harry – said to us either, what I do remember was Harry saying, "If you want to do dressage and just look good you should f**k off to the equestrian centre, but if you want to row and stay down at the lake then you need to f***ing well race." All of us were livid; we hadn't poured all our energy and dreams into this crew for countless years to throw it away at the last minute.

After a moment's silence Louis – who rarely spoke at post outing reviews – asked if anything that had been said was unfair, and if it wasn't we should shut the f**k up as nothing more needed to be said.

Next came logistics. Fred and I were told that we were wanted for a press conference. The British and other press wanted to know what had happened. We quickly agreed that the Aussies had been so cocksure and certain that they were going to win we might as well help them with their confidence and see if we could feed them some overconfidence. Our line was to be that the Aussies were really fast and they would be hard to beat; anything to 'big them up'.

Fred and I would meet the rest of the boys in the food tent and Martin gave out our meal vouchers. After lunch we'd go back to the village and the following morning we'd start to put the right things into place. We'd make the necessary changes, maybe this was the best thing that could have happened to us, it would sharpen us up, make us look for opportunities and take control.

The nine of us left Martin and Harry in the boating area and in silence we walked towards the British tent, with a bow wave of anger clearing people out of the way in front of us.

This was not a time to be depressed; yes, we'd lost the heat; yes, we'd humiliated ourselves; yes, we'd rowed badly, yes, we now had to race the repechage, yes it was a f***ing disaster, but being depressed wasn't going to achieve anything. We needed energy, vigour and passion to put this right and, by God, we were going to put it right.

As we left the boating area, Fred and I peeled off from the rest of the group and nodded to the PR person who was hovering nearby. Without a word she led us to the 'mixed zone', where press meet the athletes, and into a big white tent. While the press conference before ours finished up Fred and I stood in silence and waited, this was the last place we wanted to be.

Our turn came and we were ushered to the front of the tent, up on to the stage and we sat behind a long table with a number of microphones on it. We were introduced and with a supreme effort Fred and I tried to be civil.

"Yes we are disappointed."
"No, we didn't row very well."
"We don't know what our chances are because the Aussies seem really fast."
"Yes, we've beaten them twice before, but they were really fast today."
"Yes, we will have to race in the repechage the day after tomorrow."
"Yes, the Aussies would go straight through to the final." "Yes, they will be very hard to beat."

All we really wanted to say was that we were going to take the bastards apart and they didn't stand a hope in hell, but we didn't want to talk bollocks to Basil, so we played the game.

Thankfully we were out of there soon enough. We were back into the athletes' area walking along beside the fence when my parents, my sister and brother-in-law appeared in the other side of the fence with Isabella (my fiancée). They all looked bitterly disappointed, upset and worried. They were watching another Olympic campaign unravel. My mother looked hardest hit. I assured them that nothing was unravelling, we had messed up, but it didn't matter because we would win, the Aussies didn't have a chance when we rowed well. If they looked at the time of the two heats, our time was the third fastest overall, and we could and would go much faster.

I left them to it. Fred and I went to get some food and to be with the boys. After an unappetising lunch that I didn't want to eat we headed back to the Village. We travelled in silence; an angry silence. I was knackered, too knackered. I thought that we'd done too much the day before and gone into the race feeling knackered, but that wasn't an excuse.

Back in the village the other rowers didn't know how to treat us or what to say so most said nothing. There must have been an angry pall that hung over our flat.

The following day we had a bit of a lie-in, which was really nice, it meant that when we did get out of bed at around eight we all felt renewed and ready for action. After breakfast we headed down to the lake and went upstairs to the meeting rooms. Martin had booked us a room and showed us videos of the two heats.

The first heat was the USA, reigning World Champions, unbeaten for three years, and the Croatians. The US was the top seeded crew, but they hadn't raced in Europe all year. They'd sent some of their guys to Lucerne 12 weeks before and we'd seen them off pretty easily, but they hadn't raced as a crew and for the last year they'd been the target, the crew we had to be faster than.

As we watched the video the US were taken apart by the Croatians. The US looked rubbish and Kieran even made a comment about them and started to laugh, until he got a severe tongue lashing from Martin who was quick to point out that the US were three times World Champions and we had never won anything and judging by yesterday's performance we were in no position to laugh at anyone. Kieran had not had a good birthday the day before and today wasn't looking any better.

Watching the video of our heat, we looked shit; truly shit. We hadn't worked so hard for so long only to row so badly when it really mattered.

A few things had happened. We had been nervous and had stopped talking to each other. We thought that we'd been rowing around the lake with purpose, but gradually without noticing we'd taken our foot off the gas. We'd gone out to race wanting to row technically really well – we'd spent months and months learning to row better than anyone else so that's what we tried to do – but we forgot about one thing. We were here to race. As Harry had said we weren't doing f***ing dressage, we were supposed to be racers.

There is only one reason to row technically well and that is so you can lay down as much power as you possibly can and every ounce of that power has got to make the boat go in the right direction. In the heat we hadn't put down any power and there had been no aggression until it was too late. We now had a very simple choice, get depressed and accept the fact that the Aussies were better than us or figure out what had gone wrong and what we needed to do to put it right and then go and put it right. It was an easy choice.

Thirty minutes later we were standing around the boat and Martin briefed us on what we were going to do. We were going to work on applying power and accelerating the boat every stroke; that's what every stroke had to do, accelerate the boat. We were going to do power stokes, four of us would row at a time at set stroke rates (the number of strokes a minute) while the other four boys would sit still and keep the boat level. Rowley would monitor our speed on the boats speedometer and we would race each other. Grim faced we carried the boat down to the water, put it in and got ourselves ready.

From the very first stroke that I took, Rowley started to tell me that I need to get my oar closer to the water. He told me on the 1st stroke, the 2nd, 3rd, 4th, 10th, 11th, 20th, 21st, 28th and 29th, 40th, 41st and 42nd, the 50th etc.

The little git had obviously had a conversation with Martin and I obviously wasn't rowing well enough, which must mean that I was a lot of the problem the day before. Why hadn't anyone told me and more importantly why hadn't someone made me aware of the fault before the heat so that I could put it right and we wouldn't have lost? I was really confused and angry. I wanted to improve and put my faults right, but at the same time I was really pissed off that Rowley had waited until after we lost to help me improve. Why the f*** hadn't I had this input before we'd lost? I was livid – again!

We started the power strokes, pulling as hard as we could. Doing sets of 10, 20 or 30 strokes all at a rate of 20 to 26 strokes a minute. Stern four would row and Rowley would call out their speed then bow four, Andrew, me, Simon and Louis, would take over pulling our rocks off… and still Rowley wanted more. More speed and better rowing from me. “Stern four were faster. I want more speed, more acceleration. Ben get your oar down. That’s better. Oar down again Ben. More speed come on, accelerate, more power, more acceleration. Ben oar down again. Accelerate…” and on it went.

I was knackered, absolutely knackered, and still the little bastard wanted more. More speed and my oar lower. He was really pissing me off. More power? I didn’t have more power. Rowley still wanted more. Stern four had been faster and Rowley wanted more. More power and more speed. I was knackered. He still wanted more. Fifteen strokes to go. More speed. He wanted more speed from me. He was telling me to do more. That was it – something snapped and I was in my own red fog. I went for it.

I went from 22 strokes a minute to about 40 strokes a minute, everyone else tried to keep doing what they should be doing as I took off. They couldn’t carry on and soon I was the only person rowing at 40-odd strokes a minute with everyone shouting at me to stop being an idiot and to stop. I just saw red; Rowley swore at me and told me to get a grip.

That was it. I was going to drown the little bastard. I stopped rowing, my legs, lungs and head pounding. I’m told there was a stream of abuse pouring out of my mouth and I started to take my feet out of my shoes. I was going to get out of the boat, swim down and drown the little shit. As I started to put my feet over the edge of the boat and into the water I was suddenly grabbed from behind. A pair of thick arms wrapped around me trying to hold me still and Andrew's gruff voice was in my ear telling me not to be such a tw*t. I threw his arms off me, turned and flailed at him with my fists, but he was too quick and he got out of the way.

I don't remember what happened next. I have no idea how I calmed down. I'm not sure that I have ever been so angry before or since, but I did calm down and we did finish the session and I don't think that Rowley let me off anything.

By the time we got the boat off the water I was knackered and calmer. We'd finished the session with a flat out 500 metre sprint and we were fast, really fast. We'd done our fastest ever 500 metre piece – 1 min 17.5 sec.

Before we got the boat off the water I walked down to where Rowley was, he looked at me defiantly. We'd all had a go at him at different times and he'd never given an inch. All eight stone nothing of skin and bone and he'd stood up to a 16 ½ stone Luka and anyone else who chose to take him on. I walked down and gave him a conciliatory slap on the back before picking up everyone's oars and carrying them off the pontoon to our boat rack.

The review was good. Martin and Harry were pleased that there had been an outpouring of passion; it showed we cared, that we were angry and willing to do something about it. We discussed what had to happen, what had to be done next and how we were going to make the boat go faster.

Change is sometimes uncomfortable, I should have known that as we'd been through so much, but we would be stronger and better because of it. That was what mattered most. The next morning… we had to fight for our place in the Olympic final.

Change: Celebrate discomfort.

Ben: "Change happens, everyone knows that.
The most important thing about change is that it's all right."

Chapter summary

There are plenty of tactics for making a change easier, but most of the important work happens before we even lift a finger… how we think about change and how we talk about it.

Knowing how to navigate change is essential because:

- It happens, it's unavoidable.
- There are lots of benefits to be reaped.
- Handling change is like a muscle – use it or lose it.

How can we handle change more easily?

Section 1: Instigate change.
1a Get the crocodile.
1b Spot opportunities.

Section 2: Convince yourself/others to change.
2a Look for the upsides.
2b Don't shoot the messenger.
2c Build bridges.

Section 3: Make the change easy.
3a Celebrate discomfort.
3b Give it time.
3c Make it impossible not to.
3d Exaggerate.

What changes have been thrust upon you in the last year? A restructure at work? A new relationship? The kids leaving home? A software update on your phone?! How likely is it that there will be changes in the coming year?

When you hear about the latest change does your heart sing or sink to your boots? Research consistently shows that most of us don't like change – we don't like the uncertainty and pressure of the process, we don't like losing the comfort of the good old days and we don't like things being different.

Being able to navigate change is a key skill in all walks of life, for at least three key reasons:

- There are many instances where we have to change because we just can't go on as before. We have to leave junior school and go to big school. Lots of change happens whether we like it or not.

- In addition to these forced-upon-us changes, there are the changes we can make to reap greater benefits. For example, there's a struggling hairdressing salon in the local high street. I think the photos in the window are unchanged from thirty-odd years ago. Is the business still going? Yes, they seem to have a handful of customers. But I wonder what changes they could have made that would have made their lives easier, their customers happier and their business more profitable.
- Being able to change also appears to be a bit like a muscle. If you haven't changed anything for a while the muscle goes a bit flabby and your movement gets restricted. Do you know someone who has settled into a life of routine and goes into a tailspin because shops have stopped stocking their normal brand of shampoo?

Ben and the crew faced considerable change – relocation, change in coaching team, change in the culture of the organisation, a change in their working times, change in the technical rowing strokes they were taking. Thanks to what they learnt from navigating through all this choppy water, we can translate their lessons and apply them in our own situation to minimise the stress and make change something to relish rather than dread.

The ideas are grouped under three headings:

1. Strategies for instigating change – having the mindset to be in the driving seat rather than being a victim.
2. Strategies for communicating change – persuading yourself and others to make the transition.
3. Strategies to put change into practice as smoothly as possible.

1. Instigate change

1a Get the crocodile

I was watching some awful survival programme on telly and the survival expert was telling us all about the dangers of a crocodile swamp. His crowning line – delivered in total seriousness – was:

"The key thing about crocodiles is to get them before they get you."

I nearly fell off my seat laughing at the time, but the line has come back to haunt me again and again, and I now revere it as a pearl of true wisdom.

- Make changes on your terms.
- Don't wait until the world forces you to change or you'll get bitten on the backside by the proverbial crocodile.
- Anticipate, keep your radar up, think what might happen.

> Take the job market for example. We're not in control of whether our firm makes redundancies, but we are in control of building a network of people who know what we can offer, we can take control for making sure our skills are up to date, we can take control of having a sensible budget… and so on.

How can you get the crocodile before it bites you? The crew found that it was largely a mindset thing – making the decision to take control. The questions they asked and the time they spent on reflecting as a group helped, as well as the fact that they looked beyond the day-to-day and focused on their ultimate goal.

1b Spot opportunities

Ben: "Will it make the boat go faster? Then do it!"

Ben and the crew went further than anticipating when they might have to change; they were actively on the lookout for changes that would make the boat go faster. The momentum chapter looks at how they did this with small everyday habits. They also did it with the big stuff.

Martin was revolutionary in that he worked backwards from the goal. He didn't look at how things were currently and tweak them a bit; he took the goal of gold as the starting point and figured out the best route from there. If the answer was something very different from their current approach, then so be it.

Ben: "Traditionally we'd cram training sessions into the morning so that some rowers could work or study and Pinsent and Redgrave could play golf in the afternoon!! Martin realised you do the best quality training when your body is fed and rested, so he put in place an all-day training programme with plenty of rest time and eating built in."

It seems obvious now, but at the time it was a big change. Most people were either accepting the status quo or figuring out how to make the status quo a little bit better.

The new timetable had big consequences: Louis had to give up his law course, Simon had to go part time on his course, it made everyone's social lives more difficult, but it was an opportunity to make the boat go faster.

Use your goal as the starting point and work backwards – what changes would make your boat go faster?

2. Convince yourself and others to change

Martin had spotted the potential, but he had a job on his hands to convince everyone.

Ben: "We wanted to change as long as it meant not doing anything differently!"

Sometimes change requires buy-in from other people, sometimes it requires us to convince ourselves.

2a Look for the upsides

The very word *change* conjures up fear and negativity. If we were told we needed to change our behaviour, we'd probably assume we needed to stop doing something we liked and replace it with an uncomfortable new activity that we'd find difficult. However, change can also mean *adding to.*

When we get a new gadget or go on holiday or get a new car – that's a change we love. Because we love it, we probably don't mind that it takes a bit of time to sort it out. Go on a mini break to Barcelona and the fact that we don't know what we are eating for breakfast is quite funny. When we see it in a useful way we get useful stuff.

We've just had a new IT system put in at work, to replace a largely manual one. My instinctive response was 'urgh!' this will mean I can't do it my way anymore, it will be extra bureaucracy and pain. It was fascinating how instantaneous and negative my reaction was. Maybe you're thinking 'that's just you, Harriet!' but – in my feeble defence – research suggests the 'default negative setting' is pretty common.

It took *conscious effort* to look for the upsides. I had to ask myself, "What's the benefit? How is this helpful?" Answers included: I'll have access to way more useful information; yes, there'll be a short-term learning curve, but after that it will be a lot quicker to do. None of these answers popped into my head naturally.

We usually compare changes with how things are currently and focus on the downsides, or we make up terrifying stories about what might happen in the future, and thereby make things harder for ourselves.

Ben: "Going on a training camp was a change it was easy to feel negative about. Being away from your partner for three weeks, eating appalling food, training your arse off with not enough air to breathe, sharing a bed with a hairy Croatian, having only one TV for 30 people and the other 29 people wanting to watch MTV. But you don't get the best out of the camp if you're feeling negative. What's the upside? You don't have to do your washing or cooking, you are in the most amazingly beautiful landscape, you can convince a horse to take a walk through your accommodation block, have facial hair growing competitions!"

You can train yourself to habitually look for the upsides by asking questions like the ones the crew regularly asked themselves:

- What's the upside?
- What could be good about this?
- What is this adding?

2b Don't shoot the messenger

Ben: "During the changes in 1998 there was a bit of time when I was in Henley with Jürgen and some guys were with Martin in London. We heard that Martin was doing one session a day in the water and one on the ergo, rather than the normal two in the water. We all thought they were doing this to get really good at the ergo to get through the ergo tests for team selection. I thought they were cheating and fumed about them being bastards, trying to beat me."

In fact, the only reason Martin was making his guys do a session on the ergo was in order to ringfence the variables and work on very specific elements. You can't blame your performance on crosswinds or bumpy water when you are sitting on an ergo machine in a dry (ish!) gym with four walls.

Ben: "When Martin explained why he was doing what he was doing I thought it was quite funny how we'd responded in Jürgen's group."

We find this a lot in our corporate client work. When people feel nervous about a change they tend to assume the worst of their colleagues and bosses. They imagine all kinds of horrible motives and Machiavellian plans. I'm not saying there aren't dastardly deeds being done in offices across the land, but I am saying that decades of combined consultancy experience suggests they are far fewer than we think.

I used to be a Samaritan volunteer, befriending callers in emotional distress. One night I was sitting next to a fellow volunteer and although I couldn't hear what her caller was saying I could hear that he was really angry, shouting down the phone at her. At the end of her call I checked with her to see if she was OK. Her reply has stuck with me:

"He's going through a tough time and anger is all he can access right now."

In other words, why would a reasonable, rational person do this? Because that's all he can access right now.

How can you avoid these kinds of misunderstandings in the first place? For example, if you are a team member having change inflicted on you from above, perhaps it means asking for an explanation of why it's going ahead and what the benefits will be. Perhaps it means stepping into the messenger's shoes and understanding their point of view, so we can access a better response.

2c Build bridges

By the same token, if you are the messenger – e.g. if you are a manager leading your team through change, encouraging your peers and bosses to change, can you clearly describe *why* the changes are taking place and crucially what the benefits will be – *for them*?

Do you do the 'what, why, how, how?' check with every communication you make – do you check that you've explained what is happening, why it is happening, how it is happening and how they can feedback and ask us questions? The best ideas can get rejected because they are presented in an aggressive light.

For a time there was bad blood between the national squad and the Cambridge University crew. As Ben explains, in a totally objective and unbiased way:

Ben: 'They were evangelical in their approach. They were right and everyone else was wrong. They were God's chosen ones and they pissed us off. For example, there was one bloke I rowed with in the British team and then he went to Cambridge and became really opinionated about how to row. He told us that the national squad had just taught him to pull hard and that Cambridge had taught him to actually row. It wound me up that he thought he was right and we were all wrong."

But what happened next?

The crew's new assistant coach was Harry, a Cambridge man!

Ben: "What that guy had said was absolutely right. When Harry and Martin coached me, I started to learn to row."

What convinced Ben to change his point of view 180 degrees? If we want to get people on side, we need to build bridges. However right we are, few people respond well to being *told* they are wrong. They start to shift their thinking when they *experience* the benefits of doing it another way. This might be actual experience or it might be a description of the benefits that is so vivid and so engaging the listener can mentally experience them.

Ben: "Harry was a really nice guy. A quietly spoken Kiwi with a reputation for brilliance. He had a clear idea of what was right and what wasn't – every stroke he would say if it was right or not, but he had no arrogance about him, no ego. When he taught you it wasn't in an 'I'm the best' kind of way."

3. Make the change easy

3a Celebrate discomfort

Ben: "We knew we needed to change and we wanted to change, but we didn't like changing."

Try changing something right now.

Put your watch on the other wrist, or a ring on a different finger, or clasp your hands together and move the fingers of your right hand one notch. Go on, research shows only 20% or so of readers will actually do this rather than reading it, but the 20% who do will remember this chapter more and be more likely to act on it.

How does it feel? Weird and uncomfortable? What do you want to do? Change back to normal?

It is usually useful to us that our mind and body find normality comfortable. Can you imagine the time and effort it would take to get dressed in the morning if we had to invent how to do it each and every time? "Wow, we need to get our legs into this pair of trousers, let's brainstorm some options."

Because we have our normal, comfortable way of doing it, we don't have to think about it and we can conserve our precious mental power for worrying about the day ahead. This human trait is not so helpful when it comes to change. It's easy to confuse the *this is uncomfortable* feeling for *this is wrong and stupid.*

Expect discomfort, celebrate discomfort, it's just a message telling you to think about it for a while, until you figure out how to do it in your sleep.

3b Give it time

Don't expect progress to be a smooth progression forward.

Ben: "Trying to improve the score on a rowing machine didn't happen every single session. Of course you're looking for an improvement to motivate yourself, to stick at the change – improvement keeps you going, keeps you motivated. But to make the change happen it's about repetition."

Change takes time. Go easy on yourself. Don't beat yourself up when it doesn't happen in 24 hours. Have you ever had a cold and had to blow your nose every two seconds? Gradually it gets better and then, one teatime, you realise you haven't blown your nose all day? It's only in retrospect that you realise you've made the change from ill to well.

3c Make it impossible not to

Ben: "When you pull on the oar you are meant to have one hand holding it and the other like a claw, guiding it. I got into the really bad habit of actually letting go of the oar with one hand in order to stretch as far as I could and get the longest stroke. The way I stopped it was by getting the boys to tape up my fingers – so I literally couldn't let go of the oar even if I'd tried to."

How can we make the new change the *norm* and therefore make it impossible – or at least an effort – to revert back to the old way of doing things? Examples we've seen clients use include:

- Throwing away unhealthy food in their cupboards to make their diets stick
- Giving their partner their computer game console – so they have to have permission to use it!
- Booking meeting times with colleagues to discuss topics that otherwise never get attention
- Have an automatic agenda item in team meetings (e.g. at Will It Make The Boat Go Faster? we review our team rules as part of the weekly team meeting agenda)

- Asking a colleague to call it out publicly if we don't do what we said we would

3d Exaggerate

Exaggeration is another useful strategy:

Ben: 'It's easier to make an exaggerated change and scale back, than to be clever and not really make a change at all."

For example, Ben had a bad habit of rowing with his head tilted to one side. He exaggerated it the wrong way in order to end up with it up straight.

I was coaching a Chief Executive recently, who was high on entrepreneurial energy and drive, but tended to dominate meetings and steamroller ideas. His growing, successful company had reached a tipping point: unless he could let other people take the initiative he was going to stop the growth dead in its tracks. He needed to become a better listener, so he exaggerated the skill, to make sure he really did change, for example:

- He let everyone know what he was doing and why (as per the first two sections of this chapter)
- He put a visible timer in meetings to measure the time he spoke vs listened
- He 'over-used' certain phrases, such as 'I hear what you are saying'
- He exaggerated his listening body language – dialling up the nodding and the eye contact

After exaggerating for a few weeks he was able to settle into a new 'normal'. By signposting what he was doing and why, he also benefited from what researchers have dubbed the 'halo effect'. Staff could see he was genuinely trying to change so he got credit for his efforts and they felt motivated to support him.

Conclusion

We're living in a period of dizzying change. We can either get the crocodile first or let it nibble our backsides. We can let potential customers walk past our hairdressers and into a rival salon, or put up some pictures that don't have horse and carriages in the background.

We tend to assume change is a bad thing, but change can make our boat go dramatically faster. We also worry that change is difficult, but the crew's experience shows that there are some very simple ways to make change easier and even enjoyable.

Some of it is to do with mindset – putting ourselves in the driving seat, not being a victim. Some of it is to do with communication – building bridges and looking for the upsides – and the final bit of the jigsaw is taking simple actions to put the change into practice.

So the next question is: how does this all work when we hit severe setbacks and our world goes pear-shaped? The next chapter is all about building *bouncebackability*.

CHAPTER 12

BOUNCE-BACKABILITY

The Repechage

Bouncebackability: Control the controllables.

The Repechage

Wednesday 20th September 2000

Our last chance to get into the Olympic final was to come first or second in the repechage. We had to bounce back from our disappointment at losing the heat; we had to deliver. It also felt like I had to bounce back from two previous Olympic defeats and eight years of history.

In 1992, my first year in the national team, we'd come sixth – out of six in the final. I was the youngest person in the crew and I was the only person who was new into the National Team. The training had nearly killed me, both metaphorically and literally. I was shattered the whole time, whenever I sat down I fell asleep, which caused real problems while I was driving. I was constantly looking for different ways of managing the drive to and from training without killing myself.

Even being as young, naive and stupid as I was I knew that our preparation for the Olympics was a disaster. The way the crew was selected was appalling, we were dogged with injury and illness and some of the decisions that we made were diabolical. Finishing last in the Olympic final was horrible and I was gutted, but I knew that I would do better next time; I'd have four more years of proper training behind me, we'd be better prepared, better selected, we'd be a better crew. I was immediately looking forward to the Atlanta Olympics and I was dreaming about winning. I'd train harder and I'd go faster.

I did train harder. For four years I trained harder; I trained my arse off. I was more focused and more determined that these four years would not be a waste. I poured everything I had into them.

In 1993 I was selected for the 4- along with Tim Foster. Tim dropped out three months before the World Championships, needing a back operation. We rowed with eleven different people filling Tim's seat, trying to find the right sub. Again, bitter disappointment.

1994 I ended up back in the 8+. It was a crap year and we didn't even make the final at the World Championships; we finished eighth with Jürgen telling us that we were soft, the ultimate insult.

1995 promised much more, we were a better crew, more organised, we rowed better, it was going to be a better year. At the World Championships we made the final and thought that perhaps we could finish fourth – or maybe even third. This was going to be the year when the training paid off and we got the results we wanted and deserved.

The final was a farce. There was a very strong cross wind making the course ridiculously unfair. Most crews finished according to their lane number. We were in lane six and we finished sixth. We were all gutted. We just hadn't had the chance to show how fast we were. It was really unfair and there had been nothing we could do. We had so much promise, such high expectations and we had nothing to show for it. It was devastating. We would bounce back; we would get it right the following year.

1996; Olympic Year. This was the culmination of four years' work and dreams. It did not go well. In April we all got personal bests on the rowing machines. We were in good shape and the boat seemed to be going fast – then illness and injury struck. The second and third regattas were appalling. We lost our stroke man and struggled to get the order right in the boat after that.

Three weeks before the final we settled on a line up and we started to get it together. We started to get faster and our hopes soared. With four years' toil behind us, it had to work. We convinced ourselves that we would go fast. We'd make the final and then we'd have everything to play for. We didn't. We lost the heat, and then in the repechage we were third. We had a great row, the best of the session, but we were too slow.

Four years' work. Four years training. Four years dreaming and it had come to nothing. Absolutely f*** all.

Before going to the Atlanta Olympics, I'd decided that if we didn't do well I'd call it a day, I'd quit; I just couldn't do it all again. It was too hard, too painful and losing was too soul-destroying. We didn't do well; we couldn't have done any worse. It was the worst day of my life, we had lost the repechage by 0.4 of a second. Four years of work and I had nothing to show for it. Over five minutes thirty seconds and we were 0.4 too slow.

That was it, it was over; I'd had enough.

I remember sitting on the ground next to my mother, my head on her shoulder, my shoulders were shaking and tears were streaming down my cheeks. I couldn't believe what had happened. I'd wasted four years of my life. The thousands of kilometres I'd done up and down the river, the days spent in the gym, the things I'd missed out on – the weddings, the parties, the holidays, the friends I'd sacrificed. That was it.

Then the Russians were there. The Russian 8+ who had just denied us a place in the final were wandering around. They were in the Olympic final. They looked no different to me. Some were slightly taller, some were slightly shorter, some heavier built, but they were pretty much the same and they'd done it. If they could do it, why couldn't we? If they could do it, we would too. I knew that I had to do it again, I had to go through the whole thing again and next time it would be different.

I could either blame myself for every defeat and admit that I wasn't good enough, or I could blame the defeat on the fact that Sean, our coach, hadn't been allowed to do what he wanted to do. I could blame our lack of speed on the fact that Roy Rogers, our stroke man, had had to drop out with a knackered back, I could look for loads of reasons why we'd lost, but none of them would be because I couldn't do it because I could do it and I would do it.

So here I was on Wednesday 20th September 2000. Was this going to be a re-run of the 1996 rep? It was GB, Netherlands, Italy, and Canada; almost exactly the same as '96. In '96 we'd lost. We'd lost out on a place in the final by about four feet.

It couldn't happen again. We wouldn't let it happen. The sense of history was still there, but I knew that this was different, we were a completely different crew, the crews we were racing were different and this was a different Olympics. I kept focusing on the job in hand, so that I could banish '96 to the back of my mind, and I could row with power, acceleration and passion.

We had to win the repechage and demonstrate that we were the crew to beat. We had to prove to ourselves and the rest of the world that we were fast. We had to put the heat behind us and bounce back.

I was still livid about the heat, as I got out of bed slightly before 5 a.m., the anger of losing hadn't subsided. We'd let ourselves and everyone who had supported us down and we weren't going to do the same again. The tension in our group could probably be felt from a mile. We were all angry and nervous, there were no second chances now; we had to get it right. Everything we did we did with purpose.

I struggled with breakfast, but forced some cereal and toast down my throat. Some of the other boys struggled as well.

We arrived at the lake, had a short briefing and put the boat on the water for a short purposeful paddle. It was good – strong and powerful. We came off the water satisfied. To all those people who'd written us off after the heat, we'd show them. We'd made a mistake and we'd learnt and we were now back as a crew to be reckoned with. We'd spent so much time learning and getting over setbacks and this is what we had to do again. We had to bounce back as we knew we could. It was simple.

We were ready, my God we were ready. We sat on the start line champing at the bit to get on with it. We'd had a short briefing from Martin, it was very short, we knew the situation and we knew what we had to do. It was time.

"Italy ready?" We had to put them away. We had to show who was in charge.

"Great Britain, ready?" It might be a similar line up to four years ago, but that meant nothing. If we had any dreams or aspirations of winning an Olympic gold medal we had to be in the final and we had to make that happen now.

"Canada, ready?" We had to be long and strong. Focus on the first eight strokes.

"Netherlands, ready?" My bony left elbow was straight and just over the top of my bent right knee. My back was straight. As the traffic light changed colour I was going to slam my legs down flat as hard and quickly as I could. I was going to throw my back towards Andrew and the finish line as fast as I could, forcing my hands to my body as I did it. I'd then roll forward a short distance on my seat, lifting my hand and drive back again as fast as I could. The third stroke would be slightly longer again and the fourth longer still.

"Attention!" Lift my hands to make sure the oar is buried in the water.

Ready, ready, ready, power, power and more power.

"Beep" split the tense silence and I was hammering my legs down. Ripping the smooth laminate handle towards me as fast as I could. Next stroke, short, next longer, next really moving my back. Anger. Fury. Passion. We had to do it. We were already jumping out in front of the field. Bastards who thought that they could beat us. Anger, an almost blind anger – and more length.

Getting my oar down to the water, power; oar down to the water, acceleration – and on it went. Rowley was driving us on, he was telling us we were getting it right, that my oar was getting down to the water properly, that we were accelerating the boat, it was good, but he wanted more.

We jumped out to a length's lead in the first 300 or 400 metres. It had been a great start, but Rowley wanted more. We worked to deliver more. All that passion and anger and desire to show that we were the crew to beat was going into the water, it was accelerating the boat. We pulled our arses off and we maintained the length's lead.

In the last 500 the Italians and other chasing crews were making desperate sprints for the line to make sure that they got through. Again Rowley urged us to keep moving and sprint for the line. We worked and worked, but we had nothing more to give. I was knackered as we crossed the line nearly three seconds up on the field.

We were in the Olympic final.

We could now focus on winning.

It hadn't been the perfect row, but it had been a step up from the heat. We lacked the finesse that we needed, but we definitely had the passion and the acceleration needed to move the boat. We now had four days to find the finesse. We had had what most people thought was a disaster in the heat, people had written us off, but we had bounced back. We had had to do it countless times before and this was no different.

Bouncebackability: Control the controllables.

Ben: "Setbacks happen, often there's nothing we can do to stop them and we've just got to make sure we get back to making the boat go faster as soon as we can."

Chapter summary

Setbacks are inevitable, so build a launch P.A.D to re-launch yourself towards your goal. Prepare in advance, Accept setbacks when they happen and Do something – take action to turn the situation around.

Stage 1: Prepare
1a Look after yourself.
1b Plan in advance.
1c Get help.
1d Strengthen your beliefs.

Stage 2: Accept
2a Make excuses.
2b Remember this will pass.
2c Be bloody-minded.

2d Focus on the goal.
2e Turn it to your advantage.

Stage 3: Do
3a Get on with it.
3b Control the controllables.
3c Reflect and learn.

I was sent a cartoon by a client recently, comprised of two pictures. One had the caption, "How you think it will go..." and showed a picture of a mountaineer looking confidently at a steep, but clear path leading up a mountain towards the summit. The next picture had the caption "How it will actually go..." and showed the same path, but from a different angle. From here you could see boulder fields, crevasses, even a herd of sharp-toothed cartoon Yetis. The climb was going to be way more challenging than the mountaineer realised.

Ben: "We only had 24 months, we couldn't afford to let our performance dip. We needed to build bouncebackability so that we would stop as many setbacks from happening in the first place as we possibly could – and then minimise the timespan and severity when unavoidable setbacks hit."

The term 'bouncebackability' became popular when Crystal Palace football manager, Ian Dowie, used it as he described how his team came back from being behind to win 3-1 against Wimbledon in 2004. We've all got bouncebackability; it's just that for most of us it is rather erratic. Sometimes we manage to pick ourselves up after a knockback and get on with things. Sometimes we don't.

So what do we do - as we're staring up our own 'mountains' towards our crazy goals? Ben is in the unenviable position of enduring 12 years of setbacks on the route to gold, so he has strategies aplenty we can copy on this one. We've organised them into three categories:

1. **Prepare** before setbacks happen. Imagine the preparations that mountaineer in the cartoon could make. Part of this preparation is about general strength and resilience – you wouldn't climb Everest without being fit and healthy and mentally strong. Part of the prep is about anticipating specific setbacks – packing an ice axe for slippery bits.
2. **Accept** the setback when it happens, as opposed to being in denial. Not the 'roll over and give up' kind of acceptance, but an acknowledgement of the situation. 'OK, Fate has vomited on my duvet, this has happened… now what?'
3. **Do** what needs to be done to turn things around.

The first letters of each heading conveniently spell 'PAD'. These strategies are your launch pad to renewed performance levels.

Stage 1. Prepare

1a Look after yourself

Brace yourselves for a rant…

Look, doubtless I'll come across as a stereotypical nagging mum on this one, but for the love of bananas, *look after yourself.* There is a HUGE and GROWING body of research showing our bouncebackability nosedives if we don't practise self-care. It's incredibly frustrating that the modern cult of busyness, the western obsession with alcohol, the confusion of 'commitment to the firm' with 'available to answer emails at every hour of the day and night including on holiday' or 'getting a good night's sleep' with 'being a weakling' prevails. When we are strung out, tired, hungry, hungover, don't exercise, don't get sunlight and fresh air… we reduce our bouncebackability. Even worse: we saw in the 'performance under pressure' chapter that if we don't look after ourselves we won't perform well when stressed. In other words: Poor self-care not only means we are worse at *bouncing back* from setbacks... we are also more likely to *create* setbacks in the first place.

…Sigh…

This stuff is not rocket science, but how do you turn common sense into common practice? There are lots of ideas in other chapters about how to create useful habits, how to make changes, how to keep motivated. Here are some real-life examples:

- I'm currently using a meditation app to make meditation a habit. I signed up to their challenge to meditate 15 days out of 21 and used a habit tracker to celebrate success. I use the app if I'm commuting by train and I've also configured it to send me a reminder to meditate before bed.
- You want to go to bed on time? Why not set an alarm for time to go to bed in the same way you'd set one to get out of bed in the morning?
- I am working with a board member of a major retailer. She keeps a bottle of water at her desk and fruit and nuts

in her handbag to maintain hydration and blood sugar levels throughout the day.

- The company, 'Will It Make The Boat Go Faster?', was running a performance programme with a marketing team. They opted to have their daily 'huddles' outside to get fresh air and exercise.
- Another client firm set clear rules that although people could send emails whenever (e.g. it suited some to leave earlier in the afternoon to pick kids up and then do emails when the kids were in bed) there was absolutely no expectation to reply to them except within office hours.

Rant over.

You're welcome.

1b Plan in advance

Steve Redgrave was once asked how he dealt with unforeseen setbacks and his reply was along the lines of, 'There's no such thing as an unforeseen setback.' In other words, if you reflect on what might happen, you can always plan for it. What might throw you off course? What events might discourage you? What are the chinks in your personality armour?

Planning in advance might mean making sure you have the right kit: if you think it's going to rain, you might pack an umbrella; if you know you always cry at weddings, pack a tissue. It might mean having certain conversations, building a support network. It might also mean building your belief, motivation and bullshit filters.

For example, Ben and the crew had plenty of 'What if…?' conversations prior to the Sydney Olympics when they would be racing a day after Redgrave was attempting to win his fifth gold.

Ben: "We talked about what would happen if Redgrave's crew lost. They were the top crew in the team, they should win, but what if they didn't? We all knew that if he won we'd be delighted and feel fantastic, but we couldn't afford to feel down if his crew lost. So we prepared our bullshit filters and found useful interpretations ahead of time. If he lost we'd have to remind ourselves that we hadn't done the same training, we weren't in the same boat, and their boat speed had absolutely no impact on ours."

The crew also didn't completely buy Redgrave's view that there's no such thing as an unforeseen setback. One of the team rules for Sydney was "expect the unexpected – you can deal with it"!

1c Get help

What support network do you need? A healthy network contains different kinds of support. For example:

- Someone who will constructively challenge you – to offer a different point of view when you're stuck and can't see a way forward.
- An unconditional cheerleader who supports you because of who you are, not because of your achievements.
- Someone going through a similar experience who can sympathise with what you're feeling.
- Someone removed from the situation, who can help you to put things back in perspective…

Ben: 'I was lucky I always had a number of people who could give me a kick up the backside and tell me that things would be different and that I could do it. I also had my family who told me that, whatever I decided to do, it would be the right decision and they would support me."

What kind of support do you need to achieve your goal – and who can you get it from?

1d Strengthen your beliefs

Strong beliefs help bouncebackability. The belief chapter gives plenty of strategies for doing this, such as:

- Remember personal references: When have you bounced back from setbacks in the past? Remember what happened, what you did to turn things around. If you did it then you can do it again can't you?
- Use analogies. What language are you using? If you feel stuck in a hole then what might be a first step on the ladder out of the pit? If you feel all at sea then who could throw you a life raft?

If you don't believe in yourself you're more likely to give up when things get tough. If you do believe in yourself, you can focus your attention on how to overcome the challenge and move forwards.

Stage 2. Accept

2a Make excuses

We're often told that excuses are a bad thing. But Ben challenges us to take a deeper look:

Ben: "If you pour everything into a goal and you don't get it and take full responsibility then you could shatter your self-belief. Therefore, you have to find excuses to justify what's happened…"

Ben freely admits to using excuses and blaming other people in order to give himself some distance from disaster. But isn't that denial? Shouldn't we face up to reality, take it on the chin, take accountability for the real reasons?

Ben: "Maybe they are reasons, maybe they are excuses, just use the information usefully to help you move on to the next thing; take responsibility for turning it around."

If you look up reason and excuse in the dictionary, the entries are pretty similar:

Excuse: reason put forward to mitigate or justify offence.

Reason: motive or cause or justification.

The difference is the intention behind it. Ben wasn't intending to wallow in misery; he just wanted to move on.

Have you seen people use this approach with their kids? Lots of parents do.

"Never mind that you lost the football match, darling, the other team were really good." Do they go on to say "so we'll just give your kit to Oxfam and you can stay inside and watch telly next Saturday"? Of course not, they're more likely to say something like "better luck next time", or "let's do loads of practice this week, then".

Isn't it funny that we'll use excuses to help other people move on, but we don't use this strategy on ourselves? So go on, make excuses – just as long as you take responsibility for turning things around.

2b Remember this will pass

The Spanish have two verbs for our one verb *to be*. This is mightily annoying when you're trying to cram a GCSE in a year, but useful for providing a richly different perspective. *Ser* is the verb for permanent states; *Estar* is the verb for temporary conditions. In English, if we say 'I am stuck' or 'I can't do this' it sounds permanent, doesn't it? Permanent and overwhelming. It's easier to bounce back when we take a Spanish point of view and appreciate that the situation is temporary.

- I am temporarily upset
- I am having a fleeting few days of ineptitude
- I am speeding through a difficult patch
- I am feeling lousy today, but it will pass.

For example, over Christmas 1999 Ben's back was knackered and he couldn't row. After a three-kilometre training swim he couldn't even get out of the pool for about 20 minutes. He then couldn't get changed because his back hurt so much. He ended up pulling on his top and walking home in the snow in his wet trunks.

Ben: "Having given up so much there was no way I was going to let a few weeks off training get the better of me!"

Whether we are running a marathon, going through childbirth, weathering being under-staffed at work, missing a sales target, losing out on a promotion… reminding ourselves that 'this will pass' can help us battle through it. It's not permanent; it's just a temporary situation.

2c Be bloody-minded

Ben: 'In 1998, the year that was going to be different, the year when the eight was going to break through, we finished an appalling 7th. Each and every one of us was gutted. Did I quit or keep going? Did I believe all the mounting evidence that I couldn't do it, that I wasn't good enough or did I grit my teeth and believe that things could change?

As I had done so many times before I got on with it. I was going to show all those bastards that I was good enough, that I could beat them, that I could win. Was this arrogance? Stubbornness? Bloody-mindedness?"

Ben's emotional reaction was the first step on the ladder out of a very dark hole. What emotions will help you to bounce back? Is it your passion about your goal? Is it anger about an injustice that needs to be rectified? Is it a serenity that 'these things come to try us'? Whatever it is, when you tune in to your emotions they will help to drive you forwards.

2d Focus on the goal

When we get caught up in the present we can lose sight of our ultimate goal.

Have you ever gone to a restaurant and had a poor meal, but then got so caught up getting annoyed about it that you forget your original goal was to have a good night out? You end up ruining the evening by focusing on just one element of an enjoyable evening.

Or have you ever got so stressed being stuck in a traffic jam that you get to the business meeting all flustered and mess it up? It's incredibly unhelpful – the only reason you were worried about being late was because you didn't want to mess up the meeting!

Reminding yourself of your original goal will help you to bounce back and get back on track. What if your setback means it's not possible to achieve your original goal?

Ben: "In 1994 I wanted to be in the four but the selection decision didn't go my way. I couldn't achieve the goal I wanted, so I set myself a new one to row in the 8+ and compete in the World Championships."

If you really can't achieve your original goal, then ask yourself what is the best outcome you can achieve, given the circumstances?

> The traffic jam is so severe I'm definitely going to be late for the meeting. What's the best outcome I can achieve given that this is the case – call to postpone, make the most of this congestion-inflicted me time; make sure I get to the meeting calm and relaxed?

2e Turn it to your advantage

There is good in pretty much every situation, we just have to look for it. Sometimes it's heavily disguised – it might even be dressed up as a problem and we have to take off the false beard and glasses to find the helping hand.

For example, in the 1999 World Championships there was a raging tailwind for much of the Regatta. The Dutch broke the world record in the semi-final, and they absolutely believed they would win in the final. However, in the morning of the final the wind had changed by 180 degrees.

Ben: "The Dutch were broken. They had lost before they'd even left their hotel that morning."

The British crew made it a habit to look for the usefulness in any eventuality.

Ben: "If it was sunny we'd think 'brilliant, we've done warm weather training'. If it was windy or rainy we'd think 'fantastic, typical British weather, we can do this'. That might sound completely bollocks and completely contradictory, but in reality what is the point in seeing things as bad?"

When we are struggling to see the good in a situation, we can ask ourselves some searching questions:

- How can I use this?
- How can this help us?
- What might be positive here?
- What's the gift I haven't noticed yet?

Our brain's first response might well be: 'I can't! Nothing! Nowhere!' so ask yourself a few times to uncover the silver lining in the cloud.

Ben: "A lot of stuff is contradictory and you have to compartmentalise it in your head!"

My son had a serious eye injury in 2018. I'm not going to sugar coat the experience. He had a really painful, unpleasant time. He'll never see out of that eye as well as he used to; he adores sport and now he'll always have to wear protective goggles for many activities, which other kids take the piss out of him for.

But… there are elements of the experience he can use to his advantage. For example, he found other ways to keep busy when he was off sport – like learning to cook or learning to paint with acrylics – which I hope will stand him in good stead throughout his life. He now has a level of empathy for others in distress which is beyond his years. He's also had an early experience of what it's like for an athlete to deal with injury – relevant if he pursues a sporting career, but more broadly relevant in terms of bouncing back from life's curveballs.

Am I saying these advantages outweighed the negative impact of the injury? Absolutely not. It was a supremely crappy accident and I wish it had never happened. But did turning elements to his advantage help him bounce back better? Absolutely.

Stage 3. Do

3a Get on with it

We all know people who let one setback ruin their day. A bad journey to work and they write off the next 24 hours as a lost cause.

Ben: "Get over it! I had a saying when I was first in the team along the lines of: 'there is no point in worrying about it, because if you are worrying about it then you will do something about it and if you are doing something about it then there is no need to worry. If you are not working on it then clearly you aren't that worried about it!!'"

OK, some might say there is the odd hole in Ben's logic, but the point is that it helped him let go of worrying and start refocusing on action, getting the ball rolling again. When disaster initially happens, what is going to help you restart that all important momentum that the team prized so strongly? Getting on with it means being there in body and spirit. When you've had a rubbish meeting at work you can turn up to the next one miserable and ruin that one too, so this strategy is all about pressing a reset button and attending the second meeting with drive and commitment.

Ben: "When your back goes initially that's when you need bouncebackability to do the training, when I did really badly in trials and was put in the 8+ instead of the 4- I needed bouncebackability to get up the next morning and get to the boathouse and row with people who, to be brutally honest, I didn't want to row with."

As a result, making bouncebackability into a habit is incredibly useful. Imagine if you didn't have to think about how to bounce back, imagine if you just automatically used the strategies outlined here – what would the benefits be?

3b Control the controllables

Brian Muller was the sports psychologist in 1992 who first introduced Ben to the idea of *controlling the controllables.* It is a simple, but powerful, concept. We all have limited time, energy and headspace, so devote these precious resources into dealing with things inside your control and let go of anything you can't do anything about. How many people do you know who whinge about things they can't control – the rain, their boss, global warming, and yet do precious little about it – like carrying an umbrella, flexing their communication style or turning their thermostat down?

Ben learnt the *control the controllables* lesson back in the early 90's, in a coxless four in Duisburg Regatta.

Ben: "On the word 'Go' we pulled the boat off the start as hard as we could and there was a dull thud as our rudder got ripped off. The rules state that in this situation you are allowed to restart, so all the crews had to hang around while our coach was off hunting for a replacement rudder and we got the boat out of the water.

We had a conversation about it, about how the outcome of the race was going to depend on who dealt with this situation the best. There was absolutely nothing we could do about the rudder being ripped off – it had happened. What we could control was our thoughts and actions from that moment on."

There was plenty the British crew could control: what they ate, how they looked after themselves when injured, the beliefs they built. The *village code of conduct* they drew up to guide their behaviour at the Sydney Olympics is all focused around controlling the controllables.

A great way to control the controllables is to simply ask yourself the question: 'What can I do?' The beauty of this bouncebackability strategy is that there is always an answer.

The market is tough and I'm struggling to hit my sales target… what can I do?

- Collaborate with other sales people
- Partner with another firm
- Reach out to my network

There are hundreds of answers. OK, it might not be easy to pick one strategy from the list to try out, but it is an awful lot more fulfilling than wallowing in the mire moaning that 'there is nothing I can do'. Controlling the controllables not only makes us feel more motivated, it increases our chances of succeeding.

3c Reflect and learn

When the dust has settled, make sure you find the time to reflect on what happened:

- Might this kind of setback happen again?
- How can I prevent that happening?
- Am I happy with the way I dealt with it, or what would I do differently another time?
- What lessons am I going to take forward – about this specific type of setback and about how I can deal with general setbacks in the future?

It is a recurrent theme in this book that Ben and the crew talked a lot, to the point where other crews commented that they spent less time on the water and more time chatting. The point that keeps emerging in chapter after chapter is that this wasn't just idle banter, it was focused conversation. After every training session, in the crew's performance review, they would ask themselves what went well and what they would do differently another time to make the boat go faster.

How can you build in time to reflect and learn? Make it an agenda item on each team meeting? Set aside five minutes every day to jot down some thoughts? A small investment in reflection time can create massive savings in terms of mistakes avoided, time saved and improvements identified.

Conclusion

We are all human, if we don't care when things go wrong then we probably don't want the goal strongly enough to achieve it, so feeling low is a good sign. Building a bouncebackability muscle just makes that low a bit quicker, easier to get through and – counter-intuitively and wonderfully – extremely useful.

When we prepare in advance we can avoid obstacles altogether or at least minimise their bad consequences. The next step is accepting setbacks when they do happen – looking for the upside rather than wallowing in the downside.

Finally we need to take action, control the controllables and learn from the experience. This bouncebackability launch PAD speeds us back on course towards our goal.

So now we've got the goal, the mindset, the team, the approach – the final bit of the jigsaw is the ability to feel comfortable taking massive risks.

CHAPTER 13

RISKS

25 hours to the Olympic Final of the 2000 Sydney Games

Risks: Let the goal be your guide.

25 hours to the Olympic Final of the 2000 Sydney Games

It was 9.25 a.m. and we had just got back to our flat. We'd done our last training session before racing. We'd have a warm-up outing tomorrow morning, but no more training sessions before the big one!

It had been awesome: we'd done 250 metres off the start and we were fast, really fast. The row down the lake had been strong and full of purpose; this was our lake and we had stamped our authority on it.

We'd then practised the last 250 metres sprint to the finish line. As we started to build into it, the stroke rate was rising, 36 strokes a minute – 39 – 41 – 42 – 43. It must have looked pretty impressive. Some Brits in the grandstand, which was already two thirds full, had started shouting "Go GB! GB! GB! GB!"

Those voices were immediately drowned by chants of "Aussie, Aussie Aussie Oi! Oi! Oi! Aussie, Oi!" as we flew down to the finish line. We were quick, really quick, phenomenally quick. We finished the session with the Aussie chanting still filling the air.

The hairs were standing up on the backs of our necks as we rowed around to the boathouse.

A few minutes later we were standing in a group to review the session. We stood still, serious, quietly confident, taking turns to speak. The tension was palpable. We'd had an amazing session, everything was in place – and now there was the crowd. To beat the Aussies in front of that crowd tomorrow was going to be incredible. This was the place to beat them, in front of that crowd.

We went back to the Village, with 25 hours to go before our Olympic Final and the 2- crew now on the starting line for theirs. Ed and Greg could win this. Was it going to be the first GB rowing gold of the Games? The first of three? They would win, then the 4- would win, then we would win. The nine of us sat in the living room of our flat and we watched the TV.

They were off.

They got out of the blocks quickly and started to establish a lead. Greg and I were exact contemporaries, we'd raced each other since we were 15. Greg had always come out on top. He was an under 18 World Champion for two years. At 19 he was a World bronze medallist and at twenty he was an Olympic Champion. With the exception of the last two years, when he'd been in the single scull, he'd got a medal every year since 1991. He was an awesome athlete. Ed was also outstanding. He'd won gold at the World Championships the year before, in the 4-, and both he and Greg had beaten all of us in every trial.

By the time they'd completed 500 metres, they were in control of the race. In the second 500 metres they extended their lead slightly and looked good and in full control. They were going to win. This was to be GB's first rowing gold of the Games. Through 1,000 metres, in control, looking strong and good. 900 metres to go.

The French were – what were the French doing? They had gone berserk. They had taken the rate up by about 6 or 8 stokes a minute and they were piling through the field, but you can't sprint from 900 metres, not in a pair. They were mad. Yes, they were making up ground, yes they were catching Ed and Greg, but they wouldn't sustain it. They couldn't sustain it. They would die. You cannot sprint 900 metres in a pair, it's just too far.

Unbelievably, they were still going. They were hammering it along, through to second, still going. They were level with Ed and Greg and still going. They passed Ed and Greg and were still going.

The French crossed the line and collapsed close to passing out; how they avoided capsizing I had no idea. How they managed to pull off that plan I had no idea; it was the most impressive race I had ever seen. Ed and Greg were fourth. The sheer courage of the French was incredible and the look on Ed and Greg's faces was horrendous. They looked shattered and in total disbelief about what had just happened.

It had taken 900 metres of racing to completely change the atmosphere in our flat. Ed and Greg; the look on their faces. They had been dragged across to the pontoons and Steve Rider was holding a microphone in Ed's face asking him how he felt. It was pretty obvious, what a stupid question! Ed and Greg still looked stunned, shocked, amazed, gutted; their dream had been shattered. How they missed out on a medal I don't know, it was extraordinary.

We sat round marvelling at the courage of the French and bloody sure that we wouldn't look like Ed and Greg after our race. We decided to watch the next race downstairs in the Team GB HQ where there would be a crowd of people and a TV with BBC commentary. At about 10.20 a.m. we wandered down the three flights of stairs to the basement. The HQ was quite small and it was packed full of athletes and coaches who had come to watch Britain's greatest Olympian, Steve Redgrave, win his fifth Gold medal.

At 10.25 the 4 were on the start; the room was silent and tense.

At 10.30 they were off. Into an early lead; commanding and dominating.

Through 500 metres; 1,000 metres; 1,500 metres; no one had challenged them. They were in complete control.

The Italians were coming back. The Italians were coming back; the Italians were eating into their lead.

We were going to win, the Italians couldn't get past – or could they?

Flat out for the line. Our guys were flat out, and the Italians were still getting closer.

"Just!" the commentator's voice shouted as Redgrave won his fifth Gold, Pinsent his third and Cracknel and Foster their first.

The HQ was in complete commotion. Everyone cheering, hugging, shouting, there were wet eyes and the look on the faces of the boys in the boat – Matt, Tim, Steve and James – was incredible!

The nine of us made our way quietly upstairs and back to our flat. Stiff with excitement, goosebumps on our arms. There was a feeling of – I'm not sure – excitement, fear, terror; of wanting something so much it hurt.

We had less than 24 hours to go. We'd just seen our teammates – our mates – lose and win. What a difference. The tiniest of margins made such a big difference. We had to be on the right side of the margin. We sat down and discussed the next day.

We could do what we normally did, what the 2- and 4- had just done, a fast start, a really strong middle 1,000 metres with a push here or there and a sprint to the line. Or we could risk all as the French had done. Sprinting from halfway wouldn't work for us. For a pair the difference between a flat out sprint and cruising speed was significant, but because an 8+ is so much bigger and faster the difference is much smaller. We'd have to sprint from the start, but that was a huge risk. Would we be able to maintain it? Would we have the energy and courage to sprint so far or would we run out of juice and see everyone row past us?

Just before we arrived in Sydney Chris Shambrook, our Sport Psychologist, had given us a sheet of A4 paper with a simple one-word title; RISK. Below it, it had four neat lines and that was all:

Risks you can afford to take
Risks you can afford not to take
Risks you can't afford to take
Risks you can't afford not to take.

We had been discussing risks for a good 18 months. We had taken so many risks over the last few years: we'd changed our programme, the training we did, the coaching team we had, where we trained. They had all been risks. There were also the things we hadn't changed, the backbone of the training programme – 20-kilometre sessions, many of the winter training camps, these had been risks too.

We were all sure that sprinting from the start for the Olympic final was what we had to do; in fact, it was a risk that we couldn't afford not to take. Having put so much in for so long we couldn't fail at the last hurdle. We discussed the plan to make sure it was a well thought-through, considered risk, until it was clearly etched into our heads. If we had the courage it would work. When I give a speech, a frequent question is, 'But how can you justify doing all that planning, only to change your mind at the last minute? Wasn't that daft and rash?!' My answer is no. It was a quick decision, sure, but the framework we used and the discussion we had meant it definitely wasn't rash.

On Fred's instructions we sat and started talking about why we wanted to win. I can't remember anything that the other boys said, but I vividly remember going through the reasons why I needed to win.

I sat with my back to the glass doors which led to the balcony of our flat's living room. Through the window the Olympic stadium was about half a mile away. I would have seen that the Olympic flame was burning in its cauldron on the left of the stadium had I chosen to look over my shoulder, but I didn't. I sat facing the rest of the crew trying and failing to control the tears welling up in my eyes and rolling down my cheeks, concerned that they would all think that I had lost the plot as I talked about wanting to prove a point and wanting to get some respect from other people in the rowing world.

With the amount of passion we were going to throw at this next race and the technical skills that we'd developed it would work.

It had to.

Risks: Let the goal be your guide.

Ben: "In order to win you have got to risk losing."

Chapter summary

Every action and every inaction carries risk – it's unavoidable. If we let go of worrying about risk we can more usefully focus our attention on figuring out which risks are crazy and which are useful.

How to take useful risks

1. Unskew the scales
2. Know that fear isn't a stop sign
3. Ignore others
4. Talk it through
5. Let go of knowing; let your goal be your guide
6. Have faith in your resourcefulness
7. Know what type of risk it is:
    a. Risks we can afford to take
    b. Risks we can't afford to take
    c. Risks we can afford not to take
    d. Risks we can't afford not to take

Do you ever wish you had a crystal ball – one that would tell you whether it's worth taking a risk?

- the risk of humiliation when you ask for promotion
- the risk of financial loss when you make an investment
- the risk of losing the match when you field a new player
- the risk of losing a client when you increase your prices

With 24 hours to go before the Olympic final the British eight decided – unanimously – to take a massive risk and try a new, completely untested strategy for the race.

Ben: "We knew if our gamble went wrong we would probably come away empty handed, but it was still one of the easiest crew decisions we ever took."

Why would they do such a crazy thing? After years and years of hard work what on earth possessed them to throw caution to the wind? With the benefit of hindsight we can label their decision courageous and brilliant, but in a parallel universe, where they didn't magic up that lead of 0.8 of a second, wouldn't we be calling them a bunch of reckless idiots? And how could it possibly have been 'one of the easiest crew decisions they ever took'?

Why take risks at all?

The first clue to answering these questions is the crew's belief that we need to take risks simply because we have to – there is no getting away from it.

The dictionary definition of risk is *the possibility of bad consequences*. This made us chuckle; it highlights that every action and every inaction is risky; we just forget that this is the case.

- When you cross the road you risk being run down by a maniac.
- When you don't check out every single shop you risk not finding the cheapest option.
- When you scratch your nose you risk doing it slightly too hard and it being uncomfortable.

Knowing that you have taken risks every millisecond of your life so far and that you will continue to do so until your final breath, should help you to see things a little differently. Ben's experiences show how you can channel your energy into figuring out useful risks as opposed to crazy ones and this gives you an immediate advantage over the anxious majority who have their fingers in their ears saying "la, la, la; go away nasty risky stuff".

How to take useful risks

There are seven key lessons we can take away from the crew's approach:

1. Unskew the scales
2. Know that fear isn't a stop sign
3. Ignore others
4. Talk it through
5. Let go of knowing – let your goal be your guide
6. Have faith in your resourcefulness
7. Know what type of risk it is

1. Unskew the scales

We'd like to think we carefully weigh up the pros and cons of possible courses of action and make considered decisions, but our scales are typically skewed in favour of inaction.

Usually we only start thinking about risks when we are considering doing things *differently*. When someone suggests merging with another company or buying a new IT system or changing uniforms we are pretty good at thinking about the possible bad consequences. But how often have we attended meetings about thinking through the risks of carrying on exactly as normal and changing nothing? We tend to ignore the risks of the status quo.

Ben: "Every decision is a risk to some degree. Every action has possible bad consequences and crucially every inaction has possible bad consequences."

By definition, every time Ben and the crew entered a regatta they risked losing. That's blindingly obvious and the whole point of a race: one boat wins, the other boats lose. But if they'd sat in the boatshed, twiddling their thumbs and didn't enter a race they guaranteed losing. In the same way, every time we make a pitch to a potential client we risk losing, but if we don't pitch to them we definitely won't get the business.

The other pitfall to avoid is exaggerating how bad it will be if things go wrong. What if we give that presentation to the whole team and it's dreadful? Everyone will laugh at us, we'll never get promoted, we'll have to leave the company and end up sleeping on a park bench. Our imaginations go bananas and in no time we're picturing total disaster.

Will it really be so bad? Probably not. Are there actions we can take to lessen the potential negative consequences? Almost certainly. Can we learn from the experience? Absolutely.

So how can you unskew your scales and have a much better chance of identifying useful ways forward? Ask yourself:

- What are the downsides of not doing anything?
- What's the worst that can happen? Is that true? Can I handle that?

2. Know that fear isn't a stop sign

Have you ever tried to communicate in a foreign language when you only know a few words? Perhaps you tried to order a sandwich and were given a bar of soap, or asked for a room for two and opened the bedroom door to find that you are sharing with two other people. Frustrating isn't it?

Our emotions are messages. Take fear for example. We've got a key meeting in the morning and we're anxious. What is that churning in our belly, the sweaty palms and the nightmares of walking down Oxford Street in our pyjamas trying to tell us? It's saying, 'Think this one through! Do some preparation, get some support.'

Sadly, the message often gets lost in translation. Many people interpret it as a sign to *stop*. That might be an option, but it's certainly not a foregone conclusion. Stopping at the feeling of fear is like giving ourselves that bar of soap when what we actually want is a sandwich.

Ben: 'I threw up most mornings in Sydney. The hours before racing were a nightmare. When the boys saw me being sick they'd say, 'Great, he's ready!' All I wanted to do was run away and not have to do it, but I knew that I couldn't because it would mean giving up my dream."

When you feel fear about taking a risk hit the pause button not the stop button. Take time to reflect on what's driving that fear and therefore what can you do to allay it. Then you can decide whether to halt or to feel the fear and do it anyway.

3. Ignore others

Winning means doing something different from other people. There is loads of research to suggest we look to other people to guide our behaviour and we mistakenly think it's risky if we act differently from others. Advertisers capitalise on this the whole time – how many times have you seen an advert along the lines of, *Every six seconds someone switches to our broadband package* or *Britain's favourite airline*? The marketeers know that we will unconsciously reason 'if everyone else is doing it, I'd be crazy not to'.

Ben's experience shows that we should be guided by our goal and what is the most sensible strategy for achieving that; not by what other people are doing.

Ben was fascinated by Sarah Webb and her crewmates' strategy for the Yingling sailing at the 2008 Beijing Olympics. There are normally 11 races in the Yingling event. Competitors get points according to how they do in each of these races and gold goes to the crew that wins the most points.

Ben: "The normal strategy in Yingling is to aim to win every race. This means you push yourselves and the boat to the edge, you take risks and often get penalty points or even get disqualified for infringing others, but this risk is considered worth it because you get lots of points for winning.

In the run up to 2008 the crew thought about their goal and worked backwards from that. They decided to do the opposite of this and aim never to get a single penalty point. It would have been easy to think of this as risky in the sense that it was totally different from other competitors. The crew got a podium place in every race for four years – and got gold at the Beijing Olympics."

Of course we can look to others for inspiration and ideas, but ultimately we need to make our own way, not blindly follow the herd. When we concentrate our attention on our goal and what will work for us we massively increase our chances of success.

4. Talk it through

Many moons ago as a fresh-faced graduate I used to work in the project office on big change programmes and one of my jobs was to keep the risk log. I had a natty little spreadsheet where I recorded all the bad things that might derail the project and how we could mitigate the risk or deal with them if they arose. I'd get very excited and carefully colour code things in red, write priority next to them, raise them at the next project meeting and feel pretty damn important. In retrospect, I realise that the spreadsheet itself was utterly pointless – it was the conversations around it that were valuable.

Have you ever got lost when driving or walking? Have you ever been with someone who simply marches off going, "It's this way! Come on!" without discussing it with you? At best it's really irritating and at worst it's downright scary. When you're included in the discussions it feels much more comfortable to sign up to a course of action.

Risk assessment is very subjective so talk things through with teammates to ensure everyone pulls in the same direction. Even when we are working on a solo goal it can be massively useful to discuss options with someone else – just to get things clear in our own mind. This clarity helps us to be more efficient and effective.

5. Let go of knowing; let your goal be your guide

Ultimately, we are never going to be sure of the right thing to do (unless Hell involves Satan sitting us down with a video of what would have happened if we'd done things properly). In fact, there usually isn't one right thing to do, just different useful options.

Ben: "Martin put a second fin on the boat in Sydney. He thought there would be a cross headwind. It meant drilling holes under Andrew's seat. Andrew was livid. There wasn't a crosswind so the fin came off. The holes were filled in again and Andrew was pissed off that the boat wouldn't be quite as good as before. Why did Martin do it? Because he thought it would make the boat go faster."

When we are stuck and not sure whether it's riskier to do option A or option B, or nothing at all, we can ask ourselves, 'What will make our boat go faster?' or, 'What's a useful way ahead?' When we're stuck our momentum stops, but if we use the goal as our guide we are more likely to keep moving forwards.

6. Have faith in your resourcefulness

The crew shared their worries that they wouldn't push themselves hard enough; they wouldn't have the courage to put themselves through the pain. Brian Miller, the crew's sports psychologist before Chris Shambrook, gave the team some totally extreme examples just to prove what resources they had:

Ben: "Brian talked about Shun Fujimoto in the Olympic gymnastic final in Montreal in 1976. During his floor routine Shun fractured his knee cap. Japan and the Soviet Union were battling it out for gold, so Shun carried on. He did the pommel horse and did a perfect dismount. He finished on the rings and, again, did a perfect dismount – from a height of eight feet. Not only that, he achieved a personal best of 9.7 – despite dislocating his knee on the dismount. Japan won gold and Fujimoto walked unaided to get his medal."

I'm certainly not offering Shun up as a role model for sane people – personally, I'd hesitate to challenge him to a game of Scrabble – but what I do find useful is the idea that I can probably do much more than I think I can. When the chips are down it's amazing what we humans can do and yet all too often we pretend to ourselves that if things go wrong we won't possibly be able to cope.

Remind yourself – what have you achieved or endured when at times you wondered if you'd get through it?

- A horrendous traffic jam?
- A tough time at work?
- The break-up of a relationship?

You've faced many, many challenging things so remember you'll find the resources to overcome other obstacles too. I'm not saying that you have to, just that you could do if you needed or wanted to. It would be a shame if you don't take a useful risk purely because you've underestimated your amazing resourcefulness.

7. Know what type of risk it is

Once we've challenged the unconscious biases outlined above, we can make a healthier evaluation of the risks we are facing. Chris – the crew's sports psychologist – gave the crew a sheet about ten days before the Sydney Olympic final describing four types of risks. The four categories aren't objective – you can argue what goes under which heading – what made the headings valuable was that they provided *a framework for team discussions.*

1. Risks we can afford to take
2. Risks we can't afford to take
3. Risks we can afford not to take
4. Risks we can't afford not to take

On first glance these might seem baffling, but the explanations are more straightforward:

a. Risks we can afford to take

These are actions that can be taken because, even though it's quite possible that some bad consequences will happen, the bad consequences are small.

Ben: "The 1999 Vienna Regatta was where the Romanians led off the start and, although we closed on them in the middle, we couldn't catch them. Tim Foster was in the crew and he really pushed us to take risks. In order to win we had to risk losing so we decided to take a big risk at the next regatta. At Lucerne we threw everything into the first 1,000 metres to see what happened. We didn't win, but we learnt a huge amount. The Romanians never beat us again."

An everyday example of this might be a salesperson asking a client for business. What's the worst that's going to happen – that the client says no? That's unpleasant, but, as bad consequences go, it's tiny; it's a risk we can afford to take.

b. Risks we can't afford to take

These are where the potential consequences are so grave that we want to avoid them at all costs.

Ben: "Rule breaking, illegal boat weights, taking drugs all fall into this category. From a moral point of view no way, but even putting that to one side you'd get banned, your career would be screwed."

I once ran a workshop on optimising pallet retention (oh the glamour!) at a manufacturing plant. One participant suggested all the company lorry drivers should pick up any pallets they found on their travels across the UK. Genius, but potentially illegal. A risk the company couldn't afford to take.

c. Risks we can afford not to take

These are where there are other routes we could take to achieve our goal.

Ben: "When we were doing weights sessions there was an exercise called deep squats that strengthened the leg muscles. It tended to knacker my back and there were other ways I could strengthen my legs, so I did those exercises instead of taking a risk I didn't have to take."

If, for example, we wanted to raise our profile in our company but hate public speaking then a risk we could afford not to take is presenting to the entire company. We could write an article in the company newsletter instead, or volunteer for a high-profile project. Sometimes it comes down to timing. Maybe it would be good to present to the whole company at some point, but in the short term there are plenty of stepping stones such as making a presentation to our team or department, or going on a course to hone our communication skills.

d. Risks we can't afford not to take

These are strategies that give us such an amazing potential payoff that we are prepared to risk the possible downsides. I watched *Who Wants to Be a Millionaire?* once where the contestant took a complete guess at – if memory serves – the £250,000 question. The host, Chris Tarrant, reminded him that he'd lose hundreds of thousands of pounds if he got the question wrong, to which the contestant replied something like,

"When am I ever going to get this chance again? It's a risk I can't afford not to take…"

Which is why, with only hours to go before the focus of four years' hard work, a now or never moment, the crew decided to try something they'd never tried before in the 2000 Olympic final. It wasn't rash, it was a calculated risk. They analysed what they knew about their own strengths and weaknesses – and those of their competitors. For example, they knew the Croatians were fast at the start and hard to get past, but would struggle to get past GB. They knew the Aussies would have the crowd on their side, were the fastest in the last 500m – the very place where the crowd would be most concentrated. The eight GB oarsmen, the cox and the coaches all agreed that if they wanted gold, then sprinting all the way was a risk they could not afford not to take.

What does this mean for you? It means accepting the possible bad consequence. Say you take a gamble by going to an outlandish holiday destination or applying for an 'out there' job. Of course you're going to be unhappy if it turns out to be rubbish, but can you live with that? It also means being very clear on what exactly your goal is and how much you want it. The crew talk before the Olympic Final made it clear to the boys that their goal was gold – not silver or bronze – and they wanted gold so badly it hurt.

What specifically do you want? Does the holiday have to be kayaking with Killer Whales or are you really after adventure and could an alternative option tick that box? How badly do you want that experience? What will it give you if you go for it? What will it cost you if you don't?

Conclusion

The most conservative, boring person living the greyest of lives is taking as many risks as the adrenaline junky free climbing on a high rock face. The difference is the *type* of risks they are taking.

Once we've rid ourselves of the unhelpful belief that risk = bad and recognise that *risk = unavoidable* we can channel our energies into figuring out the risks that are absolutely worth taking for us to lead happier, more successful lives and to achieve the goals we are passionate about.

CHAPTER 14

THE FINAL CHAPTER

The Olympic Final

10.25 a.m. Sunday 24th Sept 2000

"Five minutes," came a flat, heavily accented voice over the loud speaker system.

We took our white Team GB T-shirts off and pulled our blue racing all-in-ones up over our shoulders. We passed our T-shirts down the boat so Rowley could throw them onto the pontoon behind us. We had our last sips of water and chucked our bottles back onto the pontoon as well.

I turned around and squeezed Andrew's ankle just behind me. We eyeballed each other. Andrew's eyes were hard and bright, full of anger and commitment. I slid forward and slapped Simon's side. He grabbed my ankle in a huge hand and squeezed it.

This was it.

The plan was simple. The plan had been born the day before. The classic race plan over the 2,000 metres course was to go off hard and fast for the first 500, maintain the rhythm through the middle 1,000 metres, with a push here and there, and then sprint for the line in the last 500.

Our plan was different. It was bold, it was risky and it would work. It maximised our chances of winning and if we trusted ourselves and each other it would work. We'd come up with our new plan almost exactly 24 hours before and it would work. We were prepared to risk all to win and we were going to attack, attack, attack and keep on attacking all the way – not giving any of the bastards who sat alongside the smallest sniff of a chance.

On either side of us people got themselves ready. Far over to our left I could hear the Romanians shouting and banging the side of their boat. This is what I had been preparing for. For ten years this had been what I lived for. This is what it was all about.

All I had to do was get the first eight or so strokes right and the rest would follow. I could see them in my head. I could feel the way my back was going to move.

We knew that to maximise our chances we had to be one of those crews who threw caution to the wind, risked all and wanted it more than anyone else and my God we wanted it. We'd poured so much into this we had to make it happen when it mattered.

We would sprint the whole way. There was to be no cruising, no consolidating, no sitting on the lead. We were to increase it all the way. We were to go and to keep going, never being relaxed or being satisfied with the lead. We had to extend it with every stroke that we took. We would nail every single stroke. This was to be a five-and-a-half-minute sprint!

The first 500 metres was to be the hardest, fastest 500 we'd ever done. The second 500 was going to be kick-started with a 35-stroke sprint;

it would be harder and faster than the first 500m. The third 500 was to be faster again. As we hit the halfway mark we would lay down another devastating 35-stroke sprint. At 1,250 metres there would be another 35-stroke sprint. The last 500 we'd be on our knees, but we knew that we'd still have to build into the line. We were going to lay it down with every drop of passion within us. We were going to make it happen.

We were going to row the way we'd been practising, with the intent that we'd been practising with. We were going to do what we had trained for.

I can't remember every stroke. We had tried hard to make sure that we could remember every stroke so that we could then analyse what we'd done, but I'm afraid that my memories are porous. I've watched the race countless times as I've made speeches for schools and businesses, government departments and sports clubs. It's hard to know what I remember of the race and what I know because I've seen it on a big screen.

I do remember the start, lifting my hands on the "Attention". I remember driving my legs and moving with real speed as we nailed the first few strokes. As we started to move out to length we were rowing the rhythm we needed. We were moving.

From watching the film I know that we did move; we were the first crew on to the second, third and fourth strokes. Our bow was the first one to move ahead. Afterwards, Martin and Harry said that, as they sat in the minibus with the other coaches, they saw our bow move first, they saw our bow jump out in front and by the time we were on the fifth stroke they knew that we were going to be unstoppable.

We were nailing it. Moving with speed and power. Hands rising, backs moving, legs powering down. I didn't look at how we were doing, but, in my peripheral vision, I could see that we were moving on the Italians and the Aussies.

As we powered towards 500 metres Andrew, who sat behind me, barked at me that he wanted more. My legs were on fire, my lungs hurt, I forced my back to move faster.

Rowley was calling for the blades to come down to the water and warning us that we were approaching 500 metres and we were going to hammer it for 35 strokes to ensure that we kept moving. He wanted five long strokes to set it up. I slid as far forward as I could and made sure my hands were rising so that my oar was slipping into the water as far forward as possible.

"NOW!" and he wanted power, every drop of power that we had. Forcing my legs down harder, and again and again. Counting the ten strokes in my head. 5. 6. 7. 8. We had to be ready to move our backs to accelerate the boat further. Opening them now, now, 3, 4, 5, 6, 7, ready for the last ten.

Powering both legs and backs together. "Go". 1, 2, 3, 4, 5, 5, 5, 5. F**k it – as I got tired I was less and less able to count – 6. 7. Keep moving. Keep moving on them.

Rowley told us we were through 750. He was calling my name. He wanted me to keep moving my back. I stole a glance across to the left. We were up. We were approaching 1,000 metres. We were approaching the next 35-stroke push.

He wanted five long strokes to set up the next 30. I checked my hands on my straw, the straw that was taped to the side of the boat as a marker of where I needed to be reaching in order to put my oar in the water. I was touching it every stoke. I was rowing long. Now for the power.

"Ready."
"Go."
"Legs, Legs, Legs."

...4, 5, 6, 7, getting ready to move the backs.

"Now" 1, 2, 3, 4, 4, 5, 5, 5.

Legs and back with everything we've got. I was roaring inside my head. We were going to take the bastards apart. I looked across. We were up. We were going to be Olympic Champions. Going to be an Olympic Champion, going to be an Olympic Champion, going to be an Olympic Champion was going through my head with every stroke.

The next 35-stroke push was upon us, we were at 1,250 metres. My hands were still going out to the straw, now for the power. Legs. Legs. Legs. Going to be an Olympic Champion. Legs. Legs. And back. Back. Back. Going to be an Olympic Champion. Back. We were going to f**k them. They were going to pay for every bit of pain I'd had to endure. More distance, more distance, f**k them. Backs and legs. Make them pay.

Every training session I'd had to endure, every 20-kilometre ergo session, every review, every planning session, the learning, the change, the constant drive for improvement, every two-kilometre ergo test, every weights circuit, every wedding I'd missed, every race I'd lost, every time I'd been so tired I'd had to take a chair into the shower because I couldn't stand up; it was because of them and now they were going to pay.

We were approaching 500 metres to go. I felt OK. I still had some juice in the tank. Here we go; we had nearly a length, but Rowley wanted more. When we got to 500 metres to go he wanted another 35 from us.

Here we go. We would give him more.

"Five long, ready, GO!"
My hands were touching the straw. Long. Long.

"10 on the legs, POWER NOW!"
1, 2, 3, 3, 3, 3, 3, f**k. I was knackered. I was out of power.

"10 on the backs, move NOW!"
1, 2, 3, 3, 3, my legs, my back, my arms were killing. My lungs. 3, 3, 3.

"10 legs and back. NOW"
3, 3, 3, 3.

I was f**ked; my tanks were empty. I had nothing more to give. I wanted to stop. We'd been hit by a wall of noise from the spectators and I had to focus on hearing Rowley, I managed that, but I'd also hit the wall of pain.

I was out of energy.

I was out.

Andrew swore at me: I couldn't let him down. I wanted to stop; I needed to stop.

I could not let Fred down. I'd had it.

For Harry. I had to do it for Harry.

Steve, he wasn't going to let me down. More power. 10 more strokes. 1, 2, 2, 2. Keep going. Legs down.

The Aussies were coming. So were the Italians. They weren't going to take it away from me now. 2, 2, 2. Everyone was coming back. Rowley was screaming for more; I had no more. How could I make it all go away?

2, 2, 2. I needed to stop. For Martin, for Simon, 2, 2, 2. Rowley was begging for more.

"250 to go."

F**k. I couldn't do 250. They were coming back. More, I needed more.

For Kieran. For Steve. I needed to stop. I'd had enough. I had to stop.

They weren't going to stop. My head. My head was killing me.

"Last push."

I couldn't let them down. The Aussies were piling back. They won't get past us. More power. They would pay. My head; it was going to explode. I needed to stop.

Rowley was demanding more. They were still coming. There was nothing I could do. I wouldn't let them past. 2, 2, 2, 2, 2, 2, 3. Could I make the line? More. My head. Someone was hammering in my head. No, my head was in a vice getting crushed. Things were starting to get cloudy and grey, they were crushing my head. And the Aussies were coming back. Could I make it?

I'd had it. I couldn't go on.

The buoys marking out the lanes changed colour. We had 100 metres left. I could do 100 metres. Power. Power. Speed. My head. 2, 2, no stopping just power. They were coming. Power. My head. 2, 2, 2.

We'd done it. Relief.

We'd done it – some arms went in the air. Some bodies slumped forward. We'd done it. Relief.

It took me a couple of seconds to work out what we'd done. We'd done the Olympics. Thank you, God! Thank you!

We'd done the Olympics.

We'd won the Olympics!

What followed was amazing; there were people in the water swimming out to us with Union Jacks. We were Olympic Champions. We'd done it. We slapped each other on the back. Louis and Kieran were standing up. Rowley was climbing into the boat from a safety launch – when had he fallen out? Someone gave me a flag.

We'd done it. So many years, so many defeats and now we were Olympic Champions. It was f**king amazing. Where were my parents and sister and brother-in-law? Where was Isabella? We were getting married in a few weeks. Where was she in the stand? We were Olympic Champions.

The boat was almost surrounded by swimmers holding onto the sides of the boat, congratulating us, slapping our legs and backs. Someone was throwing us bottles of water from a safety launch. How long we sat there in a stupor I don't know. We'd done it!

Eventually someone told us to row over to a press pontoon. Harry and Martin were there. We'd done it. There were some BBC people, Matt Pinsent – with a big bear hug – Harry and Martin who had guided us every step of the way. There was confusion; not knowing what to say, half sentences, lots of swearing.

Princess Anne was there; she'd come down to watch us. Half sentences with her. The women's Quad had got a silver 30 mins before our race!

The Croatians joined us on the pontoon, they'd got the bronze. We congratulated each other. I don't remember if the Aussies were there. At some point someone told us to row over to the medal pontoon 100 metres away. I think they probably told us lots of times, when finally we started moving towards the boat Louis called us all around.

We stood in a tight group, arms around each other's shoulders and he told us that the last thing we were going to do together was sing. And we did. On the medal podium, with our medals around our necks, we sang our hearts out.

I can't describe how I felt. Proud? Elated? I don't know. Much later I saw some BBC footage as Luka got out of our boat and approached the camera, he told them that we were supermen. And maybe that's how it felt as we stood, a few of us wearing Union Jacks like capes, arms around each other's shoulders and singing our hearts out.

We were Olympic Champions! It had worked. All the work, all the effort, it had worked. All the heartbreak, the stress, the constant pushing to be better, the anger, the fights, the arguments, the disappointments. It had all been worthwhile.

The Final Chapter: Now what?

Even though I know the outcome, reading Ben's description of the Final still gives me goosebumps.

We said at the start of this book that Ben's goal is a pretty extreme example of a goal. He could only achieve it at 10.30 a.m. on 24th September 2000 and the chance would be over in less than five and a half minutes. So which of the crew's strategies will help you get your gold – whether that's running a successful business, nailing a project, raising a family, living a happy life?

Writing this feels a bit like standing on the pavement waving you off on a road trip – watching as you put your keys into the ignition and start up your engine. The destination is keyed into the satnav, the wheels are pumped up, and the engine is finely tuned. Now it's time for action.

The feedback we consistently get about the crew's strategies is that they are simple to put into practice. For example, early on in my career I used to get so annoyed when people would come up with blinding flashes of the patronisingly obvious like "you need to believe in yourself" without explaining *how*. Doing tangible things like creating an evidence wall makes that much easier.

- What are the key things in this book that have leapt off the page for you?
- What actions are you going to take?

Take a couple of minutes to look through the first page of the coaching section of each chapter – each one has a quote, a summary and a list of the headings. Ask yourself:

- What strategies did I already know and have been re-enforced?
- What was new, intriguing or challenging??
- What would it be useful to try on for size – to experiment with in real life?

A couple of suggestions for making the information stick are:

- Annotate the book. If you haven't already, then scribble in the margins, highlight important sections, put book marks in key places.
- Talk about it to someone else. When we have to explain things to others we understand it better ourselves.
- Experiment – apply the strategies in your context and do contact us via the website if you've got any follow-on questions.

For me, there are a few key themes that keep popping up throughout the book.

1. Simplicity. The question 'Will it make the boat go faster' is incredibly powerful. It cuts through confusion (should we sprint at

500 metres or from the start?). It guides behaviour (should I raise that concern or bite my tongue?) and it focuses attention (Rice Krispies or Shreddies?). Time and again the crew used the question to move forward.

What is your version of the question? Perhaps it's:

- Will it make me happier?
- Will it grow the business?
- Will it get the result I want?

2. Controlling the controllables. Whether it was bouncing back from setbacks, or dealing with negative comments or making the 'impossible' happen, the crew focused their attention on what they *could* do and forgot about the rest.

How much stress would disappear from your life if you controlled the controllables and let go of the uncontrollables? For example if you focused on how you could flex your communication with your boss, rather than focusing on what an idiot he is, or spent time preparing your presentation rather than worrying about it.

3. Talking. The team rules stuck because the team talked them through, the team took a massive risk in the Olympic Final and it was the easiest decision they'd ever made, because they talked it through. The crew spent so much time talking that eyebrows were raised in a sporting culture where 'doing time' (the physical training) was valued most highly.

- Whatever your 'doing time' is (maybe it's selling, or childcare or number-crunching), how can you take time out to reflect?

- Who do you need to talk to in order to make your boat go faster? How? And how often? (Or if you work very much by yourself then perhaps this means personal thinking time, or time with a coach.)

4. Getting emotional. Ben got really angry, upset, and irritable. Whereas most of us have been taught that these are negative or unproductive emotions, Ben seemed to listen to the underlying message and act on it. If he was pissed off at himself for a lousy regatta it would motivate him to train doubly hard; if he was passionate about winning the Olympics then – although he felt a right numpty for crying in front of the crew – he used that as what we've called emotional rocket fuel to spur him on.

- What is your emotional rocket fuel?
- What are your emotions trying to tell you to do? (E.g. anger – might be advising you to change something or fear to do some preparation, or ask for support.)

5. Challenge. They focused on the facts rather than succumbing to the stories that most of us tell ourselves. They looked for what was possible or desirable rather than accepting the status quo as most of us do. Why not raise £36k to get a new boat? Why not change the training day and the yearly timetable? Why accept bullshit at face value when you can put up your bullshit filters?

- What stories have you convinced yourself are true?
- What is the truth that you are pretending not to see?

6. Finding the value. Linked to challenge is the way the crew looked not just for the facts, but the *useful* interpretation of the facts. It's raining? Fantastic! It's sunny? Fantastic! There are upsides to both. We've just lost Henley? That's really painful, but what's good about it? It's a wake-up call to focus on rhythm.

- How can you make it a habit to look for the usefulness in more situations?
- What question could you ask? (E.g. what's useful? What's helpful here?)

But that's my summary, not yours. Have fun putting the ideas into practice. We'd love to provide ongoing help and to hear how it is going. Get in touch via willitmaketheboatgofaster.com.

Whatever you want to achieve, to be, to have – whatever your definition is of a happy, worthwhile life – the very best of luck and enjoy the journey.

The Cast List

Lots of people appear in the book – perhaps so many it's easy to lose track of who's who. With some occasional nicknames thrown in to the mix as well, we thought it would be useful to give you a thumbnail sketch of each of the main players.

The British Men's 8+ oarsmen

Andrew Lindsay, Bow

Andrew was the short arse of the crew; he was only 6'2". He was the last guy to get selected and fought every day to prove his point. He had been in the crew in 1998, he then chose not to trial in 1999 so he could concentrate on his degree. He got a First from Oxford; quite a smart lad. He was an incredibly aggressive and brilliant racer. Nickname: Raffles, the gentleman thug.

At the time of writing he is CEO of Telecom Plus, which owns The Utility Warehouse.

Ben Hunt-Davis, 2

I was the oldest person in the crew and I'd been in the team longer than anyone else. I was the only person who had been to an Olympics before. This meant that I had lost more races than anyone else and I had more bad habits than anyone else!

I'm running Will It Make The Boat Go Faster? Ltd.

Simon Dennis, 3

Simon was the biggest guy in the crew; a real gentle giant, I think I only saw him angry once. He had been in the crew in 1998, he went into the 2- in 1999 and forced his way back into the 8+ in 2000. He was incredibly powerful and when he was on form everyone could feel his 'gold medal strokes'. Nickname: Donkey Dennis.

Simon is a Biology teacher at Marlborough College.

Louis Attrill, 4

Louis was from the Isle of Wight. He was incredible; thorough and methodical. He thought everything through and was very performance-driven. He started rowing at Imperial College because he didn't think the rugby club was organised well enough! He had been a national BMX champion, national kick box champion and played county rugby and cricket. He was just good at everything.

He is the General Manager at Graham Attrill Civil Engineering on the Isle of Wight.

Luka Grubor, 5

Our Croatian import, Luka, was a brilliant rower who 'studied' at Imperial College and then Oxford. He was normally pretty relaxed and laid back, his way of thinking things through was to talk them through. The end of session debriefs were often incredibly painful as Luka talked and talked until he worked out whatever it was he was trying to get straight in his head. He was also one of the hairiest men alive.

Luka works as a coach and event organiser in Split, Croatia.

Kieran West, 6

The youngest guy in the crew by a couple of months and also one of the tallest at 6'8". Kieran was one of the guys who had more nicknames than most other people. He was a key person in the crew, he was strong and rowed really well. His rhythm was brilliant and I rarely remember him getting much coaching. We did need to manage him properly to keep him healthy and on track.

He is currently the strategy director at BUPA.

Fred Scarlett, 7

Fred is the most sarcastic, sharp-witted bloke I know. His ability to cut anyone down to size in less than 30 seconds is incredible. Fred was one of the key people who challenged what we did, he was always questioning, challenging, pushing and keeping most of us laughing, although very often at some else's expense.

Fred is Sales and Marketing Director at Clivedale, a property development company.

Steve Trapmore, Stroke

Steve was a very thorough workhorse, really committed and methodical. He was physically the weakest person in the crew, but he was the key; he set a rhythm that enabled us to work hard. Steve was a brilliant strokeman, he had a really good feel for the boat and when he spoke, we all listened. Steve's only problem was steadying his hands enough so he could get a cup of tea to his mouth without spilling it everywhere.

Steve is a rowing coach for the GB National Team.

Rowley Douglas, Cox

The cox's role was to coach us as we trained and raced. A cox can never be short of things to say and Rowley fitted this role perfectly. There was never a moment when he wasn't talking, and there weren't many moments off the water when he wasn't getting stick from us, but he could give as good as he got! Like most coxes he couldn't steer, but he had an excellent feel for the boat and coached us brilliantly as we trained and raced.

He is currently the Chief Revenue Officer at CloudSense in the US.

Our Coaches, Managers and Support Staff

Martin McElroy, Crew Coach

'Macca' had learnt to row at University in Dublin, he then worked as an engineer for a number of years before going to Imperial College to do an MBA where he started coaching. He brought his business-minded approach to rowing and he was the driving force of the changes that we went through. Martin managed and drove the programme every step of the way. He was an incredibly good coach and manager, but he realised that he couldn't do it alone so he brought Harry and other experts into the team to help him. Just as we weren't the finished article, nor was he; he made mistakes, got things wrong and he learnt and developed as he went along. Some of his Irish pronunciations could reduce most of us to tears at any point. He must have been a saint to put up with us.

Martin is still involved in coaching and runs his own consulting business FirstR8.

Harry Mahon, Assistant Coach

Harry was a genius; he was probably the best technical coach in the world. He was a straight-talking Kiwi who had coached around the world. He couldn't organise a piss up in a brewery, but was brilliant at what Martin asked him to do. He would come in for a couple of outings or a couple of weeks to get us to improve certain areas. He was also Martin's steadying hand, reassuring and guiding him through the difficult times. He was diagnosed with cancer in 1997 and between bouts of chemotherapy, with some hair, no hair, looking green and yellow, stinking of whatever medication he was on, he ran his first marathon and coached us. Harry was an inspiration. He died in May 2001.

Chris Shambrook, Sports Psychologist

Known affectionately as 'Shambles', Chris was a key part of the team. He came to us as a university lecturer with a huge tool kit of things to do with us and ended up using very little of it. All he wanted us to do was build the right culture and approach to what we did. Chris was a completely sound and reliable bloke who fitted into the group brilliantly.

He left the British Rowing Team in 2016 and is a founder of K2 Performance Systems.

Steve Ingham, Sports Physiologist

'Hot buns' had an amazing ability always to be upbeat and smiling, even at the crack of dawn when he was checking our urine samples. While we were cursing him as he tried to drain our ears of blood at the end of a piece of work, he would be taking the piss out of us and making us laugh and smile.

Steve left the English Institute of Sport in 2016 and set up and runs Supporting Champions.

Jürgen Gröbler, Chief Coach

Jürgen had to be one of the most successful coaches in the world. He has coached crews to win at every Olympics he has been to since 1972. He came to the UK from East Germany in 1991, by 1993 he was the GB chief coach and in 2020 he is still in charge of men's rowing. There were many areas where we didn't see eye-to-eye, but he had a good sense of humour and you could tell how much he'd drunk the night before by how neat his hair was; if it was perfect, he'd had a big night!

Jürgen is still Men's Chief Coach and has also taken on being Women's Chief Coach for the GB Rowing Team.

David Tanner, Team Manager

David had been involved in GB rowing since the 70s as a coach and in various management roles. He was a school headmaster until there was funding for him to become the Team Manager in 97. He was a ruthlessly efficient organiser; when David was around, planes weren't late, hotel rooms were ready, food was good(ish), everything worked or God help whoever's fault it was.

Sir David retired from British Rowing in 2018.

Other Rowers

Steve Redgrave

I don't need to say much about Steve, nicknamed 'Reders', Britain's greatest ever Olympian. He was someone we were always trying to beat. Steve had a massive influence on the team, not by getting involved in what other crews were doing, he focused solely on his crew, but his presence and achievements were an inspiration and helped to keep us focused on what was possible.

Matt Pinsent

Four times Olympic Champion and 10 times World Champion. Matt was the strongest person in the team – a giant of a man. Often you could beat him in training, but never in racing unless he was in a single scull. He and Steve were very close and, like Steve, he didn't interfere with other crews, but still had a big effect on us.

Tim Foster

An incredible boat mover, really rhythmical with great timing. In rowing it's really hard to describe what talent is, but Tim had loads of it. He appeared very laid back and relaxed, but beneath it all he was incredibly driven and ruthless. I think Tim was liked and respected by everyone.

James Cracknell

One of the most driven people I've ever met. We raced each other from the age of fifteen. There were two or three years where I got the upper hand, but by 1997 he was miles ahead of me. We had a couple of set-tos, but on the whole we got on well.

Greg Searle

One of the most talented athletes in the team; Greg had been beating me since I was fifteen and we were good friends. He managed to wind up some of the boys, but I think it was because Greg had very high standards and in his eyes his standards were right. He retired in 2001 and got back in the team in 2010!

Ed Coode

Ed was liked by everyone, he had been in the 4- in 1999 when Tim dropped out to have his second back operation, and he just missed out holding on to his seat when Tim came back. He came fourth with Greg in 2000 and got his Olympic Gold medal in 2004.

Other Support Staff

There are numerous other people who played really important parts in our progress and development, I haven't been able to mention many of them in this book but it doesn't mean that they weren't crucial. The medical staff headed up by Dr Anne Redgrave and Mark Edgar kept us healthy, fit and helped us recover from injuries as quickly as possible.

The staff in the British Rowing Office who worked tirelessly to make sure we had what we needed where we needed it.

There were other coaches, physiologists and boat design and building experts who all did what they could to help us. I hope that they all know how much they helped us and how grateful we all are.

Chronology

The numbers in the boat column refers to the number of oarsmen so "8" is the eight and "2" would be the pair. The plus or minus sign refers to whether the boat has a cox "+" or is coxless "-" .

Year	**Event**	**Location**	**Boat Ben was in**	**Race result**
1989	Coup de la Jeunesse	Italy	4+	1st
1990	World Junior Championships	France	2+	4th
1991	U23 World Championships	Italy	4-	2nd
1992	Barcelona Olympics	Spain	8+	6th
1993	World Championships	Czech Republic	4-	5th
1994	World Championships	USA	8+	8th
1995	World Championships	Finland	8+	6th
1996	Atlanta Olympics	USA	8+	8th
1997	World Championships	France	2-	5th

Year	Event	Location	Boat Ben was in	Race result
1998	Pre World Championship training camp	Varese, Italy	8+	N/A
1998	World Championship	Cologne, Germany	8+	7th
1999	GB V France, along the Seine	Paris, France	8+	2nd/ last
1999	World Cup	Hazewinkel, Belgium	8+	2nd
1999	World Cup	Vienna, Austria	8+	2nd
1999	Henley Royal Regatta (Not world cup)	Henley, England	8+	2nd/ last
1999	World Cup	Lucerne, Switzerland	8+	2nd
1999	Training camps Ely	Ely, England	8+	N/A
1999	World Championships	Canada	8+	2nd
2000	GB V France, along the Seine	Paris, France	8+	1st
2000	World Cup	Munich, Germany	8+	2nd
2000	World Cup	Vienna, Austria	8+	1st
2000	Henley Royal Regatta (Not world cup)	Henley, England	8+	2nd
2000	Training camp in Sarnen	Sarnen, Switzerland	8+	N/A
2000	World Cup	Lucerne, Switzerland	8+	1st

Year	Event	Location	Boat Ben was in	Race result
2000	Training camp	Ely, England	8+	N/A
2000	Training camp	Gold Coast, Australia	8+	N/A
2000	Sydney Olympics	Sydney, Australia	8+	1st

Recommended Further Reading

There are plenty of amazing books out there. Here are a handful of examples of our current favourites:

Authentic Happiness – Martin Seligman
The Pressure Principle – Dave Alred
The Power of Habit – Charles Duhigg
Grit – Angela Duckworth
Peak – Anders Ericsson and Robert Pool
Thank You for Being Late – Thomas L Friedman
David and Goliath – (and countless other books by) Malcolm Gladwell
Crucial Conversations – Joseph Grenny, Ron McMillan, Kerry Patteson, Al Switzler
Difficult Conversations – Sheila Heen, Bruce Patton, Douglas Stone
Team of Teams – General Stanley McRistal
Drive – Daniel Pink
Good Strategy, Bad Strategy – Richard P. Rumelt
Rest – Alex Soojung-Kim Pang
Leaders Eat Last – Simon Sinek
Black Box Thinking – (and all the other books by) Matthew Syed
Why We Sleep – Matthew Walker

About the Authors

Ben Hunt-Davis

Ben spent ten years chasing the Olympic dream. He came sixth in the Barcelona Olympics and did not even make the final in Atlanta. Since winning gold at the Sydney Games in 2000, Ben has continued to be heavily involved in both rowing and the Olympics.

He was Chair of the Junior World Championships when they were hosted in Britain in 2011 and is on the organising committee for the Henley Royal Regatta. He has played a number of different roles in the last three summer Olympic Games (Beijing, London and Rio). He worked at the British Olympic Association on the run up to the London 2012 Games, running athlete education heading into a home Olympics.

Ben is also a highly popular keynote speaker, inspiring business audiences around the world to make their boat go faster.

Harriet Beveridge

Harriet is a coach, keynote speaker and comedian. As a comic, Harriet was UK Funny Women Award semi-finalist, has written and performed three critically acclaimed shows at the Edinburgh Festival Fringe and published the spoof nanny advice book 'Turnip-Led Weaning'. Her BBC Radio 4 talk on taking humour seriously was nominated 'pick of the week' and her TEDx talk on the transformative power of humour was streamed live globally.

Harriet has coached leaders, teams and organisations for twenty years – helping them to unlock their potential and navigate change. She is a sought-after keynote speaker, combining powerful, practical messages with irresistible warmth and energy.

About the Company

First there was a gold medal… then there was a book… next came the company. 'Will It Make The Boat Go Faster?' started in 2012 and is dedicated to helping businesses define their own crazy goals, and then ensure they embed the Olympic-winning strategies described in this book, – the habits, attitude and momentum – to make those goals a reality.

If you run a business or a business team and want high quality coaching or consultancy to help your 'boat go faster' get in touch via willitmaketheboatgofaster.com.